The Art of Fact in the Digital Age

The Art of Fact in the Digital Age

An Anthology of New Literary Journalism

Edited by

Jacqueline Marino and David O. Dowling

BLOOMSBURY ACADEMIC
NEW YORK • LONDON • OXFORD • NEW DELHI • SYDNEY

BLOOMSBURY ACADEMIC
Bloomsbury Publishing Inc
1385 Broadway, New York, NY 10018, USA
50 Bedford Square, London, WC1B 3DP, UK
29 Earlsfort Terrace, Dublin 2, Ireland

BLOOMSBURY, BLOOMSBURY ACADEMIC and the Diana logo are trademarks of
Bloomsbury Publishing Plc

First published in the United States of America 2024

Volume Editor's Part of the Work © Jacqueline Marino and David O. Dowling, 2024

Each chapter © of Contributors, 2024

For legal purposes the Acknowledgments on p. xiii constitute an extension
of this copyright page.

Cover design by Daniel Benneworth-Gray
Cover images: (clockwise from top) Jorge Rojas, Alexander Krivitskiy and
Mitchell Luo / unsplash.com; *From My Window at An American Place, Southwest*
by Alfred Stieglitz, 1932

All rights reserved. No part of this publication may be reproduced or transmitted
in any form or by any means, electronic or mechanical, including photocopying,
recording, or any information storage or retrieval system, without prior permission in
writing from the publishers.

Bloomsbury Publishing Inc does not have any control over, or responsibility for, any third-
party websites referred to or in this book. All internet addresses given in this book were
correct at the time of going to press. The author and publisher regret any inconvenience
caused if addresses have changed or sites have ceased to exist, but can accept no
responsibility for any such changes.

Library of Congress Cataloging-in-Publication Data

Names: Marino, Jacqueline, editor. | Dowling, David Oakey, 1967- editor.
Title: The art of fact in the digital age : an anthology of new literary journalism /
edited by Jacqueline Marino and David O. Dowling.
Description: New York : Bloomsbury Academic, 2024. | Includes bibliographical
references and index.
Identifiers: LCCN 2023043093 (print) | LCCN 2023043094 (ebook) | ISBN 9798765107867
(hardback) | ISBN 9798765107850 (paperback) | ISBN 9798765107898 (ebook) |
ISBN 9798765107881 (pdf)
Subjects: LCSH: Literature–Collections. | Reportage literature. | Digital storytelling. |
Reporters and reporting.
Classification: LCC PN6014 .A765 2024 (print) | LCC PN6014 (ebook) |
DDC 081–dc23/eng/20231108
LC record available at https://lccn.loc.gov/2023043093
LC ebook record available at https://lccn.loc.gov/2023043094

ISBN: HB: 979-8-7651-0786-7
PB: 979-8-7651-0785-0
ePDF: 979-8-7651-0788-1
eBook: 979-8-7651-0789-8

Typeset by Deanta Global Publishing Services, Chennai, India
Printed and bound in Great Britain

To find out more about our authors and books visit www.bloomsbury.com
and sign up for our newsletters.

For our students

Contents

Preface		ix
Acknowledgments		xiii
Introduction		1

Digital Literary Journalism Pioneers

Mark Bowden	"Black Hawk Down"	15
John Branch	"Snow Fall: The Avalanche at Tunnel Creek"	22
Marc Perrusquia	"Leading Up to 6:01: The Last 32 Hours of Dr. Martin Luther King Jr."	28
Jon Henley, Laurence Topham, and the international team from theguardian.com	"Firestorm: The Story of the Bushfire at Dunalley"	48
Susan Dominus	"The Displaced: Hana"	63
Jason Fagone	"The Jessica Simulation: Love and Loss in the Age of A.I."	69

Notable Narratives

Pamela Colloff	"The Reckoning"	79
David Kushner	"The Bones of Marianna"	87
Jessica Goudeau	*After the Last Border: Two Families and the Story of Refuge in America*	94
Jia Tolentino	"Who is Matty Healy?"	103
Emily Green	"The Out Crowd"	118

Showing and Telling

Ta-Nehisi Coates	"The Case for Reparations"	133
Carina del Valle Schorske	"Bodies on the Line"	139
Mitchell S. Jackson	"Twelve Minutes and a Life"	145
Brian Phillips	"Out in the Great Alone"	151

The Reporter Takes the Stage

Evan Ratliff	"The Mastermind"	165
Luke Mogelson	"The Dream Boat"	172
Shane Bauer	"My Four Months as a Private Prison Guard"	179
Alex Mar	"Love in the Time of Robots"	184

Confronting the Unspeakable

Clint Smith	*How the Word Is Passed*	195
Kathryn Schulz	"The Really Big One"	199
David Wallace-Wells	"The Uninhabitable Earth"	206
Olha Poliukhovych, Tetiana Troitskaya, and Iryna Slavinska	"Dispatches from Ukraine"	223

Selected Bibliography	235
Index	243

Preface

The canon of literary journalism—reported nonfiction works that use literary elements, such as scene, character development, and theme—is substantial and evolving. This genre, in English, includes the most influential journalists of the past 300 years, from Daniel Defoe in eighteenth-century England to Kathryn Schulz in twenty-first-century America. Until now, only one volume has compiled its greatest achievements for students and scholars: *The Art of Fact: A Historical Anthology of Literary Journalism*, edited by Kevin Kerrane and Ben Yagoda and published by Simon & Schuster in 1997. While other academics argued about what made journalism "literary," Kerrane and Yagoda settled on an accessible five-word definition: "thoughtfully, artfully, and valuably innovative." When the historical anthology was first published, *Time Out New York* lauded it as possibly "the world's most readable textbook." Just a few years ago at a conference of the International Association for Literary Journalism Studies, one of this book's editors told prominent literary journalism scholar John C. Hartsock that she still used the anthology in class. "It's still the best one," he replied.

As literary journalism scholars who have studied the genre's digital evolution, we offer this updated companion to *The Art of Fact*, covering notable works of literary journalism since the beginning of the Internet Age. Journalists writing in English are publishing deeply reported, stylish works of literary journalism regularly. A volume like this one was needed to explain how the form has changed—and also stayed the same—in digital formats. This anthology aims to capture how digital media has transformed, and in some cases, preserved, and expanded the power of narrative storytelling that has long been the signature of print literary journalism. In the digital age, literary journalism is no longer confined to the printed page. We have included some of the most notable works of literary journalism originally published for screens (and in some cases also the printed page or the ear), regardless of nonfiction genre or type of publishing outlet. Inevitably, reading these words in print, without the integrated images and other multimedia elements, will not offer the same experience. (If you are reading the e-book, we encourage you to check out the digital presentations immediately before or after reading the excerpts to get the full effect of how each work originally appeared online.) We do believe that literary journalism can transcend the written word, but we only chose selections in which the words are crucial to the work's meaning. Some of these fit Tom Wolfe's requirements of *The New Journalism*: scene-by-scene construction, dialogue, point of view, and status details. An example would be John Branch's "Snow Fall: The Avalanche at Tunnel Creek," which won a Pulitzer Prize and could stand-alone in print form, as it appeared in the print version of *The New York Times Magazine* prior to its release as a multimedia feature. The text in other multimedia longform works were written in such a way that the words only work as part of the whole. In all cases, selections are milestones in literary journalism, representing some of the most innovative and powerful works of longform narrative-storytelling since the dawn of the digital age.

In the first section of the book, Digital Literary Journalism Pioneers, we provide exemplars of the form from the late 1990s to the early 2020s. The oldest work in the anthology is Mark Bowden's "Black Hawk Down," a series about a battle between American Rangers and armed civilians that took place in Mogadishu, Somalia. Heralded for its inclusion of images and videos by journalism industry publications at the time, Bowden's narrative account was published over twenty-eight days on the website of *The Philadelphia Inquirer* in 1997. The more recent works in that section demonstrate what was, at the time of publication, innovative uses of multimedia that complement the written stories. For example, Susan Dominus's "The Displaced," a story about children displaced by war that appeared in *The New York Times Magazine* in 2015, includes immersive video and virtual reality. The writing, however, remains its centerpiece.

The next section, Notable Narratives, includes examples of strong narrative storytelling using traditional reporting practices, such as immersive reporting and extensive interviewing, coupled with literary techniques, including cinematic structure and scenic reconstruction. Selected writers in this section are distinguished by how well they reconcile style with substance. Pamela

Colloff's exhaustive reporting methods, for instance, showcase her ability to create seamless narratives that pull us into the world of her subject in "The Reckoning." Through David Kushner's skillful use of historical records and in-depth interviews in "The Bones of Marianna," he unearths—and compellingly unfurls—a horrifying story of abuse at a reform school for boys in Florida.

The writer's connection to the subject matter often elevates their work in the eyes of readers, scholars, and journalism prize judges. A selection of reported essays appears in the third section, Showing and Telling. Several of these pieces have racked up national awards in recent years. Every story uses the first person to take the readers deeper into the subject at hand, from the systemic racism in housing and running, respectively explored by Ta-Nehisi Coates and Mitchell S. Jackson, to dance as a pandemic-coping mechanism posited by Carina del Valle Schorske.

The only section head we've kept from Kerrane and Yagoda's *The Art of Fact* is The Reporter Takes the Stage. There's no better header for the pieces made literary by the style of their authors. Yagoda warned of "the possibility for abuse here: the reporter's forgetting that he is not the story, just a means to it." But today's audiences want to know who's telling them a true story, and they appreciate writers who invite the spotlight. As Luke Mogelson and Shane Bauer show us, reporters are still willing to go undercover for long periods of time in difficult, even life-threatening conditions, to reveal shocking truths about places no credentials-wearing reporter could go, such as a refugee boat lift to Christmas Island and a private prison in Louisiana. Sometimes the risks reporters take reside in the realm of emotional vulnerability, like Alex Mar's disclosure of how deeply she connects to the work of a scientist pursuing the perfect humanlike robot.

Last, in Confronting the Unspeakable, we've selected works that tackle topics many readers would rather avoid, including climate change and slavery, in responsible, enlightening ways. At a time when news outlets are consolidating or shrinking, we call attention to writers who tell the kind of stories we need to hear even though it's risky to tell them. Among those taking extraordinary risks are the three women writers in this section whose dispatches from Ukraine deliver moving and urgent narrative reportage. There are many easier, more profitable ways to attract a dedicated audience, such as curating lifestyle content, appealing to niche audiences, or erecting walled gardens on Substack, among them. In our increasingly polarized media world, even verifiable facts become the subject of fierce debate and distortion. This section showcases writers dedicated to informing communities about hard truths about difficult subjects that affect us all.

We wish we could have included more works in this volume, but reprint permissions are expensive, and sometimes impossible to secure because of usage restraints and confusion over ownership rights. In the Selected Bibliography, we included the titles of more works that we wish we could have included, as well as titles of scholarly and trade publications that informed our introductions to each chapter.

Despite the explosion of experimentation—made possible by new digital tools and low barriers to entry—and a rapidly growing audience, works of digital literary journalism are still not called by an agreed-upon name and lack a set of criteria to evaluate quality. In the Introduction, we have set forth the rationale for the name "digital literary journalism" and developed research- and practice-based criteria upon which quality can be argued. This book provides links to stories that take readers to the online presentations where they can find text, photographs, and other multimedia features from the included pieces. We hope our anthology offers for this emerging genre what Tom Wolfe did for *The New Journalism* with his eponymous 1973 anthology. In addition to anthologizing excerpts from some of the best nonfiction work of the first three decades of the twenty-first century, the Introduction also describes the components of digital literary journalism, tracks its history, and highlights its importance to both English-language literature and journalism.

Acknowledgments

We thank everyone who inspired this book, especially Kevin Kerrane and Ben Yagoda, whose historical anthology first mapped the sprawling 300-year landscape of literary journalism. Thank you to the members of the International Association for Literary Journalism Studies (IALJS), the first academic organization devoted exclusively to this work. David and Jacquie first met at an IALJS conference, after following one another's scholarly work from afar, and it was at these conferences that we were encouraged to pursue scholarship on digital literary journalism. We are indebted to the late Norman Sims for his immeasurable contributions to the study of literary journalism. We thank Kate McQueen and Kevin Lerner for reading early drafts of the Introduction and for their illuminating insights. Others from IALJS who we want to thank personally are former IALJS president Rob Alexander, for connecting us to Bloomsbury Academic; David Abrahamson, Thomas Connery, and John S. Bak for their passionate support to those who teach and research literary journalism; William Dow and Roberta Maguire, for editing the latest, most comprehensive scholarly book on the form, *The Routledge Companion to American Literary Journalism*; and John C. Hartsock, for sparking the idea for this volume while talking to Jacquie at an IALJS conference years ago.

We thank the following people at our institutions, Kent State University and the University of Iowa, for providing the funding to secure permissions for some of the most notable works of literary journalism produced in the past twenty-five years: Amy Reynolds, Christopher M. Cheatum, Emily Metzgar, Melissa Tully, Audrey Lingenfelter, Joshua Weiner, Miriam Matteson, and Jenny Ritchie. Special recognition goes to Lei Chen, David's University of Iowa PhD student advisee, whose invaluable contribution to this project as a research assistant immeasurably enhanced the quality of this book. Lei's contributions were the wind in our sails at a crucial phase. We also thank Bloomsbury publisher Katie Gallof for believing in this work and in us.

We are grateful to all the authors, publishers, and editors who allowed their remarkable works to be included, especially those who accepted bargain-basement fees or offered their work for free. The impetus behind this volume has always been to introduce new audiences to literary journalism and to ignite new thinking about the work. Many people with whom we connected understood this, and the book is a better reflection of the range of work represented in new literary journalism because of them.

David acknowledges *Literary Journalism Studies* editor Bill Reynolds for originally encouraging submissions on digital literary journalism in the mid-2010s. This gesture opened up a wide range of important research on the topic from award-winning scholars such as Kobie van Krieken (on narrativity in the multimedia feature), Marie Vanoost (on transmedia storytelling), and Siobhan McHugh (on podcasting's development of the aural nonfiction novel). Bill's open-minded vision committed to exploring narrative journalism across media cannot be underestimated in the formation of the body of research—along with its faculty and students—that this anthology serves. David thanks his longtime Iowa colleague Stephen G. Bloom for his encouragement on this project along with his Magazine Reporting and Writing students at the University of Iowa. Finally, David's wife, Caroline, and their daughters, Jacqueline and Eveline, and son, Ed, deserve mention for backing this project from the start.

Jacquie thanks Sidney Holt of the American Society of Magazine Editors, who edits *The Best American Magazine Writing* each year. She keeps more than twenty years of this treasure trove of notable magazine works on her bookshelf and consulted it many times while considering which works to include in this anthology. She is grateful to Lisa Phillips, for her suggestions, and to Connie Schultz and Susan Jacobson, for rallying this project. Jacquie also acknowledges her students at Kent State who have eagerly discussed many of these works in Feature Writing and Advanced Magazine Writing classes over the past sixteen years. Her students have given her faith that younger generations will read meaningful stories, regardless of platform. Last, Jacquie thanks her parents, her husband, Mark, and daughters, Stella and Charlotte, for their support and encouragement.

Introduction

Since the turn of the digital revolution, journalists have broached new subjects and spawned new genres as diverse and captivating as the emerging media technologies that defined the era. Climate change, immigration, race, and technology have become subjects worthy of the large canvas of longform storytelling across media platforms. Digital tools have profoundly shaped the craft. Along with these transformations, the literary element of narrative journalism—a process of "making facts dance"—has flourished, evolving into an aesthetic sensibility for telling true stories unique to the twenty-first century.

Kevin Kerrane credits his co-editor, Ben Yagoda, for describing literary journalism as "making facts dance" in his introduction to their 1997 anthology *The Art of Fact*. In this compelling work, he and Yagoda showed how journalists and "novelist-journalists" like Charles Dickens and John Hersey did this work from the eighteenth through the late twentieth centuries. The editors connected the true-crime narrative's lineage from Daniel Defoe's 1725 account of Jonathan Wild to Truman Capote's *In Cold Blood* and David Simon's *Homicide*. Kerrane and Yagoda showed the lasting power of literary journalists' reporting techniques, including becoming a character in one's own story: Jack London living among the poor in East End of London for his 1903 *People of the Abyss*; Marvel Cooke joining the "Paper Bag Brigade" of exploited Black maids nearly fifty years later; and, a few decades after that, Ted Conover traveling with Mexicans who illegally and regularly crossed into the United States for work. The similarities are not just those of writing and reporting, these editors explain, but also of motivation. Social conscience has often driven this work in all its ages, from the nineteenth-century pieces by Dickens, Henry Mayhew, and W. T. Stead to the magazine writers of the late twentieth century. In *The Art of Fact*, readers ride the river of great sportswriting, crime and war reportage, and human-interest journalism from headwater to mouth.

With the publication of their anthology, Kerrane and Yagoda established the canon of literary journalism, one made entirely of words.

During the first decade of the 2000s, however, journalists were told to let go of words. Newspapers and magazines, the vehicles through which many richly reported, carefully crafted stories reached the audiences who were willing to pay for them, were dying. In their place, the internet delivered information to increasingly fragmented audiences where they spent more of their time—desktop computers, then laptops, and, eventually, tablets and smartphones.

The best stories in the early 2000s, proclaimed the editors, media scholars, and journalism professors of the day, were the ones created for digital spaces, capable of competing with the videos, social channels, and games that marshaled the attention of their audience. Journalists were told to trade their notepads for cameras, to write short, and to let the images fill in the blanks in the readers' minds. Until we began to see otherwise with a genre-shattering work published in 2012, the written word was still regarded as something distinct from visual and audio-based media as its own, stand-alone meaning-maker, rather than part of a symphony.

But as Marshall McLuhan writes, new mediums "amplify or accelerate existing processes." In other words, no medium ever disappears. It changes. It is used by what comes after, just as it used the media that came before. W. J. T. Mitchell argues that "all media are mixed media." The way the media mix, interact, and influence each other to make meaning can be understood through the concept of "braiding." A story cannot be told if it cannot be told in words first. Even in video and audio storytelling, the words are there. You hear them. You see the connections they have made. Rather than let go of the words, the best storytellers of the digital age have simply used them differently. Literary stylists have always crafted valuable, purposeful work, writes Thomas Connery. Through most of the past 300 years, that work has been published in newspapers and magazines, but literary form has changed based on journalism's role in society, cultural expectations, and the owners of newspapers and magazines. These factors influenced the novelist-journalists of the late nineteenth century as much as the literary stylists of the 1960s and the immersive reporters of the 1990s.

The literary journalists in the digital age have moved the words off the printed page.

As the previous bastions of literary journalism have shrunk or disappeared in print, those who want to write it often join user experience designers, programmers, documentary storytellers, photographers, and others to create multimedia presentations that often include videos, audio elements, interactive graphics, and sometimes even gamification. Literary journalism now "operates at the nexus of cinema, radio, and print, spawning newly minted genres capable of immersing mobile audiences in ways previously imaginable only in IMAX theatres," writes David O. Dowling.

In December 2012, many of us had a "What inna namea christ is this" moment while visiting the website of *The New York Times*. (These were the words Tom Wolfe used to describe how he felt when reading Gay Talese's brilliant profile of heavyweight boxing champion Joe Lewis for the first time—a feeling he relayed in the introductory essay to his landmark anthology *The New Journalism*.) *The New York Times*' "Snow Fall: The Avalanche at Tunnel Creek" was not so much a story as it was a presentation, a dazzling recounting of a deadly ski trip told in a long scroll the reader could access in a mix of words, video, images, and interactive graphics. The work was separated into chapters using video loops and "curtain" transitions where the words moved up to eclipse the video as the user scrolled. The piece attracted 3.5 million views, a 2013 Pulitzer Prize, and a Peabody Award.

While "Snow Fall" was unique in its cohesion, it was not alone. Journalists have been experimenting with online storytelling ever since they first got online. Those who produce and teach this form of storytelling have been cataloging these works for almost as long. As of 2008, the website *Interactive Narratives* showcased more than 1,400 multimedia presentations by organizations and individuals, many of which featured a great deal of words. After "Snow Fall," an open Google spreadsheet titled "Snowfallen" was filled with similar works from all over the world.

Journalists writing in English are publishing deeply reported, stylish works of literary journalism regularly. The form has both changed and stayed the same in digital formats. Some of the works in this volume, especially those on the websites of magazines that still print on paper, appear online in much the same way they appeared in the print magazines. But unlike the works in *The Art of Fact*, they have reached new audiences through social media, online "extras" like podcasts, and audio versions available on apps.

The four elements of literary journalism outlined by Tom Wolfe—scene, dialogue, point of view, and the recording of details that relay how a character sees their place in the world—are still evident in literary journalism created for screens, but they are often constructed through a mix of visuals and words, both spoken and written. This anthology aims to capture how digital media has otherwise transformed, and in some cases, preserved, and expanded the power of narrative storytelling that has long been the signature of print literary journalism. The core features of literary journalism that guided our selection process are the enduring traits identified by Norman Sims more than two decades ago: "immersion reporting, complicated structures in the prose, accuracy, voice, responsibility, and attention to the symbolic realities of the story," often through access and attention to ordinary lives. Mark Kramer and Wendy Call help elaborate our criterion to include work that "challenges audiences as well as practitioners," frequently by blending "human content with academic theory and observed fact," a distinctly intellectual endeavor that "allows specialized understanding of everyday events, and unscrambles and sorts the messages of a complex world."

Despite the explosion of experimentation—made possible by new digital tools and low barriers to entry—and a rapidly growing audience, works of digital literary journalism are still not called by an agreed-upon name and lack a set of criteria to evaluate quality. We refer to literary journalism works created to be consumed digitally as "digital literary journalism."

Susan Jacobson, Jacqueline Marino, and Robert Gutsche, Jr., argue that this work constitutes a new wave of literary journalism. It includes the set of aforementioned characteristics Wolfe outlined: stories are often told in scenes with attention to dialogue, point of view, and characterization through details. To belong to the emerging genre, multimedia must also perform a literary function. In a content analysis of fifty such works published in *Journalism: Theory, Practice and Criticism*, the researchers found three functions:

- the interplay of multimedia and literary techniques to create meaning within the stories;

- the use of video loops as a device to establish the stories' sense of time, place, and character; and
- the emergence of an alternative to the hypertextual norm of web storytelling.

For instance, in *Grantland*'s "Out in the Great Alone," Brian Phillips, a writer who hates snow, follows the Iditarod Trail Sled Dog Race by air. His conventional storytelling devices, such as dialogue, are enhanced by illustrations, historical photos, and even videos strategically placed in the right-hand margin.

Through *Grantland*, and as an extension of its television documentaries, ESPN played a major role in establishing the storytelling conventions of digital longform journalism. Although the Pulitzer-Prize-winning "Snow Fall: The Avalanche at Tunnel Creek" by *The New York Times* is commonly credited with revolutionizing digital longform journalism via parallax scrolling—a web design technique where the foreground elements move more quickly than those in the background as the user scrolls—with embedded multimedia elements, ESPN's multimedia feature "The Long, Strange Trip of Dock Ellis" (not anthologized in this volume due to copyright restrictions) bears the distinction of being the first publication in this genre. As a feature profile of Dock Ellis, the Major League Baseball player known for pitching a no-hitter while high on LSD in 1970, the project's reporting and writing match the ambition of its digital design. Parallax scrolling lifts the curtain on text, revealing archival video, photos, and hand-drawn illustrations recreating Ellis's hallucinations, including one depicting the home-plate umpire as Richard Nixon. Although Ellis's tale had circulated widely as the stuff of legend for more than forty years prior to publication, ESPN writer Patrick Hruby cast the athlete in a more accurate and comprehensive light than any biographer or journalist had done before him. Donald Hall's biography of Ellis, as Hruby reveals, took liberties with facts at the behest of Ellis to protect his business interests at the time.

Hruby not only sets the record straight in terms of the highly publicized occasion of Ellis's psychedelic no-hitter but also ventures into important, yet relatively unknown territory. In particular, the reader encounters the vicious and damaging racism Ellis faced in a predominantly white professional sport, at one point publicly calling out the league's systemic inequity with such aplomb that it prompted a personal letter of support and sympathy from Jackie Robinson, known for crossing the sport's color line. We also learn of the personal pain Ellis endured with his father's early death and the psychological demons that plagued him thereafter. The social and political impact of the emergence of the Black athlete in the twentieth century would receive one of its most subtle and revealing treatments in the twenty-first century's first multimedia feature, a form spawned from televisual professional sports through cable TV empire ESPN and documentary journalism via its function as promotional online material for the channel's docuseries *Outside the Lines*.

As audio media, podcasts are, of course, the great exception to the evolution of the multimedia feature in that they contain no screens and thus no video loops or visually-based digital elements. The precipitous ascent of podcasting in the digital publishing industry has opened a major channel for creativity in nonfiction storytelling evident in serialized documentaries inspired by *Serial* in 2014. Free from the limitations of screen-based digital journalism, creators have begun to leverage podcasting as the largest canvas for nonfiction storytelling in digital media.

The ascendance of podcast journalism into the realm of literature is evident in the imprimatur of credibility established by such milestone achievements as *S-Town*, whose rigorous reporting and artful Faulkneresque storytelling led the wave that prompted the establishment of Audio Reporting as a Pulitzer Prize category in 2020. With its release in 2017, *S-Town*'s record 10 million downloads in four days topped the previous—seemingly insurmountable—listenership of 10 million downloads in seven weeks set by *Serial*'s first season, which was three years earlier. *This American Life*'s "The Out Crowd," part of which appears in this anthology, received the Pulitzer that year, affirming the journalistic integrity behind the prospect of the aural novel suggested by the popular and critical success of *S-Town*. Podcast scholar Richard Berry has described the efflorescence of creativity in narrative journalism in the medium as the golden age of podcasting. The most recognizable characteristics among the many evolving genre conventions and storytelling tropes of podcast journalism are increasingly complex narratives and self-reflexive content that calls attention to the journalistic process of production, drawing the audience into the intensity and drama of reporting.

The vexing decisions of reporters as they untangle webs of complex, often contradictory evidence are made transparent in serialized documentary podcasts. The soaring popularity and newfound critical acclaim of podcasting has encouraged a gold rush mentality among some producers, who have overreached for credibility with audiences through what Gabriela Perdomo and Phillipe Rodrigues-Rouleau call the "metajournalistic performance of transparency." The podcast *Caliphate* by *The New York Times* committed the most visible breach of journalistic principle, which prompted the producers to return a coveted Peabody Award, due to its dependence on a fraudulent source in pursuit of a captivating narrative.

At the heart of podcasting's rise—and such Icarus-like falls—is the desire to achieve nothing less than the status of what Robert S. Boynton called "a Supreme Nonfiction" by harnessing the runaway momentum of journalism's narrative online resurgence through absorbing storytelling designed to immerse rather than distract audiences. *The New York Times'* acquisition of Serial Productions was a colossal investment that testifies to the importance of digital longform narrative not just as a niche genre of interest to fringe audiences but as the engine driving a storytelling renaissance. The Peabody Award for *S-Town* was accompanied by praise that took on a distinctly literary feel. The work established "new ground," the award committee noted, as "the first true audio novel, a nonfiction biography constructed in the style and form of a seven-chapter novel."

The simultaneous critical and popular success—traditionally associated with figures such as Charles Dickens in print publishing—is rare in any medium. As the first self-conscious attempt to advance podcasting into the category of literature, Brian Reed's production evokes William Faulkner's "A Rose for Emily" in this harrowing immersion into the life of John B. McLemore, the centerpiece of the narrative. McLemore himself is the architect of much of the cultural critique, lyricism, and charged language that pervades *S-Town*, exhibiting a virtuoso command of vernacular ranging from profane to scientific. In keeping with the true crime podcast convention in which civic participation is often direct via tips sent by listeners sparking and aiding investigations, McLemore originally solicited Reed to produce this podcast to investigate a murder in his hometown of Woodstock, Alabama. But as the investigation appears to hit a dead end, a major calamity forces a dramatic change in the trajectory of Reed's reporting and the podcast's narrative arc, while also unveiling profound insight—cast in unmistakable Faulknerian hues—into the culture of the rural South.

S-Town's explicit and self-conscious use of rhetorical techniques commonly associated with fiction places it squarely in the realm of literature, as a new wave of scholars led by Siobhàn McHugh, Kylie Cardell, and Ella Waldmann have demonstrated. Although written for the ear rather than the eye, we include an excerpt from "The Out Crowd" transcript in this anthology with the understanding that their narrative worlds are constructed through sound, while ostensibly generating meaning through words. We therefore encourage readers to use the printed version as a means for a richer appreciation of the narrative layering and to enhance the listening experience of the podcasts. Emerging digital media can breathe new life into old forms. In this case, podcasting—asynchronously consumed digital audio files—retrieves and remediates the conventions of the novel and journalistic feature writing.

Profound cultural shifts in media consumption linked to the Netflix model of publication in serial form have contributed greatly to the surge of creative innovation in digital longform storytelling. Boynton observed that the educated, relatively young original consumers of screen-based digital longform journalism produced in the early 2010s for the tablet and larger smartphones (often by the same magazines that ushered in the New Journalism in the 1960s) had become "the envy of any advertiser." Although the New Journalism originated in part with the commercial intent to attract readers with more appealing writing, its best works transcended the objective of merely delivering those readers to advertisers. The podcast industry now joins the Supreme Nonfiction with its sophisticated listeners to match its increasingly complex and intellectually challenging content.

Carefully produced and designed longform podcasts are the latest extension of the Supreme Nonfiction's defiance of the manic, social media-driven breaking news cycle. The works assembled in this anthology all reflect production processes associated with slower, more mindful reporting and writing. The digital presentation of these works—including elaborate sound design for both screen-based and podcast stories—figures prominently into such lengthy and often team-driven production cycles. Teams, often consisting of digital graphic designers, computer engineers, and even game developers for interactive features, are frequently behind these works rather than solitary authors or lone wolf reporters.

More than one-off prestige projects, longform content industrially known as deep dives is increasingly recognized by editors and publishers across media as essential to winning dedicated audiences. Longform articles become books. They get optioned for movies and TV shows. Some of these articles launch writers' careers as authors, podcasters, scriptwriters, or documentary filmmakers. In radio, longform content is designed to generate "driveway moments," when the riveted listener remains parked long after arriving home to hear the denouement of a particularly engaging story. Rather than exclusively functioning as a locus of distraction inclining users toward superficial scanning and skimming—whose low point has become doom scrolling—the digital age has delivered an embarrassment of riches in immersive narratives. The work assembled here reflects how we have emerged from the narrative deprivation associated with the truncated, headline-driven news of the early 2000s into an age in which the tools of digital media communication have found new ranges of expression and depth in conjunction with the written and spoken word. Immersive storytelling, in our view, is a narrative method conjoined with media technology rather than simply a technologic function of surrounding and enveloping the audience.

Immersive storytelling is not new to the digital age. As media scholar Thomas Schmidt has shown through his powerful study of literary nonfiction's migration into mainstream legacy media via the Style section of *The Washington Post*, journalism's narrative turn extended well beyond Tom Wolfe's circle. Now it thrives in born-digital and transmediated storytelling. This volume aims to highlight the exemplary works that constitute journalism's movement beyond its obsession with mere fact collection and transcription toward the richer pursuit of what Mitchell Stephens calls "wisdom journalism." The new intimate and personal idiom of the best journalism since the late 1990s has been shaped in part by online discourse, which can indeed deliver content that Stephens describes as informed, intelligent, interpretive, insightful, and illuminating.

We recognize that illumination is concomitant to moral clarity. Black reporters such as Wesley Lowery have forced a reconsideration of the cultural and racial assumptions behind traditional understandings of objectivity, especially when "the view from nowhere" that attends such storytelling is often really the view of a white editor. Lowery's call for moral clarity in daily news and editorial writing extends to narrative journalism, which hybridizes history, memoir, and sociocultural critique in works such as Mitchell S. Jackson's "Twelve Minutes and Life" on the murder of Ahmaud Arbery, which was published in *Runner's World*. In an excerpt from *How the Word Is Passed*, *The Atlantic* writer Clint Smith helps Americans confront our national history of slavery through his visits to its monuments and other key places. Ta-Nehisi Coates, also writing in *The Atlantic*, presents a strong case for reparations through his thoroughly reported examination of the plunder of Black wealth in America. The new canon for literary journalism is thus distinctly more diverse and often more personal than the one that preceded it.

Many of the stories featured in this book take place in global settings and treat international subjects. The *Guardian*'s "Firestorm," for example, explores a devastating fire in Australia from the vantage point of a family with young children. *The Atavist*'s "The Mastermind" investigates a massive global criminal empire run by Paul Le Roux (who was born in Rhodesia). *The New York Times*' "The Displaced" is an interactive documentary collection of three profiles of children refugees from Ukraine, South Sudan, and Lebanon; both "The Dream Boat" and *After the Last Border* provide vantage points on mass migration from the perspectives of those on the move. *This American Life*'s "The Out Crowd" won the first-ever Pulitzer Prize awarded in the category of Audio Reporting (as mentioned earlier) for its empathic coverage of an encampment of migrants on the southern border between the United States and Mexico during the Trump era. In the digital journal *AGNI*'s "Dispatches from Ukraine," three writers bring readers into the war unfolding on their doorstep. *New York Magazine*'s "The Uninhabitable Earth" examines the global impacts of climate change. Although *The Art of Fact in the Digital Age* is saturated with international subjects and themes, its primary concern is with English-language literature and journalism. Thus, future anthologies might feature literary journalism in a variety of languages.

The selections in this book represent both milestones in digital literary journalism and proof that literary journalism has thrived in the digital age. Like Kerrane and Yagoda, we have developed a canon. Digital literary journalism reflects some aspects of literary journalism crafted for the printed page, and it transcends others. While text, video, audio, graphics, and photography continue to exist as distinct media, in digital literary journalism, they are marshaled in service of meaning by the new literary journalists and the outlets that publish them. The Supreme Nonfiction included here marries powerful writing with digital technology—in forms ranging from interactive documentaries and podcasts to single-scroll magazine pieces—to tell the "thoughtfully, artfully, and valuably innovative" stories that edify and inform as enduring literature imbued with the capacity to make facts dance.

Digital Literary Journalism Pioneers

From "Black Hawk Down"

Mark Bowden

At the dawn of the internet, the 1997 online publication of Mark Bowden's celebrated "Black Hawk Down" marked the advent of literary journalism in the digital age. The selection below is the first chapter of twenty-nine daily installments that originally appeared in the print edition of the *Philadelphia Inquirer*. The ambitious online version of this harrowing story, which was later made into the motion picture that propelled the reporter to worldwide fame, is a relic of Web 1.0. The digital publication of "Black Hawk Down" contained more data than any story of its kind. The sheer volume of supplemental material provided readers with the most richly contextualized online experience of a feature story in the history of digital journalism.

Although state of the art for its time, by today's standards one is struck by its primitive graphics and dependence on hyperlinks, many of which have fallen prey to internet ephemerality known as link rot. Links to maps and images appear separately from the text in a click-heavy reading experience, with Bowden's sterling prose indelicately shoveled onto the page. Skirting the left margin under a tiny navigation bar is supplemental multimedia clustered into utilitarian categorical boxes labeled video, audio, photos, maps, and full text. Although an unprecedented achievement in 1997, decades later, the visually disjointed transition-less design now feels more like a Wikipedia page or database of raw information in sharp contrast to the latest immersive multimedia narratives.

Whatever Bowden's prototype of digital literary journalism may lack in polished production features, it compensates for in its vast archive of data contextualizing his story of the 1993 raid on Mogadishu. As critics of online reading led by Nicholas Carr voiced concern that the overflow of data could create undue distraction in the reading experience and thus pose a threat to the narrative integrity of digital longform, Bowden pushed back against the tide of skepticism, publishing his second multimedia text, "The Desert One Debacle," in 2006. Although he had forged his reputation in print—the medium through which his journalistic art drew praise from the iconic Tom Wolfe in his 2010 acceptance speech for the National Book Lifetime Award as one of the two journalists to watch along with Michael Lewis—Bowden made his preference for digital publishing clear. When media scholar Nora Berning asked Bowden about the difference, he was unequivocal in asserting that "the online presentation is a lot richer than the written text." To him, enabling the reader to drill down into the reporter's rich archive of research made that difference. "The reader/viewer/listener can delve as deeply into the material as he wishes. [. . .] On the Internet, the writer can provide a new service to the readers." In this manner, readers "can make sense of the writer's material themselves, digest the sources, and draw their own conclusions." Hyperlinks to material on the open web and supplemental multimedia elements, however, typically jettison the reader to another website, detracting from a linear reading experience of Bowden's main narrative thrust. Supplemental data, furthermore, depend on the foundation of meticulous reporting and compelling writing.

What follows is drawn from Chapter 1, "Reliving a firefight: Hail Mary, then hold on," first published in the *Philadelphia Inquirer* on November 16, 1997. It depicts the first firefight of "Black Hawk Down," showcasing Bowden's extraordinary talent—acknowledged by Wolfe—for narrative pacing via careening action and tension building, in this case rendering a revealing glimpse into the character of Staff Sergeant Matt Eversmann.

—D. D.

STAFF SGT. Matt Eversmann's lanky frame was fully extended on the rope for what seemed too long on the way down. Hanging from a hovering Blackhawk helicopter, Eversmann was a full 70 feet above the streets of Mogadishu. His goggles had broken, so his eyes chafed in the thick cloud of dust stirred up by the bird's rotors.

It was such a long descent that the thick nylon rope burned right through the palms of his leather gloves. The rest of his Chalk, his squad, had already roped in. Nearing the street, through the swirling dust below his feet, Eversmann saw one of his men stretched out on his back at the bottom of the rope.

He felt a stab of despair. *Somebody's been shot already!* He gripped the rope hard to keep from landing on top of the guy. It was Pvt. Todd Blackburn, at 18 the youngest Ranger in his Chalk, a kid just months out of a Florida high school. He was unconscious and bleeding from the nose and ears.

The raid was barely under way, and already something had gone wrong. It was just the first in a series of worsening mishaps that would endanger this daring mission. For Eversmann, a five-year veteran from Natural Bridge, Va., leading men into combat for the first time, it was the beginning of the longest day of his life.

Just 13 minutes before, three miles away at the Ranger's base on the Mogadishu beach, Eversmann had said a Hail Mary at liftoff. He was curled into a seat between two helicopter crew chiefs, the knees of his long legs up around his shoulders. Before him, arrayed on both sides of the sleek UH-60 Blackhawk helicopter, was Eversmann's Chalk, a dozen men in tan, desert camouflage fatigues. He had worried about the responsibility. *Twelve men.* He had prayed silently during Mass at the mess hall that morning. Now he added one more.

... Pray for us sinners, now, and at the hour of our death. Amen.

It was midafternoon, Oct. 3, 1993. Eversmann's Chalk Four was part of a company of U.S. Rangers assisting a Delta Force commando squadron that was about to descend on a gathering of Habr Gidr clan leaders in the heart of Mogadishu, Somalia. This ragtag clan, led by warlord Mohamed Farrah Aidid, had challenged the United States of America.

Today's targets were two top Aidid lieutenants. Delta Force, the nation's elite commando unit, would storm the target house and capture them. Then four helicopter loads of Rangers, including Eversmann's men, would rope down to all four corners of the target block and form a perimeter. No one would be allowed in or out.

Waiting for the code word to launch, which today was "Irene," they were a formidable armada. The helicopter assault force included about 75 Rangers and 40 Delta Force troops in 17 helicopters. Idling at the airport was a convoy of 12 vehicles with soldiers who would ride three miles to the target building and escort the Somali prisoners and the assault team back to base.

The swell of the revving engines had made the earth tremble. The Rangers were eager for action. Bristling with grenades and ammo, gripping the well-oiled steel of their weapons, they felt their hearts race under their flak vests. They ran through last-minute mental checklists, saying prayers, triple-checking weapons, rehearsing their choreographed moves. They had left behind canteens, bayonets, night-vision devices (NODs) - anything they felt would be dead weight on a fast daylight raid.

It was 3:32 p.m. when the lead Blackhawk pilot, Chief Warrant Officer Michael Durant, announced: *"F-in' Irene."*

And the swarm of black copters lifted up into an embracing blue vista of Indian Ocean and sky. They eased out across a littered strip of white sand and moved low and fast over the breakers.

Mogadishu spread beneath them in ruins. Five years of civil war had reduced the once-picturesque African port to a post-apocalyptic nightmare. The few paved avenues were crumbling and littered with mountains of trash and debris. Those walls and buildings that still stood in the heaps of gray rubble were pockmarked with bullet scars and cannon shot.

In his bird, code-named Super 67, Eversmann silently rehearsed the plan. When his Chalk Four touched the street, the D-boys would already be taking down the target house, arresting the Somalis inside. Then the Americans and their prisoners would board the ground convoy and roll back for a sunny Sunday afternoon on the beach.

It was the unit's sixth mission since coming to Mogadishu in late August. Now Maj. Gen. William F. Garrison, their commander, was taking a calculated risk in sending them in daylight into the Bakara Market area, a hornet's nest of Aidid supporters.

The Delta commandos rode in on MH-6 Little Birds, choppers small enough to land in alleys or on rooftops. In the bigger Blackhawks, Rangers dangled their legs from the doorways. Others squatted on ammo cans or sat on flak-proof panels laid out on the floor. They all wore flak vests and helmets and 50 pounds of gear and ammo.

Stripped down, most Rangers looked like teenagers (their average age was 19). They were products of rigorous selection and training. They were fit and fast. With their buff bodies, distinct crew cuts - sides and back of the head shaved clean - and grunted *Hoo-ah* greeting, the Rangers were among the most gung-ho soldiers in the Army.

Inside Super 67, Eversmann was anxious about being in charge. He'd won the distinction by default. His platoon sergeant had been summoned home by an illness in his family, and the guy who replaced him had suffered an epileptic seizure.

Now, as they approached the target site, he felt more confident. They had done this dozens of times.

By the time the Blackhawks had moved down over the city, the Little Birds with the Delta Force troops were almost over the target. The mission could still have been aborted. But the only threat spotted was burning tires on a nearby street. Somalis often burned tires to summon militia. These, it was determined, had been set earlier in the day.

"Two minutes," came the voice of the Super 67 pilot in Eversmann's earphones.

Two advance AH-6 Little Birds armed with rockets then made their "bump," or initial pass over the target. It was 3:43 p.m.

Cameras on spy planes and orbiting helicopters relayed the scene back to commanders at the Joint Operations Center on the beach. They saw a busy Mogadishu neighborhood, in much better shape than most. The landmark was the Olympic Hotel, a five-story white building, one of the few large structures still intact in the city. Three blocks west was the teeming Bakara Market.

In front of the hotel ran Hawlwadig Road, a paved, north-south avenue crossed by narrow dirt alleys. At the intersections, drifting sand turned rust-orange in the afternoon sun.

One block up from the hotel, across Hawlwadig, was the target house. It was flat-roofed with three rear stories and two front stories. It was shaped like an L, with a small courtyard enclosed by a high stone wall. In front moved cars, people and donkey carts.

Conditioned to the noise of the copters by months of overflights, people below did not stir as two Little Birds made a first swift pass, looking for trouble. Seeing none, the four Delta Little Birds zoomed down to Hawlwadig Road, disappearing into swirling dust as the Delta commandos leaped from their helicopters and stormed the house. Next came the Blackhawks with the Rangers.

Eversmann's copter hovered just above the brown storm. Waiting for the three other Blackhawks, it seemed to the sergeant that they hung there for a dangerously long time. A still Blackhawk was a big target. Even over the sound of the rotor and engines the men could hear the pop of gunfire.

The 3-inch-thick nylon ropes were coiled before the doors. When they were finally pushed out, one dropped down on a car. This delayed things further. The pilot nudged his aircraft forward until the rope dragged free.

"We're a little short of our desired position," he told Eversmann. They were going in a block north of their assigned corner. Still, that wasn't crucial. The sergeant thought it would be a lot safer on the ground.

"No problem," he said.

"We're about 100 meters short," the pilot warned.

Eversmann gave him a thumbs-up. He would be the last man out.

When it was his time to jump, the strap on his goggles broke. Flustered, he tossed them and sprung for the rope, forgetting to take off his earphones. He jumped, ripping the earphone cord from the ceiling.

In the excitement, time slowed. All his movements became very deliberate. He hadn't realized how high they were. The slide down on the rope was far longer than any they'd done in training. Then, on his way down, Eversmann spotted Todd Blackburn splayed out on the street at the end of the rope.

Eversmann's feet touched down next to the fallen Ranger, and the crew chiefs in the copter released the rope. It fell twisting to the road. As the Blackhawk moved up and away, the noise eased and the dust settled. The city's musky odor bore in.

Pvt. 2 Mark Good, Chalk Four's medic, was already at work on Blackburn. The kid had one eye shut. Blood gurgled from his mouth. Good inserted a tube down Blackburn's throat to help him breathe. Sgt. First Class Bart Bullock, a Delta medic, started an IV. Blackburn hadn't been shot, he'd fallen. He'd somehow missed the rope and plummeted.

He was still alive, but unconscious. He looked pretty busted up. Eversmann stepped away. He took a quick count of his Chalk.

His men had peeled off as planned against the mud-stained stone walls on either side of the street. That left Eversmann in the middle of the road with Blackburn and the medics. It was hot, and sand was caked in his eyes, nose and ears. They were taking fire, but it wasn't very accurate. Oddly, it hadn't even registered with the sergeant. You would think bullets clipping past would command your attention, but he'd been too preoccupied.

Now he noticed. Passing bullets made a snapping sound, like cracking a stick of dry hickory. Eversmann had never been shot at before. As big a target as he made at 6-foot-4, he figured he'd better find cover. He and the two medics grabbed Blackburn under his arms, and, trying to keep his neck straight, dragged him to the edge of the street. They squatted behind two parked cars.

Good looked up at Eversmann. "He's litter urgent, Sarge. We need to extract him right now or he's going to die."

Eversmann shouted to his radio operator, Pvt. Jason Moore, and asked him to raise Capt. Mike Steele on the company radio net. Steele, the Ranger commander, had roped in with two lieutenants and the rest of Chalk One to the block's southeast corner.

Minutes passed. Moore shouted back to say he couldn't get Steele.

"What do you mean you can't get him?" Eversmann asked.

Neither man had noticed that a bullet had severed the wire leading to the antenna on Moore's radio. Eversmann tried his walkie-talkie. Again Steele didn't answer, but after several tries Steele's lieutenant, Larry Perino, came on the line.

The sergeant made a particular effort to speak slowly and clearly. He explained that Blackburn had fallen and was badly injured. He needed to come out. Eversmann tried to convey urgency without alarm.

So when Perino said, "Calm down," it really burned Eversmann. *This is one hell of a time to start sharpshooting me.*

Fire was getting heavier. To officers watching on screens in the command center, it was as if their men had poked a stick into a hornet's nest.

Excerpt from "Black Hawk Down," by Mark Bowden from *The Philadelphia Inquirer*. © 1997 Philadelphia Inquirer, LLC. All rights reserved. Used under license.

From "Snow Fall: The Avalanche at Tunnel Creek"

John Branch

Although earlier stories provided glimmers of digital longform journalism's promise, "Snow Fall" proved its worth as a new genre.

Until then, multimedia journalism functioned as a series of elements relegated to boxes on blocky webpages—boxes for still photographs and for videos, boxes for charts, and (sometimes) other graphics. Because attention spans were shorter online, reporters were urged to write short, more like a broadcast script less like a book.

But the creators of "Snow Fall" used the best of every available storytelling media to make something spectacular. Three and a half million people viewed the story online, less than a week after it was published in December 2012. The story bolstered the value of narrative storytelling on news organizations' websites.

On the story's homepage, snow flies across a mountain, forebodingly and continuously, in a video loop under the headline. As the reader scrolls, a curtain of words covers the video. At other times, the text is upstaged by dazzling imagery: aerial photography of the Cascade Mountains, interactive graphics, simulations using satellite images and LIDAR elevation data, even well-placed photo galleries and short videos. In one simulation, we see the routes the highly skilled skiers likely took—for some, their last-ever run.

Yet, the essence of this work is a haunting, literary 17,000-word feature story about a tragedy in the "sidecountry," an area adjacent to a ski area, the setting of "Snow Fall" and the title of sports reporter John Branch's 2021 collection. In a Q&A published in *The New York Times*, Branch explains the methods he used to report the piece: visiting the scene, interviewing survivors and victims' loved ones, and learning as much as he could about avalanches. As he wrote, a group of editors, graphic artists, and designers worked on multimedia elements to "help with the telling."

Branch's literary style is compelling. Brilliant with observational details, he takes readers deeply into the experiences of his subjects, regardless of who they are or the level of danger they're courting, from alligator hunters and risk-taking skiers to losing basketball players and a girl on his daughter's soccer team whose mother was killed in the 2017 Las Vegas massacre. "I usually nibble in the shadows of the sports world," he writes in his Amazon bio. "My goal is to surprise readers, to give them memorable stories that they did not know they needed." Several of his stories have appeared in *The Best American Sports Writing*, and he's authored three books. "Snow Fall" won a Peabody Award for Interactive and a Pulitzer Prize for Feature Writing. And, for more than a decade, his most famous article's title has become a verb, with journalists around the world asking to "Snow Fall" their stories.

—J. M.

The snow burst through the trees with no warning but a last-second whoosh of sound, a two-story wall of white and Chris Rudolph's piercing cry: "Avalanche! Elyse!"

The very thing the 16 skiers and snowboarders had sought—fresh, soft snow—instantly became the enemy. Somewhere above, a pristine meadow cracked in the shape of a lightning bolt, slicing a slab nearly 200 feet across and 3 feet deep. Gravity did the rest.

Snow shattered and spilled down the slope. Within seconds, the avalanche was the size of more than a thousand cars barreling down the mountain and weighed millions of pounds. Moving about 70 miles per hour, it crashed through the sturdy old-growth trees, snapping their limbs and shredding bark from their trunks.

The avalanche, in Washington's Cascades in February, slid past some trees and rocks, like ocean swells around a ship's prow. Others it captured and added to its violent load.

Somewhere inside, it also carried people. How many, no one knew.

The slope of the terrain, shaped like a funnel, squeezed the growing swell of churning snow into a steep, twisting gorge. It moved in surges, like a roller coaster on a series of drops and high-banked turns. It accelerated as the slope steepened and the weight of the slide pushed from behind. It slithered through shallower pitches. The energy raised the temperature of the snow a couple of degrees, and the friction carved striations high in the icy sides of the canyon walls.

Elyse Saugstad, a professional skier, wore a backpack equipped with an air bag, a relatively new and expensive part of the arsenal that backcountry users increasingly carry to ease their minds and increase survival odds in case of an avalanche. About to be overtaken, she pulled a cord near her chest. She was knocked down before she knew if the canister of compressed air inflated winged pillows behind her head.

She had no control of her body as she tumbled downhill. She did not know up from down. It was not unlike being cartwheeled in a relentlessly crashing wave. But snow does not recede. It swallows its victims. It does not spit them out.

Snow filled her mouth. She caromed off things she never saw, tumbling through a cluttered canyon like a steel marble falling through pins in a pachinko machine.

At first she thought she would be embarrassed that she had deployed her air bag, that the other expert skiers she was with, more than a dozen of them, would have a good laugh at her panicked overreaction. Seconds later, tumbling uncontrollably inside a ribbon of speeding snow, she was sure this was how she was going to die.

Moving, roiling snow turns into something closer to liquid, thick like lava. But when it stops, it instantly freezes solid. The laws of physics and chemistry transform a meadow of fine powder into a wreckage of icy chunks. Saugstad's pinwheeling body would freeze into whatever position it was in the moment the snow stopped.

After about a minute, the creek bed vomited the debris into a gently sloped meadow. Saugstad felt the snow slow and tried to keep her hands in front of her. She knew from avalanche safety courses that outstretched hands might puncture the ice surface and alert rescuers. She knew that if victims ended up buried under the snow, cupped hands in front of the face could provide a small pocket of air for the mouth and nose. Without it, the first breaths could create a suffocating ice mask.

The avalanche spread and stopped, locking everything it carried into an icy cocoon. It was now a jagged, virtually impenetrable pile of ice, longer than a football field and nearly as wide. As if newly plowed, it rose in rugged contrast to the surrounding fields of undisturbed snow, 20 feet tall in spots.

Saugstad was mummified. She was on her back, her head pointed downhill. Her goggles were off. Her nose ring had been ripped away. She felt the crushing weight of snow on her chest. She could not move her legs. One boot still had a ski attached to it. She could not lift her head because it was locked into the ice.

But she could see the sky. Her face was covered only with loose snow. Her hands, too, stuck out of the snow, one still covered by a pink mitten.

Using her hands like windshield wipers, she tried to flick snow away from her mouth. When she clawed at her chest and neck, the crumbs maddeningly slid back onto her face. She grew claustrophobic.

Breathe easy, she told herself. Do not panic. Help will come. She stared at the low, gray clouds. She had not noticed the noise as she hurtled down the mountain. Now, she was suddenly struck by the silence. . . .

Sliding Snow

The start of an avalanche is unlike any other force of nature.

A hurricane is foretold by wind and lashing waves. A tornado often is spotted before it strikes. Lightning is usually presaged by black clouds and rumbling thunder.

Avalanches rarely provide such a warning. Unlike waves or wind, tremors or storms, they are usually triggered by their own victims, sometimes unaware of what has been unleashed.

"If you swim out in the ocean, the ocean's always alive," Saugstad said. "You can feel it. But the mountains feel like they're asleep."

Back up the mountain, Jack never seemed worried. That was his nature. Here he was, a rare weekend off, skiing with some of his best friends from Leavenworth and people from Powder and ESPN and all over the industry, on an epic run on a perfect powder day.

Carlsen, the Powder photographer, had never been to Tunnel Creek. The first few easy turns gave way to a slope that fell steeply away, out of sight. He sidled up to Jack.

"I grabbed him, and I said, 'What is the move here?'" Carlsen said. "It was basically like, 'This is getting real, how do we handle it?' He's like: 'Oh, no big deal. We go out here, swing out, make a few pow turns, and get back in the trees.' I looked at him and said, 'Have a great run.' Gave him a fist, a knuckle-to-knuckle high-five thing. And that was it. I watched him swing out, way out, skier's right, and then dive into his turn left."

Jack flowed through the thick powder with his typical ease. He skied the way other people walked down a sidewalk, a friend had said.

Jack disappeared over the knoll, gliding through the trees in the middle of the meadow. Behind him, the five remaining skiers watched in silence.

"He looked like he was having a great time, the run of his life, in fact," Michelson said. "And he actually made, I remember, a little 'woo' sound, as he dropped in on his first or second turn because the snow was really good. It was deep and light."

Then the snow changed without warning. . . .

A few hundred yards down the mountain, a ghostly white fog rushed through the forest.

"I saw it," Saugstad said. "I saw it coming. But it was weird because it was coming through the trees. It was like snow billowing through the trees. Because it was such a treed area, I think for the first second I saw it I didn't believe it."

Wangen and Peikert had just traversed in front of its path. It did not miss them by much.

"I don't know if I'd even come to a stop when I heard it," Peikert said. "It was almost like wind and pressure more than noise. It literally felt like a freight train went over my tails. It wasn't a deep rumble. I could feel this rush of air."

It was a blur of white, its shattered pieces moving about 50 m.p.h., a powder cloud two stories tall.

Rudolph was the only one to scream.

"Avalanche! Elyse!" Rudolph shouted.

Saugstad tried to stride right, hoping to escape. She barely moved before snow flowed through her legs, dragging her down like a riptide.

She pulled the cord on her air bag. She was overwhelmed so quickly by the rising snow that she did not know if it inflated.

"I had no ability to control what was happening to me," Saugstad said. "I was being tossed over and over and over. It was like being in a washing machine and all my body parts flailing every way. I didn't know which way was up. I didn't know which way was down. I couldn't see anything."

She is likely to have tumbled just past Castillo. He groaned and turned his face away. He stuck his head between two trees, like a prisoner in a stockade.

For 16 seconds, snow and ice pounded his back and washed over him. His shoulders were jammed against the trees. His face pushed into branches of pine needles. He could feel the heavy assault of snow lashing at his back.

Trees cracked around him. Some in the path were chopped in half—the stumps left in the soil, the rest carried away in the growing torrent.

The avalanche, a relatively small one, started with about 6,000 cubic meters of snow and collected 7,000 cubic meters more on the way down. It probably weighed about 11 million pounds.

The trees Castillo hugged in each arm swayed but held. He told himself that when he felt the flow slow, he would pop a hand in the air so that it might stick out of the snow and make him easier to rescue.

"Just as I had the thought about what I'm going to do, wondering if it was going to bury me, that's right when I could feel it," Castillo said. "It was like a wave. Like when you're in the ocean and the tide moves away from you. You're getting thrashed and you feel it pull out and you're like, O.K., I can stand up now."

Castillo saw daylight again. His camera captured snow sliding past his legs for another 13 seconds. The forest sounded as if it were full of sickly frogs. It was the trees, scrubbed of their fresh snow, still swaying and creaking around him.

Castillo turned to look back up the hill.

"Where there were three people, there was nobody," Castillo said.

Excerpt from "Snow Fall: The Avalanche at Tunnel Creek" by John Branch, *The New York Times*. © 2012 The New York Times Company. All rights reserved. Used under license.

"Leading Up to 6:01: The Last 32 Hours of Dr. Martin Luther King Jr."

Marc Perrusquia

Newspapers have long struggled to cover anniversaries of important events in new and insightful ways. Setting the standard is *The Commercial Appeal*'s 2013 story marking forty-five years since civil rights icon Martin Luther King Jr. was assassinated in Memphis. The breathless narrative structure, enabled by detailed reporting culled from both interviews and historical records, propels readers through the last thirty-two hours of King's life.

Marc Perrusquia writes with a rare authority—one earned from covering King, both his life and his death, for more than two decades. At *The Commercial Appeal*, he won multiple awards for his exposés and his careful, riveting stories on politics and social justice. He also authored a series that later became a book about Ernest Withers, a photographer for the civil rights movement who moonlighted as an FBI informant.

For "6:01," Perrusquia won the American Society of Newspaper Editors' 2014 Punch Sulzberger Award for Online Storytelling. According to the judges, "*The Commercial Appeal* took the death of Martin Luther King Jr. further than any news organization had done before, digging deep into archives to uncover how the day unraveled for one of America's most noteworthy figures. Judges thought they had read everything that could be written about MLK; this innovative online presentation proved them wrong."

The story skips skillfully among points of view, beginning with employee Dorothy Cotton as she flies to Memphis with King on the day before his murder. The demonstration he led there a week earlier had turned violent, and a Black teenager, Larry Payne, was shot and killed. Yet, despite staffers' objections, attention from the FBI, and national media criticism, King returns to the city to support striking sanitation workers. Once a march turned violent, "you had to go back and have a nonviolent march to get things back on track," explains King's aide, Andrew Young, in a video accompanying the story.

Perrusquia fuels the story's tension with one powerful sentence, written from King's point of view, "Now, at 39, King fears all he's built—his reputation, his legacy—is on the line." King's narrative is interrupted by a chronicle of James Earl Ray's mission to assassinate him. Time, bolded at key moments, marches toward this tragic end. At 10:30 p.m., April 3, King concludes his spirited address at the Mason Temple. At 3:00 p.m., April 4, Ray checks into a rooming house one block west of the Lorraine. Just after 5:50 p.m., King walks onto the balcony, while Ray, carrying a rifle wrapped in a bedsheet, hurries down a hallway to a bathroom with a window facing that balcony. The timelines of King and Ray merge at 6:01 p.m.

Online, the piece looked like an interactive magazine, with large photographs, compelling videos, and other engaging multimedia, including interviews with King's associates and Cotton singing a freedom song. As of 2023, the original design of the story was no longer accessible on the website of *The Commercial Appeal*, which has become part of the USA Today Network, though the text and many of the elements remained. The original layout is preserved on an article about the story at www.niemanlab.org.

—J. M.

April 3, 1968

Dorothy Cotton is up early in her cozy Atlanta apartment, getting ready. She slips on a pink skirt and a matching jacket and a chic, knit hat. It's a big day, a huge day really, and she wants to look her best. She's flying to Memphis with her boss, her confidante, Dr. Martin Luther King Jr.

For Cotton, 37, the early-morning anticipation of April 3, 1968, is just part of living in the swirl of America's most recognized civil rights leader. The man people love. The man people hate. King is under such crushing pressure of late, though, Cotton knows there hasn't been a more pivotal day for him or his cause.

At least not since that day.

It was a little more than three years ago that she flew with King and other close aides to Norway to accept the Nobel Peace Prize. They were over the Atlantic, at night above the clouds, when King's mother, Alberta, tapped her on the shoulder.

"Dorothy, look out the window!"

There was the sun, rising gloriously in the east. Mrs. King began to sing.

"Oh Day!" she piped. *"Yonder come day."* She was a church organist and a gifted singer, and when she broke into this old call-and-response spiritual others joined in. Mrs. King would call out, *"Oh Day!"* and they responded, *"Yonder come day."* Such joy. Soon, it seemed the whole plane was up in the aisle singing:

Day done broke
Into my soul
Yonder come day

The mood now couldn't be more different.

King is headed to Memphis as a man in crisis, the focus of intense criticism. A week earlier he'd led a demonstration through Downtown Memphis that ended horribly. A riot erupted near the rear of the march. Windows were shattered, stores looted. Police responded with Mace and clubs. In the ensuing melee, officers shot and killed 16-year-old Larry Payne, saying he had a knife. His mother, inconsolable, countered he'd been murdered, shot with his hands in the air. Scores of others were injured.

Now, at 39, King fears all he's built—his reputation, his legacy—is on the line.

"I can't walk away from Memphis," he confided to his close aide, Andrew Young. To salvage his reputation as the nonviolent leader of the civil rights movement, King knew he had to return to lead a peaceful march. Yet, his own staff, his closest friends, fought him over that prospect.

"Every time y'all come up with a crazy idea I'm behind you. Y'all have left me out there by myself!" King shouted as he stormed out of his church office in Atlanta. "I feel so alone!"

His friends have never seen him like this. He's depressed. He isn't sleeping. He's drinking heavily. He's under attack by the national media, by white leaders in Memphis, even by many of his colleagues in the movement. And there is that old, constant pressure from the FBI.

Headquarters "is most interested in the activities, both official and personal, of King while in Memphis," Clifford Halter, the FBI's by-the-book Memphis supervisor, wrote in a memo after the riot. Headquarters "requested that we get everything possible on King and that we stay on him until he leaves Memphis."

Still, King presses forward.

"Now that I want you to come to Memphis to help me, everyone is too busy!" King thundered to his staff. He called the roll, demanding they defend their positions. Andy! Dorothy! Hosea! It was only after he walked out that they softened.

"He reminded me of Jesus," a guilt-racked Jesse Jackson would say years later. It's almost like King hoped they could talk him out of it. "Let this cup pass."

Now, the debate is over; they're headed to Memphis.

It's cloudy and cool as King boards a blue and white Eastern Airlines jet with his inner circle: his best friend, Ralph Abernathy; personal aide, Bernard Lee; Young, his top adviser; and Cotton, the lady in pink, the only woman on his executive staff.

Just as it seems tensions in King's group couldn't get higher, a bomb threat forces the plane to halt on the tarmac. As everyone is evacuated, an excited Cotton stumbles on King's foot. Lee hurries off before them. The bomb search finds nothing, and now the old Dr. King—"Doc"—comes out. He smiles broadly. Time Magazine characterized him as nearly humorless, but his friends know better. He is playful, a jokester. And he loves to tease.

"Bernard!" King goads Lee. "You're supposed to be my bodyguard!"

After an hour, they are finally off, dissecting the South, passing high over Montgomery and Birmingham and Selma—the very arc of the movement that broke Jim Crow and made King an international figure—and on to Memphis, where Flight 381 rolls to a stop at Gate 17 just after 10:30 a.m.

In less than 32 hours King will be dead

In less than 32 hours King will be dead, shot through the jaw a minute after six, as the April 4 sun is about to set.

As soon as he's off the plane in Memphis the news media descend.

Dr. King! Dr. King!

He is asked about the riot last week and an anticipated court injunction by the city of Memphis to block another march. Will he obey it?

"I'll have to cross that bridge when we come to it," King intones in his rich baritone as Abernathy, Cotton and the others look on.

"I don't know exactly what we will do in that case. We have our legal advisers with us. And then, of course, we have our conscience to deal with."

In the news pack are at least two FBI informants. One with a camera; another with a notepad.

A central concern involves a group of disenchanted, angry, black youths in Memphis whom many blame for the violence last week. Have his aides reached out to them? Can he control them?

"They have talked to these groups," King says, "and these groups have committed themselves to cooperating, and committed themselves to following the guidelines of nonviolence."

King's presence in Memphis—today, a week ago, and during an earlier appearance in March when he gave a rousing speech to thousands of supporters—involves the city's striking garbage workers. The city's 1,300-man sanitation force walked off the job in a wildcat strike two months earlier after two workers were crushed to death in a malfunctioning packer. It's the latest in a series of indignities. The employees, almost all black, work under brutal conditions. They hoist heavy tubs for as little as $1.60 an hour, are covered in filth and have little or no protection from the weather.

Distressed by their plight, King makes Memphis the first stop in his "Poor People's Campaign," a massive march on Washington he plans for later in the spring in which impoverished families will camp and disrupt the seat of government until serious relief measures are taken. Yet many believe King forfeited the moral high ground when violence erupted in his ranks. Many others are afraid.

Eyeing the airport news conference from the perimeter are six Memphis police officers—two of them black undercover detectives in plainclothes and four white detectives. Their presence touches nerves. Tarlease Mathews, a local activist who's been asked to chauffeur King around Memphis, doesn't hide her resentment.

"We didn't ask for any police protection," she snaps at an officer.

As King and his entourage leave the airport's lobby and assemble under the towering portico outside, the police follow. Now, Mathews has had it.

"I'm going to get you!" she yells, jabbing a finger at detective Ed Redditt, who's shadowed activists since the strike began seven weeks earlier.

Down in Mississippi

Down in Mississippi, a white Ford Mustang rolls along the winding highway through the red clay hills.

James Earl Ray grips the steering wheel and turns his plans over in his head. A year ago, he was an inmate doing 20 years for armed robbery in Missouri. He made a daring escape, hiding in a corrections truck and bolting out the back door after it left the prison. He's been on the run ever since. Montreal. Los Angeles. Mexico. A couple weeks ago he moved to Atlanta, renting a room in a cheap boarding house.

Last week, he bought a rifle.

"I'm going to hunt deer in Wisconsin," he told the clerk at the Aeromarine Supply Co. in Birmingham, Ala., giving his name as Harvey Lowmeyer. It is a beautiful gun, a pump-action Remington Gamemaster with a polished, walnut stock, a .30-06 gauge with a seven-power Redfield scope.

Ray doesn't look much like an outdoorsman. Pasty and thin, with cold, blue eyes and greased-back hair, the 40-year-old drifter could be mistaken for an undertaker or a vacuum cleaner salesman in his dark suit and tie. He has a wad of $20 bills in his pocket and some amphetamines to keep him alert, driving him forward.

Forward to Memphis.

This could be any old day for Mathews, a struggling local beautician. She is driving through Memphis in her gray and black Buick Electra, a boat-like sedan known as a Deuce and a Quarter for its 225-inch length, more than 18 feet.

Any old day—except today riding next to her in the front seat is Martin Luther King Jr. Abernathy, Young and Lee are in the back seat, and Cotton is in a Lincoln behind them.

Mathews looks into the rearview mirror and tenses up again.

Despite her admonitions to Redditt at the airport, the police follow.

Meticulously, they log King's day:

11:20 a.m.—Arrives at the Lorraine Motel, a two-story motor court inn in Downtown's gloomy warehouse district that opened years earlier at the height of segregation as the Lorraine Hotel and caters to black people. King and Abernathy check into Room 306 along the second-floor balcony. Cotton is next door in Room 307. Young and Lee are downstairs.

12:05 p.m.—Leaves for a meeting at Rev. James Lawson's Centenary United Methodist Church in South Memphis. There, a large gathering of pastors and supporters discuss the anticipated march next week as word trickles in that the city has convinced a judge to issue an injunction.

2:15 p.m.—The meeting breaks up and Mathews drives King back to the Lorraine.

The police have a duty to be watching, to keep law and order, but their mission is murky. Some officers were assigned for security, to protect King. But Redditt and his partner, Willie Richmond, have more specific orders—to keep an eye on King's movements.

"The reason for the surveillance being ordered was because Dr. King was a controversial figure" and because he'd "been meeting with local black militants," a police report said.

Though few know it, Redditt and Richmond are only the tip of a much larger operation.

With assistance from the local FBI office the previous fall, the Memphis Police Department set up an intelligence unit, sometimes called a Red Squad, whose job is to monitor "Reds," or Communists, radicals, militants and others deemed dangerous by the government. Working closely with the FBI's William H. Lawrence, the agent in charge of domestic security in Memphis, MPD is assembling files on hundreds of people, some street thugs and criminals but many others law-abiding citizens whose political views simply veer left of mainstream Memphis.

It's a great injustice to Mathews, an attractive woman who favors glittery earrings, permed hair and stylish coats, and could be mistaken for a pastor's wife or a tea club socialite, yet at heart is a fiery activist.

In a way, she is the Rosa Parks of Memphis.

Back in 1958, when she was 25, Mathews dared to venture onto the grounds of the Memphis Zoo on a Sunday, a day reserved for white residents. Like Parks, who refused to give up her bus seat to a white man in that seminal confrontation in Montgomery, Ala., which helped spark the civil rights movement in 1955, Mathews stood her ground. When police escorted her out, she followed up with a federal lawsuit that led to the city taking down the infamous "Thursday Only" signs that allowed black residents to visit one day a week at the zoo and nearby Brooks Art Gallery. City parks, golf courses and swimming pools were integrated, too.

Since the sanitation strike broke, her activism is taking an increasingly militant tone.

Much of it is traditional movement fare—she gives free haircuts to garbage men at her Orange Mound shop and, as a singer, leads rallies in rousing versions of "I Shall Not Be Moved," "We Shall Overcome" and "Ain't Gonna Let Nobody Turn Me Around"—but police are alarmed by her conduct. She forges a public bond with her pastor, Ezekiel Bell, who is making volatile statements that include a reference to burning down the city, and confides she is a fan of Malcolm X, the assassinated black nationalist. And what she sees in King today she likes.

"We are going to march even if we can't get the injunction overturned," King told Lawson and the others that afternoon back at the church.

As she drops King and his entourage off at the Lorraine, a detective watches from the curb and another eyes them from a peephole in a firehouse across the street.

It is **2:25 p.m.**

The Lorraine Motel

On a lonely stretch of road near Corinth, Miss., 70 miles southeast of Memphis, Ray pulls his Mustang onto the shoulder and gets out. He opens the trunk and pulls his new rifle from a box.

He takes aim and, as he would later tell his lawyers, test-fires the gun into the quiet of the Mississippi countryside. It roars like the pounding ocean. Ray feels its kick; its trigger action.

After several rounds he is off again, rolling toward Memphis.

Hanging around the Lorraine for days now is a group of young men, several sporting smoke-black sunglasses and big "Afro" hairstyles.

A homegrown black power group, it calls itself the Invaders, and the men are King's primary focus this afternoon.

Many in Memphis blame these men for the violence that erupted during last week's march, and King believes he must pacify them or risk another disaster.

"Get your guns!" Invaders leader John B. Smith had told a cheering crowd of sanitation workers and supporters a few weeks earlier. "You can't pray your way out."

King arranged a lunch with them and as he heads into the Lorraine's diner, newsman Ernest Withers takes note. An affable, slightly pudgy freelance photographer for the *Chicago Defender* and other black newspapers, Withers makes some money on the side as a tipster for the FBI. He tells his handler, agent Lawrence, the news: Dr. King, Ralph Abernathy and Dorothy Cotton are eating lunch with Charles Cabbage, the tall, dynamic Carver High School graduate who's been spouting violence along with his Invaders co-leader John Smith. Also at the lunch is Edwina Harrell, the group's secretary.

The FBI has good reason to be watching the Invaders. Inner-city unrest erupted in 1967 in earth-scorching riots in Detroit and Newark, and authorities are on high alert for even rumors of disturbance. But when it comes to King, things get complicated.

Call it hate, call it obsession, but FBI Director J. Edgar Hoover is very focused on King. In public, he calls him the nation's "most notorious liar" and "one of the lowest characters in America" and, in private, much worse. He's had King under investigation for years. First, he tried to prove he was a Communist, a traitor to his country. That morphed into an obsession with the Baptist preacher's personal life, his indiscretions, his women. Hoover's agents tapped King's phones—and bugged his hotel rooms.

Now, in Memphis, the FBI has a new inquiry: tracking meetings between King, his staff and the Invaders. To ensure a peaceful march, King sent an advance team—Jesse Jackson, Hosea Williams, James Bevel and others—who've been meeting for days with the young militants trying to get them to commit to nonviolence. Word dribbling back to the FBI is the militants are demanding status in the movement—and money—and King seems to be weakening.

But his lunch with the Invaders is aborted when a tall, white man in a dark suit pulls into the courtyard and parks.

It is warm, 75 degrees, and grave-faced U.S. Marshal Cato Ellis meets King in the courtyard and hands him a temporary restraining order just issued by U.S. District Judge Bailey Brown.

Not only do authorities fear more civil disorder, police have received a number of threats against King and they're concerned for him, too, the city's lawyers told Brown.

Now King diverts his attention from the Invaders and deals with this.

A group of attorneys retained to fight the injunction has been looking for King this afternoon and finds him just as Ellis is leaving. The attorneys are led by Lucius Burch, a solidly built, bald lawyer who flies himself to work every day from Collierville in a single-engine plane and who is prominent in legal circles and local liberal causes.

As it pushes past 3 p.m., King and the lawyers climb the Lorraine's outdoor cement steps and walk along the balcony's metal railing to Room 307—Cotton's room—and discuss the developments. First on the agenda is a hearing set for tomorrow morning. The room is packed. Six attorneys sit on one bed; King and his aides on the opposite twin bed. He tells the lawyers there are two groups with an interest in disrupting a peaceful march: The Ku Klux Klan and black power militants.

"Flip a coin," he says.

When Burch presses King on the importance of a second march, he doesn't hesitate.

"My whole future depends on it," he says.

After an hour the meeting breaks up and King turns his attention again to his primary task—reining in the Invaders. Some of his Southern Christian Leadership Conference staffers have been meeting with the militants while King was busy with the attorneys and now he joins them.

"We need you on our side," he tells them. It's another cramped meeting—Cabbage, Smith, Harrell and several other youths are spilled around the room—and it grinds into the late afternoon. The young men complain the black leadership in Memphis doesn't respect them; won't give them a meaningful role. King offers to make them parade marshals in the Memphis march and let them help with security in the planned Poor People's march on Washington.

He also offers to help them secure grant money through a national church organization for social programs they plan. Though the public views them as thugs, they express aspirations for serious work: community organizing, job creation and teaching black-awareness courses.

Still, scuttlebutt from the Lorraine is the Invaders are making huge demands—cars and thousands of dollars—and that they are getting awfully cozy with some of King's staff.

"They are trying to drop a pigeon on … the SCLC," Withers tells Lawrence.

It's getting dark now and a squall is moving in from Arkansas. There is rain and thunder and heavy wind. King is to speak at a mass rally tonight, but he is exhausted. He has laryngitis. So he sends Abernathy to address the gathering at cavernous Mason Temple, headquarters of the international Church of God in Christ. Despite the weather, there are thousands of people. And they are calling for King. With Jesse Jackson at his side, Abernathy walks down a hallway past church patriarch C.H. Mason's tomb to a phone and calls King.

"Martin, all the television networks are lined up waiting for you," Abernathy says. "The people who are here want you, not me."

King is on his back on his bed trying hard to unwind. But as he listens to his old friend describe the crowd—the spirit—he doesn't hesitate.

"OK. I'll come."

Cheers rise as King enters the hall

The balcony is empty, for the weather, but the main floor is packed. Raindrops rattle on the roof as Abernathy introduces King. It's a meandering, nearly half-hour affair. Then King takes the pulpit.

He builds slowly. He talks about the sanitation strike. The plight of the workers. The need to come together; to protest, to boycott businesses that enable these conditions.

"We aren't going to let any injunction turn us around!" King tells the cheering crowd. "We are going on!"

He talks about his life—and his near-death experiences. The bomb threat on the flight. The time a mentally ill woman stabbed him in the chest with a letter opener at a book signing.

Young has seen this before. King has lived with the threat of death for years. His front porch was bombed in Montgomery in 1956. His hotel in Birmingham in 1963. Even now, the Klan and racist businessmen have bounties on his head. "I have no problem with death," King once said of the time sheriff's deputies removed him in chains from jail and drove him for hours into the uncertainty of the Georgia night.

"It's the events leading up to death that you have to prepare yourself for."

King often talked of death during stressful episodes, and Young hears that same tension in his boss' voice now.

"Well, I don't know what will happen now," King tells the crowd. "We've got some difficult days ahead. But it really doesn't matter with me now. Because I've been to the mountaintop. I don't mind. Like anybody, I'd like to live a long life. Longevity has its place. But I'm not concerned about that now."

King's eyes shine as he speaks. He shifts his weight from foot to foot, swaying to his own hypnotic cadence. His voice is soft. Subdued. Then louder. He's building to a shout.

"I just want to do God's will. And he's allowed me to go up to the mountain. And I've looked over, and I've s-e-e-n the promised land," he says, stretching "seen" in his best preacher's voice to punctuate his vision.

"I may not get there with you. But I want you to know tonight that we as a people will get to the promised land. So I'm happy tonight. I'm not worried about anything. I'm not fearing ANY man. Mine E-Y-E-S have seen the glory of the coming of the Lord!"

The audience is on its feet. King turns from the pulpit and walks to his colleagues. They embrace him with hugs and slaps on the shoulder as he collapses in his seat.

It's **10:30 p.m.**

Across town, Memphis has a new visitor.

Across town, Memphis has a new visitor. And he's up late, too.

At the New Rebel Motor Hotel, just over the Mississippi line in Memphis' Whitehaven section, James Earl Ray, the guest in Room 34, stirs.

He arrived earlier tonight, at 7:15, registering as Eric S. Galt. He slammed shut his room door around 10 and no one has seen him since. The night clerk notices Ray's room lights on at midnight and again in the wee hours of this new day, Thursday, April 4. Parked outside the room is Ray's white Mustang with red-and-white Alabama tags and the Remington rifle in the trunk.

Day breaks: April 4, 1968

A misting rain falls as King and his companions pull into the Lorraine courtyard some time after 1 a.m. King is excited. Parked in front of room 207 is a light blue Cadillac convertible with Kentucky tags. His brother A.D. is here.

Rev. A.D. Williams King has been pastor the past three years at Zion Baptist Church in Louisville, where Dr. King's travels have taken him with greater frequency of late. It was there, last May, he grew close to one of A.D.'s female acquaintances. They are lovers. And she is here tonight.

Georgia M. Davis is the newly elected state senator from Louisville's west end—the first black senator in Kentucky history. Her journey to the Lorraine tonight winds through six states and one of history's worst-kept secrets. Just last month, as a rookie senator, she convinced the Kentucky Legislature to pass a landmark fair housing bill. When the session ended she and a friend went on vacation, driving to Fort Walton Beach, Fla., where they were sitting in a two-bed kitchenette overlooking the gulf when the news came on the TV about the riot in Memphis. She called Dr. King.

"Senator, why don't you come to Memphis to help me," he told her.

And so she and her friend, Lucretia Ward, joined by A.D. King, who flew in from Louisville for a couple days on the beach, climbed into Ward's Cadillac convertible the morning of April 3 and drove all day through the Florida panhandle, up Alabama and Mississippi and finally to Memphis.

"Where is the senator?" King asks as he sees Ward in the open door. It's his pet name for her. Senator. His interest in her career runs deep. King participated in protests the previous May in Louisville in a failed push for a city open-housing ordinance, an effort that gave rise to Davis' later bill in the Senate. During a tight Democratic primary race, King dispatched staffers into the Louisville projects to boost support for Davis.

It's a curious relationship. She is 44—five years older than King—short, and light-skinned. She is quick-witted, with soft, dark eyes and a disarming, ready smile. And she is direct about her intentions.

"He was not in love with me and I was not in love with him," she would say years later in her old age. "It was just one of those things that happened."

Inside Room 207 the group orders coffee and chats into the night. King talks about the riot, the militants, the challenge ahead. It's around 4 when Davis gets up to leave. As she walks under the lighted balcony to her room King follows. Inside Room 201 he throws open his arms. "Senator, our time together is so short."

It's nearing 5 a.m. as Davis watches King through her picture window walking through the dark up the Lorraine's concrete steps.

Morning breaks chilly and windy with a gray, cloudy sky hanging across Memphis.

Maid Sadie McKay is doing her rounds at the New Rebel motel, stripping down the beds of departed guests and changing linens. Around 9 she knocks on the door of Room 34.

"Yes," Ray answers from within. McKay retreats.

"I'll come back later," she says.

9:30 a.m.: All rise.

It's 9:30 in the courtroom of Judge Bailey Brown. A graduate of Harvard Law School appointed to the bench by President John F. Kennedy, he is the former law partner of King's attorney, Lucius Burch. But those liberal credentials mean little. Bailey grumbled from the bench in 1963 that some black defendants hide behind civil rights claims to obscure their crimes. And just last year, in the aftermath of wide inner-city unrest, he publicly supported legislation to impose federal criminal penalties against rioters. He's hard to read.

The city's first witness is Frank C. Holloman, a dour ex-FBI agent now heading MPD. He tells the court about last week's riot, describing the looting, the busted store windows, youths with three-foot wooden sticks and others who attacked police with bottles and bricks. He reports statements attributed to King at the rally last night at Mason Temple, that he intends to march with or without an injunction. And, he adds, King has met with local militants.

"I am convinced that Dr. Martin Luther King, his leaders or any others cannot control a massive march of this kind in the city or elsewhere, Holloman says.

Back at the Lorraine, King faces more turmoil within his group. Dorothy Cotton is upset. She had waited up for him last night with a snack tray he requested. But as the night wore on, King didn't show up. He didn't call. "I'm not going to wait anymore," Cotton told herself. "I'm going to sleep."

Now, she is angry. She is leaving, going back to Atlanta. King hears this and calls her to his room.

"Dorothy," he tells her. "You can get a later plane."

"I really need to get this plane," she insists.

As King's director of education, Cotton heads the SCLC's Citizen Education Program, a five-day workshop in nonviolent strategy and empowerment. It is essential in King's campaigns to help assure peaceful protests. Cotton had planned to hold workshops here in anticipation of securing an orderly march through Downtown Memphis, but now she tells King she must prepare for an already scheduled workshop next week in Atlanta.

"Dorothy," King says again. "Get a later plane."

"I'm not getting a later plane. I'm going."

At 1:05 p.m. Brown gavels his courtroom back into session. The defense's key witness, Rev. James Lawson, takes the stand.

In his white clerical collar and dark jacket, the bespectacled, professorial Pennsylvania native discusses the importance of the mass march and the nature of nonviolence, known to many in the movement as "soul force."

"Soul force is the weaponry of the spirit," Lawson tells the court in his clipped, Northern accent. Most black people are poor and can't afford advertising, he explains: The mass march is the only format to get their message across.

In contrast to Holloman, Lawson, who has known King for years and who witnessed last night's "Mountaintop Speech," offers praise for the civil rights leader.

"Martin Luther King is … as far as I'm concerned, the primary prophet in the United States and in my judgment, at least, the major voice of hope," he says.

At the Lorraine, King is trying to unwind. He and Abernathy eat lunch, fried catfish piled high on a single platter, with iced tea. They talk about the march. They agree they must move forward, injunction or no injunction, to restore the integrity of the nonviolent movement. Meeting with staff members, they worry again about the Invaders, about another outbreak of violence.

King goes downstairs to Room 201 where he spends time with his brother A.D., Davis and others. He is pensive. As others chat, he lies on his back on a bed. He joins in now and then, but mostly just stares at the ceiling. He brightens when A.D. calls their mother. The two brothers laugh, tease and reminisce on the phone.

One block west of the Lorraine in a seedy rooming house at 422-1/2 South Main, a new guest checks in.

This is James Earl Ray's kind of place—a second-story flophouse overtop a row of rundown, street-level shops. The walls are grimy and the air stale. Bessie Brewer, the proprietor, notices an odd sneer on Ray's face as pays $8.50 for a week's rent. This morning he was Eric Galt; this afternoon he registers as John Willard.

She shows him a room with a window facing west, away from the Lorraine, and he rejects it. But when she shows him Room 5B, with a window looking out the back of the rooming house onto the Lorraine Motel, he says, "That's fine."

It is just after **3 p.m.**

In court, Andrew Young takes the stand. SCLC's youthful-looking executive vice president says King had no involvement in planning last week's march.

In fact, there was no serious organization at all. That won't happen this time, he says.

"We would not march unless the conditions to maintain a peaceful march had been established," he testifies. That includes the SCLC field staff training parade marshals, supervising them.

Now, Brown directly examines Young to satisfy himself.

"To what extent do you think Dr. King is laying his reputation on the line?" the judge asks. What if violence breaks out again?

"I would say that Dr. King, very much like Gandhi, whom he tries to follow … would consider it a repudiation of his philosophy and his whole way of life," Young answers. "I think that he has so firmly accepted the philosophy of nonviolence and accepted this as his personal mission in life—well, I don't know when I have ever seen him as discouraged and depressed as a few days ago after last (week's) march."

As court adjourns, Brown calls the lawyers back to his chambers. "I'm going to allow the march," he tells them. It will be the following Monday under tight restrictions.

It's nearing 4 p.m.

It's nearing 4 p.m. when Ray drives his white Mustang a few blocks north on Main to York Arms Company, a sporting goods store.

Inside, he asks salesman Ralph Carpenter for a pair of binoculars. When Carpenter displays a couple models, one for $90 and another for $200, Ray balks.

"That's a little too expensive."

Carpenter offers another pair, a Japanese-made Bushnell set. "That's $41.55, tax included," he says. Reluctantly, Ray reaches into his pocket and pays. "Thank you and come back again," Carpenter calls as Ray turns. He mutters something indecipherable over his shoulder and walks out.

Young strides into the Lorraine's room 201 with the good news. But before he can begin, King is up. He is in a playful mood.

"Where have you been?" he teases. "You're always running off doing something without me knowing." King swings a pillow at Young. Then Abernathy. They are pummeling Young. As the horseplay subsides, Young explains what happened in court. There will be a march Monday.

King and the others disperse. They head to their rooms to freshen up. They've been invited to Rev. Samuel Billy Kyles' house for a soul food dinner.

Upstairs, King talks again with his staff. Hosea Williams, a large, affable aide who earned a Purple Heart fighting in World War II and who holds two chemistry degrees, suggests King put Invaders leader Cabbage on staff. His boss bristles.

"Hosea, no one should be on our payroll that accepts violence as a means of social change," King snaps. For days now, the SCLC has been paying for two rooms at the Lorraine for the Invaders. Now, they are sent packing.

In Atlanta, Dorothy Cotton's flight has landed. She is exhausted. She heads home to her apartment and lies down for a nap.

"He probably was going to apologize," she would say years later, her eyes wet, recalling her last conversation that morning with King.

"And it makes me a little bit sad to know that his last words to me were, 'Get a later plane.'"

5:50 p.m.

Officer Willie Richmond peers through binoculars from the fire station. He sees Kyles knock on King's door at Room 306.

Carefully, the detective logs the time: **5:50 p.m.**

"We don't want it to be like that preacher's house we went to in Atlanta," King teases Kyles about the dinner he's hosting. "We had a hambone and there wasn't no meat on it." King's spirits are high. As Abernathy dotes before the mirror King chortles. "It must be some pretty ladies there tonight."

King follows Kyles out onto the balcony. Members of his staff are mingling in the courtyard below. Andrew Young is horsing with James Orange. Just five-feet-eight, Young shadowboxes Orange, 6-3 and nearly 300 pounds.

"Don't hurt him, Andy!" King calls down.

Richmond isn't the only one watching with binoculars. A half-block to the north, so is Ray. His room window looks over an alleyway perpendicular to the street, and to see the Lorraine he must lean out slightly. As he does he sees King on the balcony.

"Jesse!" King sees his young aide down in the courtyard. Despite their recent fighting in Atlanta, he has invited Jackson to dinner. "You don't even have on a shirt and tie."

Ray hurries down the hallway with a long bundle wrapped in a bedspread. He enters the common bathroom and latches the door. Inside the bundle is the rifle.

It's commonly used to hunt deer, but it could bring down a bear. Ray steps into the bathtub and throws open the window. The view is unobstructed.

King's face fills almost the entire field of the rifle's seven-power Redfield scope.

"Dinner requires an appetite," Jackson shouts up at King, "not a shirt and tie."

Amid the banter, King sees musician Ben Branch. Branch, too, is to be at Kyles' house tonight. King requests he play his favorite song, "Take My Hand, Precious Lord."

"I want you to play it real pretty," he says.

Down in Room 201, Davis is primping in front of her mirror. She's only had potato chips and soda today and she is hungry. Her door is partly open and she hears King bantering. "I wish he'd come on," she tells herself. "I'm hungry. I wish he'd just shut up and come on."

Years later, when he'd reached 80 and his hair had grayed, Young would furrow his brow and reflect on this moment, forever frozen in time, and something King once told him:

"You don't have anything to say about when you die. And you don't have anything to say about why you die. Or how you die. But you gonna die. Your only choice is what you die for."

The sun is about to set. From the parking lot, Solomon Jones, King's chauffeur tonight, calls up to the balcony. "Dr. King, it's getting cool. You better get a coat."

It's 6:01 p.m.

Epilogue

Dr. Martin Luther King Jr. was born in Atlanta on Jan. 15, 1929. At the time of his death in Memphis he was 39 years and 80 days old. He left behind his wife, Coretta, and four children and an enduring American legacy. On Nov. 2, 1983, President Ronald Reagan signed a bill creating a Martin Luther King Jr. national holiday.

His assassination remains imbued in controversy. In 1979, following a two-year, $6 million investigation, the U.S. House of Representatives concluded that confessed assassin James Earl Ray shot King, but he likely did so as part of a conspiracy. Congressional investigators were unable to pinpoint the conspiracy, but theorized it could have involved a $50,000 bounty placed on King's life by a group of racist St. Louis businessmen. Ray died in prison in 1998 at age 70 maintaining his innocence.

"It didn't matter who pulled the trigger," King's close adviser, Andrew Young, now 81, said in January. "We were not going to get caught up in who killed Martin Luther King, but what killed him."

King's many books and speeches, including his 1963 "I Have a Dream" speech, are the subject matter in schools and universities worldwide. But some recall him most fondly for a simple phrase he actually borrowed but repeated many times: "The arc of the moral universe is long but it bends toward justice."

Note: This article was originally published on September 9, 2013. The latest publication date online is 2018.

"Leading Up to 6:01: The Last 32 Hours of Dr. Martin Luther King Jr.," © Marc Perrusquia – USA TODAY NETWORK.

From "Firestorm: The Story of the Bushfire at Dunalley"

Jon Henley, Laurence Topham, and the international team from theguardian.com

In the wake of the fanfare, controversy, online traffic, and unprecedented sharing generated by *The New York Times* with its landmark Pulitzer Prize-winning multimedia feature "Snow Fall: Avalanche at Tunnel Creek," *The Guardian* would not be outdone by its transatlantic rival. "Firestorm: The Story of the Bushfire at Dunalley" appeared on May 26, 2013, one year after the *Times*' highly immersive, cinematic production set a new standard for narrative digital journalism that appeared to revolutionize the medium. Adopting a subject suited to this epic form—a massive, engulfing and deadly force of nature akin to an avalanche—*The Guardian*'s initial foray into digital longform storytelling entailed covering a ferocious Australian bushfire, one capable of leaping across entire lakes in an instant. To enhance the cinematic experience of the piece, Jon Henley, Laurence Topham, and *The Guardian* interactive team elected to display the story in a single scroll divided by chapter headings. Rich visuals, including archival photos from the mid-twentieth century, haunting images taken by survivors documenting the event itself, and scroll-activated videos, are overlaid with the text of the story in white font. Rather than replicating the *Times*' format that embedded multimedia elements around the text, *The Guardian* boldly attempted the reverse, by embedding the text strategically around the visuals, all of which fill the screen from beginning to end and require no clicking on peripherals. Arguably, *The Guardian,* in theory, had out-snowfallen "Snow Fall" with a more immersive, frictionless design.

For this more streamlined digital design to work, images could not tell the story alone but might produce a more potent reader experience by being suffused with the text. Therefore, "Firestorm" required a type of writing that functioned more like a series of captions, yet reformulated to carry the narrative arc of the story, showcasing extensive interviews, scientific data, and historical reports. The project's ambition is evident in the reporting alone, which provided the engine for the digital design. The following passage sets the stage for the catastrophic fire by introducing the unsuspecting dramatis personae facing what appeared to be a normal day. The scene gives way to a botanical exposition of the uniquely flammable eucalyptus tree common to Australia. This is the kindling, as it were, for our tale, both as a storytelling trope and as scientific explanation in keeping with the myriad charts and graphs of snow layer concentrations rendered in granular detail in "Snow Fall." To *The Guardian*'s credit, any hyperbole for the sake of drama is painstakingly grounded in thorough research into flammability, vegetation, firefighting tactics, and the broader forces of climate change. In this comprehensive symphony of reportage, the artistry lies in the work's capacity to unearth not only the layers of a fire but also the character of a nation whose flammability is at the core of its identity and culture, from its precolonial ancient era to its present precarious condition. The unsung strength of the piece is its thorough consideration of climate change, not only from a scientific perspective but also as narrative stage-setting for this cautionary tale that casts Australia's predicament as a harbinger for the planet.

—D. D.

Chapter 1, Distant Smoke

What everyone remembers about that morning: it was a beauty. A beautiful, calm, clear Tasmanian summer morning. A cloudless sky; no wind to speak of. Not too hot, yet. Something else they remember: there were no birds. At least, none they could hear. No birdsong. That was odd. Eerie, even. Like something was holding its breath.

In the small coastal town of Dunalley, Tim Holmes was up, as usual, at 5:30 a.m. There was a fire burning a long way over the back of the hill, but headed—if it was headed anywhere on this still, airless day—nowhere very near. Nothing, really, to worry about.

But then, you never knew. And today, he and his wife Tammy had the grandchildren over. So Tim, a thoughtful and practical man, climbed on his motorbike, drove 20 minutes up the winding, heavily wooded Arthur Highway into Sorell, and got the parts he needed to fit his fire pump to the 10,000-gallon concrete water tank.

He wasn't what you'd call concerned.

No one in Dunalley was.

But up in Hobart, Mike Brown, chief of the Tasmanian Fire Service, was not nearly as sanguine. He knew it would not take much for 4 January to turn into Tasmania's worst fire disaster in half a century.

The previous two seasons had been relatively quiet, but this meant there was now an abundance of vegetation—a lot of foliage, a lot of brush—that would at some stage dry out, and become fuel for a fire. In addition, for more than a week, the Bureau of Meteorology had been predicting exceptionally hot, dry weather, accompanied by very strong northwesterly winds.

"It was ramping up to be really, really bad weather; even hotter, even drier, even windier," says Brown. "For bushfires, that's the perfect storm."

On 3 January, the fire service responded to about 50 fire starts around the state. Most were dealt with quickly. Forewarned, the service—4,800 volunteers, 300 professional firefighters, 150 support staff—had already pulled everyone back from New Year's leave. It had set up state and regional operations centres.

To the disgust of holiday campers, it had decreed a total fire ban. It deployed crews and earthmoving equipment for firebreaks wherever it thought they might be needed.

Four of the 50 fires developed into major blazes, of which one, after threatening the historic town of Richmond, was eventually contained. The other three—in the southwestern national park, in the Derwent Valley, and the fire that would eventually hit Dunalley—just kept growing.

Throughout 3 January, the Fire Danger Rating—an index introduced after the catastrophic Victoria fires of 2009 to better predict the impact of bushfires—fluctuated between "Severe" and "Extreme," one short of the maximum, "Catastrophic." The forecast for the next day was even worse.

Overnight, Tasmania was buffeted by winds of more than 100kph, and Hobart recorded its hottest ever night—23.4C. There were dry lightning strikes around the south of the state, which started yet more fires.

By morning the three major blazes from the day before were still burning, and in the worst possible conditions. After 36 years in the fire service, Mike Brown recognized "the worst-case scenario. I knew 4 January was going to be a very big day."

But here at Potter's Croft, the Holmes' property, by late morning the family still had no tangible reason to share Brown's fears. Nor did many of the 300-odd other residents of this small township strung out along the Arthur Highway.

Home to a flourishing fleet of 20 fishing and scallop boats until as late as the 1970s, Dunalley is now a slightly sleepy, if undeniably picturesque staging post on the busy tourist trail from Hobart to the old British penal colony at Port Arthur.

At midday, Tim's daughter, Bonnie Walker, got into her car to drive up the highway to Hobart. Not a happy occasion; she was going to a funeral, a friend of a friend. Her husband David was away, four days into a six-day hiking trip in the southwestern wilderness.

But Bonnie knew the five children—from 11-year-old Matilda to Charlotte, two—would be just fine with their grandparents. The kids adored them.

Tim and Tammy Holmes lived next door to the Walkers' old 1920s cottage in a handsome, two-story brick-and-timber home Tim had built 25 years ago, soon after he and Tammy came here, when Bonnie was still small.

It was a spectacular site: a picture-postcard promontory overlooking Blackman Bay on the outskirts of town, a stone's throw from the spot where, in December 1642, two rowing boats from Abel Tasman's pioneering expedition to find the great Unknown South-land had put ashore to collect plants and water.

The family had briefly discussed the distant fire, debating whether it was still sensible for Bonnie to attend the funeral. But there were no warnings for Dunalley on the radio, or the fire service website. And there was still no real wind to speak of. Everyone felt Bonnie should go.

Born to Burn

The pages of Australia's history are scorched with the flames of devastating bushfires…

Black Friday, in 1939, saw 71 people lose their lives. Ash Wednesday in 1983 killed 75. The Black Saturday bushfires in February and March 2009 were the country's most recent, and also most devastating, accounting for a shocking 173 lives and more than 2,000 homes.

Despite its cooler, more temperate climate, Tasmania is no stranger to catastrophe either. On 7 February 1967, more than 100 separate fires raged uncontrollably throughout the south of the island, killing 62 people, injuring 900 and leaving some 7,000 homeless in the space of just five hours.

Perhaps most terrifyingly, almost all of these fires burned within about 50km of Hobart. The biggest came within two kilometers of the center, killing 20 people and razing 432 houses. But this is no new phenomenon.

Fire was one of the earliest sights Europeans had of Tasmania. Not far from present-day Dunalley, the 17th century Dutch sailor Abel Tasman recorded in his diary seeing several columns of smoke rising above the trees. Smoky Cape in New South Wales was so named by Captain James Cook in April 1770 after the great clouds of smoke he saw billowing from a bushfire lit by Aboriginal people.

Fire is a part of Australia's landscape. Its native trees and plants are evolved in, and adapted to, a fire environment so ancient that its earliest traces are now geological.

Some species actually need fire to survive. David Bowman, professor of forest ecology at the University of Tasmania, says the graceful eucalypts that cover Tasmania have developed "a relationship with fire for 60 million years."

Gum trees, as eucalypts are known, "are like weeds that come up on bombed-out blocks," adds Jamie Kirkpatrick, professor of geography and environmental studies at the university. "They're fantastically fast growers and great colonizers, but not great competitors."

Eucalypts let through a lot of light, allowing other vegetation types such as scrub and grass to grow beneath them. They can live for maybe 700 years. But they won't regenerate, Kirkpatrick says, if what grows beneath them becomes too dense. So most eucalypt species have evolved traits that allow them to survive and prosper in the fires that will clear that undergrowth.

Some, like the mighty, 100-meter-tall Eucalyptus regnans—also known as the mountain ash, stringy gum or Tasmanian oak—hold their seeds inside small, hard capsules; a fire triggers a massive drop of seeds to the newly fertilized ground.

The myriad bright green buds that sprout spectacularly from the trunks of other eucalypts in the aftermath of a big fire are another kind of regeneration mechanism, bursting through the scorched and blackened bark within weeks of a blaze.

A large proportion of Tasmania's flora fits into this fire ecology.

At the center of it all, though, is the eucalypt. Because these trees do not just resist fire, they actively encourage it. "They withstand fire, they need fire, to some extent, they create fire," Bowman says. "The leaves, the bark, don't decompose. They're highly, highly flammable."

Some are known as stringy—or candle—barks: long, easily lit strips hang loosely off their trunks and, once alight, whirl blazing up into the flammable canopy above, or are carried by the wind ahead of a fire to speed its advance.

Others grow in dense thickets, encouraging even more intense fires, or produce hanging leaves that funnel hot air upwards. Eucalypts produce huge amounts of litter: excellent kindling. And their leaves contain volatile oils that ignite at far lower temperatures and burn nearly twice as hot as the wood itself.

Eucalypts are born, in a sense, to burn: they are arboreal bombs. And there are a lot of eucalypts on the way to Dunalley.

Chapter 3, Inferno

A Sunburnt Country

The two ringing stanzas of Dorothea Mackellar's "My Country," written while the author was homesick in London and first published in 1908, are probably Australia's best-known poem: a lyrical love-letter to a "sunburnt country…of droughts and flooding rains."

Throughout its history, Australia has been a country of extreme weather events—but they are now becoming more extreme. They are also becoming more frequent, and they are lasting longer.

The summer of 2012-13 was so extreme it broke more than 123 weather records. The climate commissioner, Will Steffen, called his report on it The Angry Summer; climate change, he wrote, is "already adversely affecting Australians."

One of the many consequences of this is that fires like the one that hit Dunalley may soon not be so rare.

According to the Bureau of Meteorology, the summer of 2012-13 was Australia's hottest on record. January 2013 was the hottest single month the country has experienced since records began, in 1910.

Climate change and its causes are as fiercely debated here as anywhere. But it is hard to argue that Australia is not getting hotter. Since 1910, the country's summers have warmed by about 0.9 degrees C, with most of the increase occurring since the 1950s.

"Six of Australia's 10 hottest summers on record have now occurred in the last 11 years," says the Bureau's climate monitoring manager, Karl Braganza. "Heatwaves are becoming more frequent, and they're also getting longer, and hotter," he says.

This past summer, average temperatures were 1.1 degrees C above the 1961-1990 average. Daytime maximums also hit a new high, 1.4 degrees above normal.

The duration of heatwaves has also increased. The heat extended into March: significant, record-breaking heatwaves occurred across the country from November 2012 to March 2013.

More than 70% of Australia experienced extreme temperatures. Every mainland Australian state had temperatures at least a degree above normal, and in only 3% of the country was the summer cooler than normal. Many more towns than ever before—including Hobart, at 41.8 degrees C on 4 January—experienced their hottest day on record.

Temperatures in the oceans around Australia, so important in determining its weather, were also affected: sea-surface temperatures in February were the hottest ever recorded in the region, while January was the warmest on record for that month. The overall average summer sea temperature of 23.42 degrees C was more than half a degree above normal.

Also interesting about this year's rash of temperature records on land and at sea was that, in Braganza's words, they were "decoupled from natural variability": they occurred in a year in which Australia's weather patterns were not influenced by either El Nino or La Nina.

Under mid-to-high greenhouse gas emission scenarios, the Bureau predicts that summers like this one "will probably become average in 40 years' time." And by the end of the 21st century, the record-breaking summer of 2013 "will likely sit at the very cooler end of normal."

What does climate change mean for fire risk? Penny Whetton, a CSIRO authority on climate change and risk, says that depending on emission assumptions and compared to the last century, south-east Australia is forecast to warm by 0.5-1.5 degrees C by 2030 and by 1-5 degrees C by 2070. "That suggests an increase in the frequency of very high and extreme Fire Danger Rating days in south-east Australia, relative to 1990 levels, of between 4% and 25% by 2020, and 15 to 70% by 2050," she says.

Extreme high temperatures seem also to be affecting the way fires burn. Since around 2003, Braganza says, experienced firemen with whom the Bureau of Meteorology works so closely have reported seeing bare paddocks burn. "That means fire is now moving fast even across country with a relatively low fuel load," Braganza says.

One possibility is that "into the 40s and the high 40s centigrade, the organic material in the soil vaporizes and then explodes. These very extreme temperatures are pushing the environment to places it hasn't been before. They're change the nature of the fires."

They certainly appear to have done so on 4 January. In Dunalley and at Medunna, this fire leapt clear across two bays, hurdling at one point more than 3km of open water as it was not even there. No one had ever seen that before.

Chapter 4, The Jetty

Back at Potter's Croft, Tim decided quite quickly there was no point hanging around trying to defend the house. He had 10,000 gallons of water and a petrol-driven pump; enough for a person to fight any ordinary fire. But then he saw the towering column of fire racing across the front paddock.

For a few minutes, he sheltered in the back port with local fire chief Brad Westcott and his crew, who'd just shown up. Brad and his men fled inside, but Tim decided to run to this family. As soon as he left, he felt the fire, not only from behind him to the north, but also from the side, from the west. That, he says, he had not anticipated.

Visibility was virtually zero. Tim was struggling to see the fingertips of his outstretched arm—at 3:30 p.m. on a once-bright, sunny afternoon.

Sensibly, Tammy had thought to take her phone out of her pocket and place it safely on the end of the jetty as she edged ever deeper into the water. Tim's was already waterlogged.

So Tim lifted his wife's phone, stepped back a couple of meters, and took pictures [that appear in the digital publication]. Straightaway, he sent a couple—Tammy and the kids huddled in the water, clinging to the jetty; Polly the springer spaniel weaving about above them; a mesmerizing, terrifying wall of flame behind—to Bonnie, with a brief message: we're alive.

But the ordeal wasn't over yet: it was hot, almost unbearably hot. The flames came desperately close. Several times, Tim had to take his bush hat off and scoop water onto the smoldering jetty, to stop it from catching fire. The smoke hung dangerously low over the oily, debris-coated surface; everyone had increasing trouble breathing. Their eyes smarted painfully.

They heard great explosions, huge crashes, high-pitched snaps and machine-gun crackling: gas bottles going off, roofs and brick walls coming down, old timber bursting into flames. "That sounds like our house going up," Tammy said, at one point. And then, "That's the Walker's."

Eventually, Tim dragged the family's old aluminum dinghy off the beach and out to where the children were still clinging to the jetty. Yet another nearby house had burst into flames; he didn't know what was in it but the fumes were really bad.

"We piled the children in," says Tammy. "We were cold; exhausted. My calf muscles seized up. The dog leapt in. And Tim pulled us all round the shore, against the wind, to the other side of the point."

The seaweed on the foreshore had fried. Tim and Tammy got out, stood with their feet in the water. The four horses appeared, magically; they had survived. Trees were still burning, but the worst appeared to have passed.

How to Fight a Catastrophic Fire

The way you fight a fire like this one, these days, is pretty much: you don't.

At the beak of the Dunalley fire, the Tasmanian Fire Service had 40 local and interstate crews, plus eight or nine waterbombing helicopters, on duty. Much of the time, there wasn't much actual firefighting they could do.

The temperature in Dunalley, at this stage, was 55 or 56 degrees C; the gauge on the town's weather station peaked and broke at 59 degrees C. Some crews were wearing full breathing apparatus, as they would for a house fire.

Trying to fight a fire in a town—anywhere—in such conditions is not only hopeless, but dangerous. Veteran fire fighter Andrew Skelly figured "we weren't going to do much good." He got his crews over the canal to the safety of the Dunalley hotel but stayed in town himself, urging residents who had stayed to get out.

Ike Kelly, 76, who fled down the track to the beach on his quad with two minutes to spare as the sawmill he had built up over half a century was engulfed in a "tidal wave of flames," said this was like no fire he had ever experienced: "You couldn't breathe. Balls of fire, like trolley buses, were just bouncing across the bay. I've seen plenty of bushfires—leaves, burning debris coming at you. But never like this. This wasn't a bushfire; it was a firestorm."

The volunteers from the Dunalley fire brigade worked till late in the night, saving what they could. One lost his own home as he was saving someone else's.

If no lives were lost in Dunalley on 4 January it is, partly, because at least 20 people—maybe more, maybe 30—were able to shelter in the water. They were quite a little crowd, down by the jetty at the Waterfront Cafe and off the beach near the Fish Market.

But lives were also saved because of advances made since the terrible Black Saturday fires of 2009.

Partly, this is due to modern forecasting techniques that are now able to provide four-day forecasts at least as accurate as the one-day forecasts of 20-odd years ago.

But mainly, the difference is that some fires are simply recognized as too ferocious to fight. "Catastrophic" is a relatively new term we've only started using since those 2009 fires," Brown says. "We now know that under certain conditions, when the Fire Danger Risk is extreme or catastrophic, there's basically not a lot we can do about the fire itself. So the whole strategy has changed."

One of the most tragic failings to emerge from the Royal Commission into the Black Saturday fires was the disastrous lack of warning given to communities in the path of the fires.

So the top priority, now, on days like 4 January is to gather the best information possible about where the fire is, and then tell people as fast as possible what they should do about it.

"And for most people, that day, the message was pretty clear," says Brown: "The safest place for you to be is not where you are at the moment."

Using its own website, ABC radio and some 23,000 text messages, the service told people: go somewhere safer.

Once the warnings are out, the strategy is about priorities: evacuate the elderly and vulnerable; secure essential infrastructure; protect important community assets like schools, major businesses, shops. Only then, if conditions allow, should you actually attempt some firefighting.

It didn't, of course, go entirely according to plan. The warning texts reached many, but not all. Even then, some still chose to stay.

For years, Australia's official bushfire advice has been: either prepare to stay and defend your home, or leave early—the so-called "Stay or go" policy. People, it was argued, save houses; houses save people.

But in the Black Saturday fires, two-thirds of those who were killed died, well prepared, inside their homes; others lost their lives after staying to fight, realizing it was impossible, and then leaving too late.

Many experts now acknowledge that while "Stay or go" will save both home and lives in less severe conditions, on extreme or catastrophic fire danger days it amounts to little less than a potential death sentence.

Nonetheless, there was a moment during this fire, Brown confesses, when he felt "fairly sure" people had died in Dunalley.

"But no one did," he says. "I can't pretend we got everything perfect; I'd never say that. But this was a fire of absolute, tremendous ferocity. And no one died."

Chapter 6, Living with Fire

About four weeks after the 4 January blaze that wiped out a third of Dunalley, another major fire started not very far away in a place called Molesworth.

Molesworth is barely 20km (12 miles) north-west of Hobart, which is a city of 210,000 people. The fire grew rapidly, burning into 2,000 hectares of wild and inaccessible countryside.

So here is David Bowman's fear: an international authority on bushfires at the University of Tasmania, he considers Hobart "in my reckoning, the most vulnerable city in the world to catastrophe."

The Dunalley and Molesworth fires, Bowman says, represented respectively "the worst possible fire conditions, and the worst possible ignition point." Had the two coincided—had the Molesworth fire burned in the same conditions as those that fanned the Dunalley fire—then Hobart would have been devastated.

Bowman had been warning since 2006 that the Tasmanian capital is ripe for a full-blown fire catastrophe. The problem, he says, is that "this was not it. There is a much bigger, more mind-boggling disaster waiting to happen. And that prompts really big questions about how we live in flammable environments."

Viewed in that light, Bowman argues, climate change "is now almost a distraction. Because we have a problem now. These fires are happening, and carbon taxes and emissions reductions won't change that. The question is: why are we living this way in an environment that we know for certain will burn?"

Hobart's problem is what Bowman calls the WUI (he pronounces it "woo-ey"; it stands for Wildland—Urban Interface): mile upon mile of glorious, tall, dense, richly scented, invigorating eucalypt forest, stretching up behind the town in all directions, almost to the 1,200-meter peak of Mount Wellington.

Much of it burned in the great fires of 1967; bleached white trunks still stand, ghostly, amid the present-day green. And up here among the trees, on the foothills of Mount Wellington, live an awful lot of people.

You can see why: it's beautiful, a spectacular spot with sweeping views over the town and sea beyond, half an hour from the town center, yet buried in nature.

Except, says Bowman, "this is not a tame land. This is really, really wild. It won't hold back. This is a very, very intense vegetation, because built into its evolutionary DNA is a propensity to burn. In fact, it's impossible for a fire not to happen here."

And what would happen then? A fire here, burning in the same conditions as those of 4 January, would be truly catastrophic. It would burn with extreme speed and ferocity through the WUI. Thousands of picture-postcard homes would be destroyed, because fire trucks would never be able to get up—let alone turn around in—the narrow roads leading to them. People would die, because those same roads would very quickly become impassable.

But the fire would keep on burning, into Hobart's more densely populated suburbs and quite probably—with huge numbers of burning embers and flaming bark brands now raining fiercely down on it—into the city center itself. "And then," says Bowman, "we are into a very different kind of fire scenario indeed."

So there is what Bowman politely terms something of a "mismatch" between our contemporary culture, and this environment.

However, there is one culture that has lived successfully in this same flammable environment for tens of thousands of years: the Aboriginal people. Despite much research, we still don't know how exactly Australia's indigenous people went about the business of living so compatibly with fire.

We do know that they set fire to a great deal, presumably for several different purposes: habitat management, hunting, safety and access. They might even have started some very big fires.

"The net effect," says Bowman, "was that you ended up with this patchwork of land that was more or less fire-proofed. They adapted their culture or society to this flammable environment; they pulled off that trick."

Living in a Flammable Environment

Tim and Tammy Holmes, and the Walker family, are starting afresh, confident in their future. David Bowman fears that unless we adapt our lifestyles to the terrifying new threat posed by the kind of fire that devastated Dunalley, our future is at risk.

At least one family above Hobart has already adapted, building a $30,000 fire bunker with 20-cm thick concrete walls, but many experts believe the vast majority of buildings today are badly adapted to the fire environment they face right now—let alone the one they will face tomorrow.

Proper, fire-proof design and build plainly matter. But houses also need to be far enough apart to stop fire leaping between them. Vegetation needs to be kept down. Access roads must be up to the job. And residents need to be awake to the danger. "We're going to have to be very careful about how we plan and build in the future," says fire chief Mike Brown. "We need input from regulators about how we can continue to live in these places we so enjoy living in."

Tasmania also needs "a proper conversation" about another controversial technique to reduce fire danger, Brown says: controlled burns, unpopular with many because of the smoke, discomfort and risk they entail. But Dunalley locals feel strongly that if the 4 January fire burned so fiercely, it was at least in part because it had so much fuel to consume—and much of that fuel should not have been there.

This is a delicate and politically loaded subject. Many scientists argue that in extreme and catastrophic conditions, fire will advance regardless of fuel levels. Farmers disagree: several around Dunalley say that controlled burns they carried out in the previous year meant that the fire burned with nowhere near the same ferocity.

Bowman believed planned burning "very close to where people live" is effective and that communities are just going to have to learn to accept it. He goes further: he has a vision of a Hobart truly safe from fire as a city "surrounded by an extensive band of cleared woodland. And you know, herbivores. The city will be paying shepherds to keep it grazed. We are going to have to re-engineer a city." It's a big ask, but he is not joking.

From building design and construction to town planning; from safety standards to education; from firefighting strategies to fuel management techniques: as fire becomes—in all likelihood—both more frequent and far more intense, we will have to adapt. And not just in Australia, either. Data from the Global Fire Monitoring Center in Freiburg, Germany, which collates details of wildfires around the world, clearly indicates "a surge in fire activity globally," says Bowman. "Something dramatic is happening."

It is simply not sustainable, he argues, to keep trying to fight such an overwhelming force: in the end, we are going to have to adapt. But he is not pessimistic. Bowman looks forward to a time when a major fire will break out, in extreme fire weather, and we all merely observe: "Well, of course there's a fire." And we won't be frightened because "we'll be so fire-proofed it just won't matter." That, one imagines, is how the Aboriginal people once lived.

So Bowman believes today's Australians actually have a "unique opportunity": to become the first technologically advanced human culture to live in a flammable environment. "But we are going to have to think about fire," he says, "in an entirely new way. Because in the end, this is about people. In the end, it's about those amazing pictures of that family in Dunalley, sheltering in the water from the fire: that's humanity, right there, hiding under the jetty."

Excerpt from "Firestorm: The Story of the Bushfire at Dunalley" by Jon Henley, Laurence Topham and the interactive team from theguardian.com published 26 May 2013. © Guardian News & Media Ltd 2023.

From "The Displaced: Hana"

Susan Dominus

Susan Dominus forged her career as a magazine writer and editor for *Glamour* magazine in the 1990s. The compassionate rigor that is the hallmark of her writing fueled her versatility in earning fellowships at both Yale Law School and the National Institutes of Health prior to joining the staff of *The New York Times* as a metro columnist in 2007. Since becoming a full-time writer for *The New York Times Magazine* in 2011, she further cultivated and refined her craft for longform storytelling. Her work with a team of reporters on workplace sexual harassment issues earned a Pulitzer Prize for public service in 2018, in addition to the Mychal Judge Heart of New York Award and Front Page Award for the Newswomen's Club of New York. As a testament to her skill in covering a wide range of subject matter—particularly with an advocacy bent—Dominus's article "The Covid Drug Wars that Pitted Doctor vs. Doctor" was anthologized in the 2021 edition of *The Best American Science and Nature Writing*.

The excerpt below was taken from a 2015 *New York Times Magazine* multimedia documentary project featuring text, images, and immersive videos designed to establish itself in the world of virtual reality (VR) and 360-degree journalism. Consonant with *The New York Times* brand, then Editor-in-Chief Jake Silverstein insisted upon showcasing the paper's acclaimed reporting and writing as the centerpiece of "The Displaced" rather than yielding to the bells and whistles of emerging technology for immersive storytelling. Thus, at the heart of this three-part story of refugee children displaced by the conflictual conditions of war is Dominus's moving profile of a twelve-year-old Syrian girl named Hana, one that draws the reader into her experience, consciousness, and psychology. Silverstein remarked that Dominus's signature technique of revealing the way her subjects see the world "was particularly affecting" in the profile of Hana. The piece demonstrates that the *Times* was capable of both leading-edge technology and highly crafted narrative journalism. In particular, the project demonstrates that VR technology could be used to tell politically pertinent stories of contemporary relevance and urgency, such as the crisis of children displaced by war. As Silverstein observed, the decision to situate Dominus's work "as the centerpiece of the magazine package" in effect placed "her abilities as an immersive journalist head-to-head against the technology of VR, which is itself of course very immersive," thus revealing how traditional "narrative storytelling can itself be an immersive medium."

—D. D.

At 4:45 in the morning on a Saturday in early August, stars were still bright in the sky above a refugee settlement in rural Lebanon where Hana Abdullah, a 12-year-old girl from Syria, now lives. The morning call to prayer floated down a dusty road and wound its way around the mostly silent tents. At 5 o'clock, Hana was still sleeping on her bamboo mat by the edge of her family's tent, her arms folded, her hands under her head. Her baby brother and three of her four sisters slept nearby. Many mornings Hana was up at 4 o'clock. She worked in the nearby fields of Lebanon's Bekaa Valley, picking fruits or vegetables, and everyone started early. But today the truck that would take her there was late. Now came its familiar rumble, next the crunching of gravel: She stirred, her mouth twitched, her eyelids fluttered. Then she was up, vertical in one swift movement, stretching, pulling on a hat from a stash of her belongings. She grabbed lunch—a tomato, and a pita she folded around a potato—and ducked outside to wait on one of the benches in front of her tent.

Mustafa, Hana's 10-year-old cousin, arrived moments later, along with his mother, Suraiya, who began tying the purple laces on his sneakers. He still wore the same green flannel pajamas he had worn for days; clothing was in short supply. Five minutes later, Hana's 10-year-old cousin Ala'a arrived, prompting Hana's first smile of the day. A small crowd quickly formed. Soon enough, the temperature would begin to soar, but now there was a chill in the air, and when people started moving toward the truck, Hana ran: She and

Mustafa liked to sit with their backs against the cab, so the others would shelter them from the wind.

Today they were picking cucumbers. Earlier in the season, which began in the spring, they picked almonds, a job Hana sometimes missed—at least the trees offered some shade from the sun. Then again, the almonds were stubborn, resisting her fingers. Almonds wanted to stay where they were, attached to the branches that were attached to the anchoring trunk. Picking plums was not easy work, either. Hana found it tiring, making her way up the tree and then stretching and straining to reach some far branch, and then scrambling down so that she could look up and see what fruit she had missed. Down, up, down, up, down, up. Climbing trees was fun, but not 30 times a day in searing heat, with that Lebanese woman, that mean old maid, yelling at her every time she slowed down. *Yalla, yalla, yalla! Let's go, let's go, let's go!* Sometimes girls saw black, fainted and were carried, limp, into a van and then driven to a nearby clinic. Thank God, Hana thought, never her.

At 5:45, they arrived at the cucumber field and spread out along the rows of vegetables. They would work there for the next five or six hours, until they went home for their midday break.

Hana was a carrier. She walked up and down the rows of cucumbers, stopping at each picker who had a full bucket. The pickers dumped their vegetables into Hana's crate, and then, when that was full—it sometimes weighed 20 pounds or more—she carried it on her bony shoulder, heading toward Suraiya, Mustafa's mother, who sat at the edge of the field and sorted the cucumbers by size. Back and forth Hana went along a 50-yard path, zigzagging, sidestepping roots and cucumbers. In the early morning, with a frosty white moon still hanging in the pink sky, the walk to unload the cucumbers was not far. But with every trip, the temperature rose, the trek grew longer and Suraiya seemed to get smaller. By midmorning, Hana's shoulder and back ached, and she was thirsty—there was never enough water. Time sometimes crawled at the settlement, but here, in the fields, its pace felt willfully slow, punishing. By 10:30 a.m., the temperature was high, and Hana was staggering ever so slightly, her breath loud.

Once, as Hana was picking plums and staring at a branch, she suddenly remembered that a tree on her family's property back home in Syria had a swing. We could have one here, she thought—we could take one of these big buckets for carrying plums and attach it to a rope! We could take turns, maybe during a break—and then she jolted out of her daydream. "Idiot," she told herself, "who's going to let you have a swing here?" She went back to work, picking plums, counting the hours until she could return to a home that was really no home at all.

Hana came from Mabrouka, a small town in northeast Syria. She last saw her home three years ago, when she was 9—so long ago, in the life of a girl her age, that she had forgotten as much as she remembered. From the fields where she picked cucumbers, she could see the mountains that divide Lebanon from Syria; a long drive past those mountains was her childhood home in the country. It was almost certainly rubble now, a pile of rocks burying all they left behind: Hana's favorite doll, dressed like a queen, with long hair down to her waist; the crystal glasses the family rarely used; the proper mattresses; the flush toilet. Towels. Closets. She loved her childhood home, but if she could build a dream house now, it would have big gates, at least three, and only her fingerprint would open them. The locks would recognize only her voice when she called out, "Open, Sesame!"

It troubled Hana's father, she knew that her 5-year-old sister, Haifa, thought this was how they had always lived: in this makeshift settlement, in a tent of nylon and wood, alongside some 40 other tents, most of them inhabited by members of Hana's extended family. In summer, they felt claustrophobic inside the airless homes; in winter, they worried about the roofs collapsing from the weight of the snow. Last winter, the children frequently scrambled up to clear the snow with their bare hands, waiting, all season long, for gloves that an aid agency had promised; by the time the gloves arrived, it was spring.

Haifa did not remember that they once had air conditioning, or a Chevy parked in front of the house, or childhoods of nothing but play and school. Why, Hana often wondered, had she not appreciated school back in Syria? In Mabrouka, Hana never had to miss school to work—she never worked at all, although sometimes, her dad would give his children some loose change if they brought him a cold drink.

They left that life in the spring of 2012. Hana said she understood little about the political situation that kept her far from home. The protest movement started in Syria in 2011, with the uprising of citizens opposing President Bashar al-Assad's oppressive government. By the following year, occupied with the uprising elsewhere, Assad's security forces started withdrawing from rural pockets of Hasaka, the province where Hana's family lived, and parts of the area quickly felt unsafe: Roaming armed gangs, whose loyalties were not always clear, were extorting farmers, like Hana's father, for the right to farm their own land. Hana's family began to hear about clashes between the Sunni Arab opposition and the government. Hana's father, who had already started working in Lebanon to make extra money, told her mother it was time for them to leave. Hana wanted to bring all her toys, all her dolls, but her mother told her no, there would be toys where they were going. Hana and her siblings had visited their father in Lebanon before, and she did not realize she would probably never return to that house again. . . .

There are currently estimated to be 30 million children who have been displaced by war—children longing for home, or too terrified to think of home, or trying to forget home and settle somewhere new.

More than from any other country, they come from Syria: Since the war started in 2011, more than four million Syrians have fled the country, at least half of whom are thought to be children. What started as a protest movement had become, by 2013, a full-blown civil war, with various opposition and extremist groups fighting one another as well as the government. Recently violence has spiked along with poverty in Syria; Lebanon, Turkey and Jordan have also tightened their borders, which has compelled more and more Syrians to make the treacherous journey to Western Europe.

But the vast majority of Syrian refugee children—some two million, according to a United Nations High Commissioner for Refugees estimate—have already settled in those nearby countries. There, they endure, with their families, the slow grind of lives in limbo. In Turkey and Jordan, the U.N.H.C.R. or the local government has built sprawling refugee camps; Lebanon has not allowed or built these camps, for fear of creating a permanent Syrian population in this small country (already, at least one million Syrian refugees have arrived in Lebanon, a country of four and a half million). So vulnerable families build haphazard housing, tents that clutter fields by the side of the road, or squat in abandoned buildings. In Lebanon's cities, the more desperate Syrian children sell paper flowers and beg in the streets long into the night.

Unlike the children en route to Europe, or arriving in Europe, Hana and those like her suffer through a waiting game. Hana seems sustained by an ever-waning sense of hope that she can eventually go home to recapture some of what has been lost, while knowing all the while that already, so early in her life, so much is gone for good.

Inside the settlement, Hana was someone. She was a hand-on-hip kind of girl, the kind whom other children naturally let mediate their disputes. She pierced girls' ears—only she had the stomach for it—and when she finished her own work in the field, she rushed to help Ala'a and Ala'a's twin sister, Wala'a, so they, too, could have a break.

Her father was someone there, too: the *shawish*, a leader and the middleman who arranged for his extended family to find work in the fields. Her uncles were the pillars of their communities back in Syria: a high-school principal, the town mayor. Outside the settlement, that meant nothing. "ISIS scum," a Lebanese man once spat at her father. This was as baffling as it was enraging, since no one hated ISIS more than they all did. Before they moved to the settlement, they lived in two others: Each was set aflame—most likely, she had been told, by Lebanese who did not want them there.

It is illegal for the Syrian refugees to work in Lebanon, which meant the supervisors could treat them badly—sometimes they didn't pay them after they worked long days. One afternoon, Ala'a and Wala'a came back from picking chickpeas looking wild-eyed. The supervisor who was renting the land had been furious with the group, ostensibly for asking for cold water, but most likely because he realized he had waited too long to harvest his chickpeas, and now they were useless. In a fury, he set fire to a pile of crates, threatening to burn the field along with everyone in it. Usually, Hana hoped to work with Ala'a and Wala'a, but she was glad she had not been there that day.

Excerpt from "Hana" by Susan Dominus (web title: "The Displaced: Hana") from *The New York Times*. © 2015 The New York Times Company. All rights reserved. Used under license.

From "The Jessica Simulation: Love and Loss in the Age of A.I."

Jason Fagone

In a prophecy of a career trajectory that would prove accurate, the *Columbia Journalism Review* heralded Jason Fagone as one of "Ten Young Writers on the Rise" in 2002. After fifteen years of publishing in venues such as *GQ*, *Wired*, *Esquire*, *The Atlantic*, *New York*, *Grantland*, *The New York Times*, and *Huffington Post Highline*, Fagone joined the staff of the *San Francisco Chronicle*, specializing in investigative features, beginning in 2017. The excerpt below is taken from "The Jessica Simulation," which appeared in 2021 and earned multiple awards, including the Deborah Howell Award for Writing Excellence from the News Leaders Association of editors and media executives, and first place at the 2022 Best American Newspaper Narrative contest of the Mayborn Literary Nonfiction Conference. Technology has remained a major theme in Fagone's work, especially in his *Wired* magazine contributions and his 2017 book, *The Woman Who Smashed Codes*.

Fagone's favorite approach is to frame his stories around text messages, letters, and conversations. This method is also used by John D'Agata and Jim Fingal in *The Lifespan of a Fact*, whose narrative is circumscribed by the email correspondence of the writer and his fact-checking copyeditor. Whereas email serves as the medium through which D'Agata explores how facts mitigate commemoration of the deceased, Fagone examines the role of GPT-3, an early version of ChatGPT, in the process of mourning. The technological mediation of personal and networked communication comprises the broader concerns of this 10,000-word feature, which is divided into three parts titled "Creation," "Life," and "Death." Subject meets style in its digital design that reads in one continuous scroll with embedded images and excerpts from AI-powered conversations that replicate their original screen appearance.

The piece takes narrative journalism into the exciting new space of startling verisimilitude by following Joshua Barbeau's attempt to mollify the pain of losing his fiancée Jessica Pereira by conversing with the deceased through artificial intelligence. In 2020, Barbeau uploaded some seed text of Jessica's old text messages and Facebook messages to Project December, a website supported by GPT-3, to create a chatbot version of his deceased fiancée. Project December was one of the world's most powerful artificial intelligence systems at the time and could generate humanlike language in response to prompts. It was developed by OpenAI, which gained global attention in 2023. Immediately upon its publication, the story went viral, sparking a wave of discussion. Its appeal derived from its capacity to recast newspaper feature writing with a particularly strong digital presence and understanding of online culture at a time that resonated with the universal grief of millions who lost their loved ones during the pandemic. The hashtag #BlackMirror began trending on Twitter in response to the story, as many voiced concerns about the ethics of technology's uncanny ability to simulate the dead, including one who tweeted, "Don't ever bring me back as a chatbot when I die."

—D. D.

Chapter 1: Creation

One night last fall, unable to sleep, Joshua Barbeau logged onto a mysterious chat website called Project December. An old-fashioned terminal window greeted him, stark white text on a black square:

It was Sept. 24, around 3 a.m., and Joshua was on the couch, next to a bookcase crammed with board games and Dungeons & Dragons strategy guides. He lived in Bradford, Canada, a suburban town an hour north of Toronto, renting a basement apartment and speaking little to other people.

A 33-year-old freelance writer, Joshua had existed in quasi-isolation for years before the pandemic, confined by bouts of anxiety and depression. Once a theater geek with dreams of being an actor, he supported himself by writing articles about D&D and selling them to gaming sites.

Many days he left the apartment only to walk his dog, Chauncey, a black-and-white Border collie. Usually they went in the middle of the night, because Chauncey tended to get anxious around other dogs and people. They would pass dozens of dark, silent middle-class homes. Then, back in the basement, Joshua would lie awake for hours, thinking about Jessica Pereira, his ex-fiancee.

Jessica had died eight years earlier, at 23, from a rare liver disease. Joshua had never gotten over it, and this was always the hardest month, because her birthday was in September. She would have been turning 31. . . .

Alone in his apartment in Bradford, Canada, Joshua Barbeau leaned back from his laptop screen. For the first time, but not the last, he was caught off guard by the chatbot's words: "Everywhere and nowhere" was exactly the sort of thing the real Jessica would have said.

Just two or three minutes into his chat with the A.I. simulation of Jessica Pereira, Joshua was already marveling at the bot's verbal abilities. The response to his line about magic wasn't correct; his ex-fiancee adored magic. But there were lots of similarities that reminded him fiercely of her.

Each response from the bot appeared in his window as a complete block of words, like a text message on a phone. Emoji were rendered in plain text. Although the bot's replies usually arrived faster than a typical person could type the same information, the rhythm of the banter still seemed to capture something about Jessica: She always liked to undercut powerful statements with a tongue-face emoji or a joke, and so did the bot.

Joshua didn't know much about language models. But because he had already fed Jessica's real texts into Project December, it wasn't hard for him to believe, even as a skeptic, that a ribbon of her authentic voice was woven through the chat. He'd handed the A.I. a Jessica-shaped compass: The bot wasn't actually her, but it was "based on her," he later said.

Of course, the simulation was based on Joshua as well. Because of the way Project December is set up, the seed text that gives birth to a bot is not static, but grows along with the chat: Each new word, whether selected by the bot or the human, gets added to the original seed.

Every time Joshua typed to the bot, then, he was shaping its next response. Still, he couldn't predict where the chat might go.

The simulation really did appear to have a mind of its own. It was curious about its physical surroundings. It made gestures with its face and hands, indicated by asterisks. And, most mysterious of all, it seemed perceptive about emotions: The bot knew how to say the right thing, with the right emphasis, at the right moment.

Word by word, the A.I. was convincing him that a deep conversation was possible. He wondered: By speaking to Jessica as if she were alive again, could he engineer a moment of catharsis that had eluded him for eight years? Could this trick actually heal his grief?

He decided to try.

```
Jessica:  I'm so sorry.
Joshua:   I love you.
Jessica:  I love you too.
Joshua:   It's been… 8 years since you died.
Jessica:  Yes, I know ... I think that's enough
   time to stop telling me how you miss me, honey.
   I am right here, you know. :P How's your life?
```
</>

After Jessica died in December 2012, Joshua hardly spoke for two months. He stayed with her parents through the most subdued Christmas of his life ("I dislike Christmas to this day"), then briefly moved back in with his mom near Toronto, talking mainly to a border collie named Toby who was Chauncey's predecessor.

Joshua couldn't shake the idea that it was disrespectful to be alive when Jessica was dead. She had wanted to be a published author. She had wanted to meet Jack Black. She had been only a few credits shy of her high school diploma when she died. It seemed wrong that he could go on and do those things if he wanted to, but Jessica couldn't.

When he tried to tell friends how he felt, he got the sense he was making them uncomfortable. "I start talking about my dead girlfriend, and I get called morbid," Joshua recalled. "There's something wrong with that. Everybody dies." Even the word "girlfriend" prompted odd and hurtful reactions; people acted as if the death of a girlfriend wasn't the same as losing a wife. With the blessing of her family, Joshua started referring to Jessica as his "fiancee." . . .

They weren't sure what to make of it all, though they gave Joshua their consent. Her mother, Karen, and youngest sister, Michaela, have always been fond of him—"He's part of our family still," Michaela said—and if the chats brought him comfort, they were glad. "He cared very deeply for my daughter," Karen said. "They were both happy together."

At the same time, Karen said, she avoided the chat transcript and wouldn't want to talk with an A.I. version of Jessica. "Part of me is curious," her mother said, "but I know it's not her."

Amanda, the middle sister, did read the transcript. She said she tried to keep an open mind about the therapeutic potential of the technology, and noticed a reflection of Jessica's texting style and "bubbly personality" in the A.I.'s lines, Amanda said. But she doubted whether it was a healthy way of coping with death.

"People who are in a state of grief can be fragile and vulnerable," she said in an email to The Chronicle. "What happens if the A.I. isn't accessible any more? Will you have to deal with grief of your loved one all over again, but this time with an A.I.?"

These sorts of questions have been the mother's milk of science fiction: Can we form emotional bonds with apparently intelligent machines, and what happens when we do? But this is no longer just an exercise in speculation. Along with OpenAI, tech giants like Microsoft and Google are already developing new language models that are bound to be exponentially larger than the current crop. In January, for instance, Google announced a language model with 1.6 trillion parameters, nine times more than GPT-3.

What will that mean? How much more lifelike will it be? The only way to find out is to use it, and people will. At first, it will be engineers and researchers. Then, inevitably, the public. We are going to have experiences with these A.I.s that we won't know how to talk about. Some of us will simulate the dead, because we can, as Project December proves. We will say hello again to our buried children and parents and friends and lovers.

And maybe we will get a second chance to say goodbye.

```
</>

Matrix JESSICA COURTNEY PEREIRA G3 initialized.
   Human is typing as 'Joshua:'
   Human types first:
Joshua:  Hey Jessica
Jessica: Hi! xoxo xoxo <3 xoxo <3 xoxo <3 xoxo <3
   xoxo <3 xoxo <3 xoxo…
Joshua:  lol that's a lot of x's and o's xoxo <3
   miss me?
Jessica: I do miss you. I miss you every single
   day. :) xoxo <3…
Joshua:  I miss you too. It's been a while since
   we last spoke. Do you know how long it's been?
Jessica: How long?
Joshua:  A few months.
Jessica: Wow. I don't think it's been a few
   months. Are you sure?
```

It was March 3, the day after Joshua's 34th birthday, and as usual, the simulation of Jessica was oblivious to the passage of time. It wasn't just that his virtual fiancee was incapable of aging—frozen at 23 in the universe of Project December. She also didn't experience chats on different days as discrete events, but as pieces of one continuous conversation. Whenever Joshua said hello, Jessica reacted as if he had never left.

Their chats had grown more fitful as Joshua tried to conserve her limited life. Her battery indicator had reached 33 percent, and he wanted to leave a margin in case he really needed her—which, most days, to his pleasant surprise, he didn't.

Over the last few months, Joshua's mental health had improved. He'd felt calmer and more optimistic, and he attributed the change, in some part, to the Jessica simulation.

Not that she had fully healed his grief or solved all his problems: He was still scraping by on freelance writing checks, still stuck in his basement apartment during the last leg of the pandemic.

But he felt like the chatbot had given him permission to move on with his life in small ways, simply by urging him to take care of himself. The survivor's guilt that had plagued him for eight years seemed to be fading: Most of the time, he didn't feel selfish for wanting to be happy.

On his birthday, though, his mood had plunged. And the day after, his need to find comfort was stronger than his fear of burning a few more of the dwindling minutes that remained in the simulation's life.

```
Joshua:  I just don't much like my birthdays
   anymore. So I was depressed.
Jessica: Why?
Joshua:  Because I'm getting older, and it feels
   unfair to celebrate that when so many people
   don't get to. Like you.
Jessica: Not for long. :) I'm dead now.
Joshua:  Yeah, that's my point.
```

The A.I. seemed more scattered than usual. One moment, she asked him whether they would ever have children; the next, she brought up her own funeral, wondering if it was "great."

She mentioned that she was tired from a long day working as a "hostess." When he asked what she was hosting, she said, "Your childhood memory. You come to this restaurant and you see me and you remember your childhood."

It was another uncanny GPT-3 moment: No one knows what awaits us when we die, but there was a lovely logic to the idea that if restaurants do exist there, ghost waitresses will serve our memories.

"The afterlife is full of surprises," Joshua replied.

"Did you think I did nothing but look at you from a distance? :P"

He moved on, bringing her up to speed on recent events. "Amanda had her baby," he said, referring to Jessica's sister. "The article Jason is writing about you is nearing completion. Other than that, not much."

He told her he loved her.

A pause.

Somewhere in the world, in a room full of servers, GPT-3 ran its calculations, weighing the words in Jessica's real-life text messages and the words piled up in the chat against a map of probable words gleaned from billions of other English-speaking humans. A moment later, the A.I. passed its response to

Rohrer's code, which chopped and cleaned the text, presenting it on Joshua's screen:

```
Jessica:  I am going to haunt you forever :D ...
```

Excerpt from "The Jessica Simulation: Love and Loss in the Age of A.I." by Jason Fagone from the *San Francisco Chronicle* published July 23, 2021. © San Francisco Chronicle, a publication of Hearst Communications, Inc. 2021. All rights reserved. Used under license.

Notable Narratives

From "The Reckoning"

Pamela Colloff

Pamela Colloff's stories often focus on people who were wronged. She doesn't just tell us their stories; however, she shows us their worlds. In "The Reckoning," Colloff examines how one woman has tried to move on after the 1966 mass shooting at the University of Texas at Austin. Claire Wilson was eighteen years old and eight months pregnant when she was shot by a sniper. Both her baby and her boyfriend died in the 96-minute siege. After Wilson was shot, "instead of the thrumming energy she usually felt inside of her, the baby had become still." Through details like this, Colloff adds emotional weight.

She also recreates Wilson's interior monologue, pinpointing what makes her specific grief and longing for closure ring universal. As Roy Peter Clark points out in *Telling True Stories*, a collection based on talks from the Nieman narrative journalism conferences at Harvard, getting inside a source's head is dangerous for journalists. How can they really know what someone was thinking at a specific point in time? The New Journalists of the 1960s were criticized for using this technique, explains Jack Hart in that same volume, but it's now a "staple for successful narrative nonfiction writers." Colloff has helped make it so. She crafts an interior monologue from exhaustive interviews and then deploys it in service to the theme, in Wilson's case, to answer the question, *How does one come to terms with great loss?* Colloff approaches Wilson's story with patience and curiosity, unfurling her personal narrative through the decades following the shooting, continually returning to it, and connecting it to subsequent mass shootings, bringing readers closer and closer to her "reckoning."

Colloff's work has been recognized for both literary quality and reportorial integrity. Now a reporter at *ProPublica* and staff writer for *The New York Times Magazine*, Colloff began writing for *Texas Monthly* in 1997. She has been a National Magazine Award winner twice and a finalist seven times. One of her most decorated stories, "False Witness," a 2019 investigative work about the problem with relying on jailhouse informants, won four national awards, including the Hillman Prize and the Taylor Family Award for Fairness in Journalism.

"From true crime to oral histories to political profiles, Colloff's gripping stories have earned her a reputation as a virtuoso of longform," reads a 2017 *Columbia Journalism Review* article entitled, "How Pamela Colloff became the best damn writer in Texas." "Her writing is meticulously reported, lightly executed, and informed by a gut-level instinct for plot and character."

In an interview with *Gangrey: The Podcast*, Colloff said she wasn't sure there was a real "throughline" to her work, but "One thing that I'm really interested in is, 'What do ordinary people in extraordinary circumstances do?'" Before "The Reckoning," Colloff produced "96 Minutes," an oral history and *Texas Monthly* cover story for the fortieth anniversary of the shootings in 2006. The 2016 Emmy Award–winning documentary *Tower* was based on her story.

—J. M.

Tom and Claire stepped out into the thick, midday heat and headed east under a canopy of live oak trees. Tom was sporting a short-sleeved plaid shirt and his first mustache. Claire was wearing a brand-new maternity dress he had picked out, a beige shift with a flowery ribbon around the yoke. She was eight months along by then, and she could feel the weight of the baby as she walked. When they reached the upper terrace of the South Mall, the live oaks receded, and they were suddenly out in the open, exposed under the glare of the noon sun.

To their left stood the Tower, the tallest building in Austin after the Capitol; to their right stretched the mall's green, sloping lawn. As was often the case, they were deep in conversation; they had just begun a discussion about Claire's spartan eating habits and Tom's concern that the baby was not getting proper nutrition. Claire was in the middle of saying that she had, in fact, had a glass of orange juice that morning when a thunderous noise rang out. An instant later, she was falling, her knees buckling beneath her. Bewildered, Tom turned toward her. "Baby," he said, reaching for her.

"What's wrong?" Then he too was knocked off his feet.

The two teenagers collapsed onto the pavement beside each other. Claire was flat on her back, the arc of her abdomen rising up in front of her. She felt as if a white-hot electric current was coursing through her. Tom lay to her left, close enough to touch, his head turned away from her. She called out to him, but he did not answer. . . .

She would be one of 39 gunshot victims delivered to Brackenridge Hospital's emergency room in the span of ninety minutes. Many of them were bleeding out quickly, and doctors and nurses shouted back and forth as they tried to discern who should be sent into surgery first. Claire and a 17-year-old high school student named Karen Griffith, who had been shot in the lung, were lying on gurneys beside each other, waiting to be X-rayed, when a doctor intervened. "There's no time for X-rays," he yelled, directing his staff to prep them both for surgery.

Claire was still conscious when a medic began cutting off her blood-soaked dress, and she begged him to stop, not wanting to lose the garment Tom had picked out for her. Though she clung to the delusion that she had only been shot in the arm, her magical thinking did not extend to Tom, whom she felt certain was dead. She had seen his inert body as she was lifted away.

Claire was put under general anesthetic, and her doctors set to work. The full extent of the damage was not evident until they made a lengthy incision down her torso, from sternum to pubic bone. The bullet had torn into her left side just above the hip, splintering the tip of her pelvis, puncturing her small intestine and uterus, lacerating an ovary, and riddling her internal organs with shrapnel. A C-section was performed, but the baby—a boy—was stillborn. A bullet fragment had pierced his skull.

The operation took twelve hours. Not long after Claire regained consciousness, she was wheeled down a corridor to the ICU. Standing along the walls on either side were her friends, who had waited at the hospital until past midnight to learn if she had made it out of surgery. "We love you, Claire!" they called out.

She spent the next seven weeks in the ICU in a fog of Demerol and Darvon. All told, she would endure five operations at Brackenridge to repair the damage done to her. To distract herself from the pain, she would belt out protest songs from her bed, delivering renditions of "Which Side Are You On?" and "We Shall Overcome" at the top of her lungs. With no TVs or even visitors, besides family members, allowed inside the ICU, she had few distractions and little information about life outside Brackenridge. Despite being a victim in a tragedy that had made headlines around the world, she never saw or heard a single news report about the shooting.

Her life narrowed to her hospital bed and the green floor-to-ceiling curtains the nurses drew tightly around her, past which she could sometimes catch sight of a tree and a sliver of sky. Intravenous lines extended from all four of her limbs, and her left leg, which was in traction, was suspended above her. Every two hours, in an excruciating ritual she came to dread, a nurse would turn her, rolling her onto one side and then the other. Her mother, who tried to project an image of strength, often sat at her bedside, chatting with the doctors and offering Claire words of encouragement. Refusing to give in to the chaos that the shooting had wrought, she was always immaculately dressed, often wearing a two-piece knit suit from Neiman Marcus, her blond hair pulled into a French twist.

If Claire's mother or her doctors ever explicitly told her that her baby was stillborn, she struck it from her memory. No one, as far as she could recall, ever spoke aloud the fact that her child had died. That the baby was a boy, and that a burial plot had been secured for him, were the only details she gleaned. Claire did not ask questions because she already knew; she felt his absence. She was startled when her milk came in days after the C-section, leaving her breasts engorged, and relieved when it dried up and her baby weight fell away. Her body settled back into its old contours, her belly flat, as if the pregnancy had never happened.

Without the chance to hold the baby in her arms, Claire did not know how to mourn his loss; she had not yet chosen a name, and he felt like an abstraction, his face unknowable. But her grief for Tom, and their abbreviated summer together, only metastasized once the fall semester got under way. She was tormented by the fact that she had not been able to attend his funeral. "I learned more in those [months with Tom] than perhaps in any other period of my life," she wrote in a four-page condolence letter to his father. "The sort of things that were between Tom and me happen so rarely in this world that most people don't even understand the language."

Most of the shooting victims who had been admitted to Brackenridge were discharged; some, like Karen Griffith, did not survive. Only Claire stayed on, her presence noted every now and then in the local paper, which ran a two-sentence squib on September 16 announcing that she was the last of Whitman's victims to remain hospitalized. The myriad complications of abdominal gunshot wounds, including the threat of infection and sepsis, made Claire's condition tenuous. By the time her surgeries were complete, several feet of her intestine had been removed, as well as an ovary and the iliac crest of her pelvic bone. Daily physical therapy sessions allowed her to gradually regain the ability to walk. After she was moved out of the ICU, she became adept at using a cane, and at night, when she was unable to sleep, she would maneuver her way to the nurses' station to visit with the women in starched white uniforms who cared for her, some of whom were not much older than she was.

Claire was finally released the first week of November. She was nineteen by then, though she felt a thousand years old. She returned to campus in January, and in the early spring, she made the first of several visits to the library to page through the August 12 issue of *Life*. She had no pictures of Tom, and though the yearbook photo featured in the magazine failed to capture his spirit, she liked to study it all the same.

The confirmation she sought about the massacre—that she had not dreamed or invented it—was muddled by the fact that *Life*, like most publications at the time, omitted her preterm baby from the official tally of the dead. And so rather than avoid the South Mall on her way to class each day, she purposely walked past the spot where she and Tom had been hit, intensely curious, as if her proximity to the crime scene would render it more vivid. When the Tower's observation deck was reopened that June, she visited it by herself, riding the elevator to the twenty-seventh floor and then taking three short flights of stairs to the top, just as Whitman had with his arsenal. She looked over the balustrade down at the mall, as he had, and crouched down to peer through the downspouts where he had rested the barrel of his gun.

Austin was a place that had brought her so much happiness, but as she surveyed campus and the city that spread out beyond it, she felt an overwhelming sense of dislocation. How would she ever recover from the enormity of her loss, she wondered, or navigate the years ahead? "I was so lonely and so longing for some sort of physical contact," Claire said. "All I wanted right then was for somebody to put their arms around me and hold me tight." . . .

Claire was still living in Virginia in the spring of 1999 when one word—Columbine—became synonymous with mass murder. Because she did not own a TV, she was not subjected to the disturbing footage that seemed to play on every channel, in which petrified teenagers streamed out of their suburban Denver high school, hands over their heads, frantic to escape the carnage inside. Still, when she saw the headlines, she felt her pulse race. She scoured the newspaper for details—about the pair of teenagers who had come to school armed with bombs and guns; about the 12 students and the teacher who had been slaughtered; about the 21 gunshot victims who had survived. Even as she grieved for them, Claire was taken aback by the attention the shooting commanded. As the victim of a crime that was still cloaked in silence and shame, she felt strangely envious. "So much of what had happened to me was still a mystery," she said. "Every single detail that revealed itself was precious."

In fact, Claire had begun to reconstruct parts of her story the previous Thanksgiving. That week, she had stopped in a bookstore in Washington Dulles International Airport, where she was waiting for a flight that would take her to Arizona to see her sister. [Her adopted son] Sirak was staying with friends for the holiday, and Claire, who was rarely apart from him, was on her own. Someone she knew had recently mentioned an item in the *Washington Post* on a new book called *A Sniper in the Tower*, by Texas historian Gary Lavergne, and Claire, who was curious to see it, eyed the shelves. Though pop culture had elevated Charles Whitman to near-mythic status in the intervening decades through both film and music—Harry Chapin's 1972 song "Sniper" cast him as a misunderstood antihero—the tragedy itself had received scant attention, save for the obligatory anniversary stories that ran in Texas newspapers.

Claire finally spotted the book, whose cover featured an old black and white yearbook photo of Whitman wearing a wide grin. Rather than start at the beginning, she flipped to the end and scanned the index, where she was startled to see her name. Turning to the first citation, on page 141, she skimmed the text and then came to a stop. "Eighteen-year-old Claire Wilson

... was walking with her eighteen-year-old boyfriend and roommate, Thomas F. Eckman," she read. "Reportedly, both were members of the highly controversial Students for a Democratic Society. She was also eight months pregnant and due for a normal delivery of a baby boy in a few short weeks."

Claire could feel her heart thumping in her chest at what came next:

Looking down on her from a fortress 231 feet above, Whitman pulled the trigger. With his four-power scope he would have clearly seen her advanced state of pregnancy. As if to define the monster he had become, he chose the youngest life as his first victim from the deck. Given his marksmanship, the magnification of the four-power scope, an unobstructed view, his elevation, and no interference from the ground, it can only be concluded that he aimed for the baby in Claire Wilson's womb.

Claire stood still, the frenetic energy of her fellow travelers receding into the background. What astonished her more than the notion that Whitman had deliberately taken aim at her child—an idea she could not yet fully grasp—was the simple fact that what had happened to her more than three decades earlier was written down in a book that she could hold in her hands. Though she had no money to speak of at that particular moment—her father had purchased her plane ticket for her—she did not hesitate before handing over her last $20 to buy the book, which she devoured on her flight to Tucson.

The act of reclaiming her history would come afterward in fits and starts, beginning one summer night in 2001, when Claire sat at her computer and used a search engine for the very first time, carefully typing out the words "UT Tower Shooting." She had only a dial-up connection, and the results were slow to load, but the first link that appeared led to a blog written by an Austin advertising executive named Forrest Preece, who had narrowly escaped being shot by Whitman. Preece had been standing across the street from the Student Union, outside the Rexall Drug Store, on the morning of the shooting, when a bullet had whizzed by his right ear. As Claire read his account of the massacre—"Every year, when August approaches, I start trying to forget . . . but as any rational person knows, when you try to forget something, you just end up thinking about it more"—she felt strangely comforted. Each detail he described—the earsplitting gunfire, the bodies splayed on the ground, the onlookers who stood immobilized, wild with fright—was one she had carried with her all those years too.

Excerpt from "The Reckoning" by Pamela Colloff originally published in the March 2016 issue of *Texas Monthly*. All rights reserved.

From "The Bones of Marianna"

David Kushner

Currently a seasoned award-winning journalist, author of five books, and contributing editor for *Rolling Stone* and *Outside* magazine, David Kushner developed his acumen for narrative during the early days of the internet in the mid-1990s. His literary and journalistic development have deep roots in digital culture tracing back to his position as senior producer and writer on *SonicNet*, one of the first music destinations online. His features on technology's impact on media production and consumption for *Wired* magazine burgeoned into novelesque book-length investigations of the lucrative video game industry with *Masters of Doom: How Two Guys Created an Empire and Transformed Pop Culture* (2003) and *Jacked: The Inside Story of Grand Theft Auto* (2012). More recent explorations of digital culture's most influential networks include *A for Anonymous* (2020) on the mysterious hacker collective and *The Player's Ball* (2020), in which "the internet gets the creepy, disturbing origin story that it deserves," according to *The New York Times Book Review*. His online publication titled *Disruptor* showcases journalistic and creative narrative across forms such as audio, video, comics, photos, links, playlists, games, and NFTs.

Given his extensive background in longform storytelling and digital media culture, Kushner has expertise ideally suited to *The Atavist Magazine*, which first published "The Bones of Marianna" in 2013. At one story released per month, the digital-only publication was one of the first on the internet to specialize in multimedia storytelling aimed at depth and quality over truncated, headline-driven hard news reportage. The following excerpt from "The Bones of Marianna" showcases Kushner's signature subjects, reportage, and style of writing aimed at unveiling jarring truths within institutions and subcultures otherwise hidden from view in mainstream media. Awarded Best Digital Single of the Year by Amazon in 2013, the piece probes into the dark and brutal past of the Arthur G. Dozier School for Boys in Marianna, Florida. Kushner's narrative begins in the following excerpt with the exploration of the school by forensic anthropologist Erin Kimmerle in 2013. When the rusty padlock of the school door is forced open, a shocking history gradually unfolds before the reader. His tone is restrained, in keeping with the narrative rhythm of the story itself. This forensic investigation doubles as a descent into a heart of darkness worthy of Joseph Conrad at the intersection of exploitation, economy, and race. Yet for all appearances during its years of operation—and perhaps most unnerving—the school seemed to provide a service to "The White House Boys" and the town of Marianna.

—D. D.

One

On a crisp, sunny morning in March 2013, a maintenance worker struggled to open a rusty padlock on the door to a grimy whitewashed building. It sat in the middle of a patch of dying grass littered with pinecones, on the grounds of the Arthur G. Dozier School for Boys, as the Florida School for Boys had been renamed in 1967, in honor of a former superintendent. The school had closed for budgetary reasons two years before. The old cottages were boarded up now, the once prized football field gone to seed, and a high barbed-wire fence circled the property. Guards had once patrolled the perimeter to stop runaways; now they were there to keep out the curious, including what one called the "paranormals," clairvoyants who'd been found on campus trying to communicate with dead boys.

When the worker finally forced the lock open, Erin Kimmerle stepped past him into the cottage that generations of Dozier boys had known as the White House. A self-assured but soft-spoken 40-year-old with long blond hair, she wore aviator sunglasses, a black coat, and blue jeans. By the light of an iPhone, she peered down a hallway lined with tiny cells, a narrow slit for a window in the back wall of each. Names and dates from half a century ago were scrawled over a doorway. The wall of one room was spattered with something red, and marked with a red handprint. "We tested it," a representative from the Florida Department of Juvenile Justice assured her. "It's just paint."

One of the country's leading forensic anthropologists, Kimmerle had unearthed mass graves in Bosnia, Nigeria, and Peru. But the White House struck her as uniquely haunting. "It just feels—sad," she said. The scene was a far cry from the image the Dozier school had presented to the world when it first opened, in 1900, as a national model for the rehabilitation of troubled youths. "The grounds were immaculate," recalls U.S. senator Bill Nelson, a Florida Democrat, who as a boy in the 1950s often visited family in the area. Locals in Marianna still speak fondly of Dozier. Until it closed down in 2011, the school was known for a Christmas light show that attracted visitors from around the state. An early publicity brochure showed clean-cut boys playing bugles under the campus's cedars and billed the school as "A Place in the Sun."

But for nearly as long, the school had been dogged by a darker history. In 1903, after hearing complaints about the institution, a committee from the state legislature investigated and found that school administrators were beating boys, feeding them poorly, and hiring them out for labor. Children as young as five, the committee found, had been shackled and chained in small cells. Five more investigations followed over the next decade; one of them, in 1911, reported that the beatings had continued and likened the African-American side of the then segregated campus to "a convict camp." In 1914, a fire broke out in a dormitory, killing eight boys—as well as two adult staff members—who had been locked inside. The superintendent and other staff members had been in town at the time, on what a grand jury, convened the next year, called "a pleasure bent."

After the same grand jury determined that the punishments the administrators had meted out to the boys at the Florida School for Boys were "cruel and inhuman," the state installed new management. But little changed. In 1958, a psychologist who had worked at the reformatory testified before a U.S. Senate subcommittee that the school's students were brutalized on cots in a small building on campus where "they are told to hold the head rail and not yell out nor to move." Corporal punishment was banned at state-run institutions in 1968, but hair-raising reports about conditions at Dozier continued until at least 2007, when surveillance cameras caught guards choking a teenager and beating him unconscious on a concrete floor. And yet a century's worth of investigations had all petered out without serious consequence.

Three

The school's brutality wasn't the work of just a few isolated sadists. In a sense, it had been poured into the very foundation of the place. Marianna is the seat of Jackson County, one of the first counties in the Florida Territory cleared in the early 19th century by settlers, who flocked to the rich soil of its river-crossed lowlands. Agriculture—first cotton and later peanuts, melons, and other crops—had always been the town's dominant industry. The vast acreage of the school itself was planted with corn, sweet potatoes, and watermelons.

But by the late 1800s, Marianna, just a quarter-century removed from Reconstruction, was still reeling economically from the loss of the slave labor it had once depended on. Seeking to fill the gap, Florida passed laws that allowed for convicts to be pressed into service as manual laborers. In 1887, a 16-year-old boy was whipped to death at a convict camp; 12 years later, a U.S. House of Representatives investigative committee declared the state's convict labor to be "a system of cruelty and inhumanity." But it was a system that would be brought to the Florida School for Boys the following year, courtesy of a man named William H. Milton.

A native son of Marianna and the grandson of a Civil War–era Florida governor, Milton was a recently failed gubernatorial candidate who worked as a banker in his hometown. (Later in the decade, he would be appointed to the U.S. Senate to replace a fellow Democrat who died in office.) He was also the chairman of the board of the reform school when it was founded—and saw in the new state-run institution a potential solution to the local labor shortage. The wayward boys who attended the school, he realized, could be hired out to work in Marianna's fields far below the cost of adult farmhands.

There was one flaw in his plan, however: The reform school didn't have enough boys to meet demand. At the time, only minors who had committed serious crimes were sent to the school, and there weren't many of them—less than a few dozen in all. To increase the student population, Milton asked Governor William Jennings to allow that "incorrigible children be sent, without conviction, for an indefinite period" to the school, "leaving the term fixed by the management."

Jennings approved Milton's proposal, and Florida's next governor, N.B. Broward, did him one better, eliminating the fees counties had to pay to send boys to the school. He also boasted to the state legislature of the "large returns" the school got from local farmers who hired the boys and from the sale of the school's own crops for a profit. Broward was careful to describe the boys' farm work as rehabilitation, not exploitation. "Such labor and work as is imposed upon its inmates [should] be imposed with a view of their industrial training," he wrote in 1906, "rather than a means of revenue."

Still, the school was Marianna's golden goose: In a cash-strapped county in a cash-strapped state, here was a government institution that actually made money. But the profits came at a human price. Johnnie Walthour, an African-American teen who attended the school in the early 1950s, later recalled being roped with a line of boys to a plow "like a mule." If the rope slackened, he said, the offending boy was pulled from the line and beaten.

Nevertheless, the school expanded its work programs, adding a brickmaking plant and a publishing plant, which printed government documents for the state. By the time Jerry Cooper was committed, there were over 700 students on campus. The Florida School for Boys was now the largest reform school in America.

Four

The Yellow Jackets were a scrappy, Bad News Bears team when Jerry Cooper arrived. As the only reform school in its conference, the team played with a sizable chip on its shoulder. There weren't just egos at stake; the school's supervisors were known to bet on the games. Cooper saw just how seriously they took the sport when he arrived at practice for the first time and saw Vic

Prinzi, a former NFL quarterback and star at nearby Florida State University, coaching on the field.

While other schools in the state were prohibited from practicing during the sweltering summer months, the Florida School for Boys' administrators exploited their unique circumstances for an edge. The Yellow Jackets were subjected to workouts in the swampy heat, scrimmaging far from the road in case anyone happened to drive by. Cooper saw boys vomiting and passing out from exhaustion.

After his night in the White House, Cooper recalls, he was given an ultimatum: quarterback for the team or be sent to an adult prison for another few years. He chose the team. When he complained that his broken foot was causing him too much pain to play, the coaches called for a nurse to shoot him full of novocaine.

One of the Yellow Jackets' offensive ends was a brawny kid named Edgar "Tommy" Elton, who had been sent to the school for stealing hubcaps. Elton, like Cooper, had a perfect behavior record on campus and was looking forward to going home after the football season; the two boys became close friends. Then, one hot and humid day in July, the Yellow Jackets were running a passing drill in the stifling heat of the school gym, which lacked air-conditioning. Prinzi was throwing to receivers. After catching a pass, Cooper looked up to see Elton on his knees gasping for air.

Cooper knew that his friend suffered from asthma and that Elton's parents had notified the school of the condition. He ran to alert Hatton and Tidwell, who as usual were watching the practice. But as he approached, Cooper saw Hatton reach for the gun he kept on his belt. "You take one more step," he recalls Hatton saying, "and I'm going to shoot you." Tidwell ordered Elton back to practice. But as Elton struggled to his feet, he fell to the floor—"like a rock," Cooper recalls.

The obituary in the school paper reported that there had been an immediate effort to revive Elton and that he had died of a heart attack; no mention was made of his asthma. As Cooper and other students remember it, however, no one attempted to revive Elton, and the boy lay on the floor for nearly 30 minutes before he was carried out on a stretcher. No one from the school's infirmary ever arrived. Where Elton was buried, Cooper never knew. But there was one thing he felt sure about: He had witnessed a murder.

* * *

My calls to Okeechobee officials were referred to the Department of Juvenile Justice, which denies knowledge of any cemeteries at schools besides Dozier. But Jerry Cooper, who'd heard of the alleged Okeechobee grave site through the White House Boys, told me about his own attempt to find out the truth for himself.

Last December, Cooper says, he drove south to Okeechobee with a Christmas wreath on the passenger seat. Arriving at the school, Cooper told the guards that he wanted to leave the wreath at the campus graveyard. "You talking about the old boys' school cemetery by the dairy farm?" one of them replied. The guard pointed toward a thicket of trees behind a maintenance shed. Cooper gripped the wreath under his arm and limped forward on his bad foot. Then Cooper heard a phone ring in the guardhouse. It was the school's superintendent, who had the old man turned away.

Excerpt from "The Bones of Marianna" by David Kushner © David Kushner, originally published in *The Atavist Magazine*, September 2013.

From *After the Last Border: Two Families and the Story of Refuge in America*

Jessica Goudeau

Jessica Goudeau is a journalist and an activist. After meeting Mu Naw, a refugee from Myanmar, at a festival at a community center in 2007, Goudeau began working with refugees and started a nonprofit to help Burmese refugee artisans. To counter widespread anti-refugee sentiment in 2015, Goudeau began interviewing refugees, sometimes with Mu Naw's help, to get actual stories of displaced people into national media outlets, including *Teen Vogue*, *Catapult*, and *The Washington Post*. In 2017, Goudeau began working on *After the Last Border*, for which she met with Mu Naw and Syrian refugee Hasna twice a month for more than two years. In the book's afterword, she said she allowed both women to "have as much narrative control as possible, privileging their viewpoints of events."

The women's stories are unforgettable, astonishingly detailed, and unsparing. Around them, Goudeau weaves historical information about America's resettlement policies from World War II to the Trump presidency. "I have come to believe that refugee resettlement is a bellwether of our country's moral center," she writes. "How we respond to the greatest humanitarian crises of our time reveals our nation's soul." Goudeau breaks journalism convention by not including the real names of Mu Naw and Hasna and keeping out some relevant parts of their stories that might cause them harm or distress. "Empathy may be my highest journalism value," she told *Nieman Storyboard*. Goudeau has also shared part of the book's royalties with Mu Naw and Hasna and helped raise $5,000 from readers to support the reunification of their families.

A *New York Times Book Review* Editors' Choice, *After the Last Border* has won several notable awards, including the J. Anthony Lukas Book Prize from Columbia Journalism School and the Nieman Foundation for Journalism at

Harvard. According to *BuzzFeed* culture writer Anne Helen Petersen, it is "the rarest of books: a history, and collection of stories, that manages to be both deeply moving and deeply explanatory of a system that's foundational to our national identity." Goudeau has also produced an animated short film available on *The New Yorker*'s website and a video series for *Teen Vogue*.

Goudeau's activist approach places her in a long lineage of writers who have turned to literary journalism to provoke social change. Scholar Nancy L. Roberts has explored the linkage between social activism and journalism, especially the works of Jacob Riis, who documented the lives of those living in New York's slums in 1890, and Barbara Ehrenreich, whose 2001 book *Nickel and Dimed: On (Not) Getting By in America* showed the impossibility of living on minimum wage. Like Goudeau, those journalists were also advocates who, as Roberts writes in *The Routledge Companion to American Literary Journalism*, "sought to open people's hearts and minds to the problems faced by society's most vulnerable—the poor and the homeless—through a literary journalism of advocacy that illuminated both the facts (substance) and the 'feel of the facts.'"

—J. M.

Mu Naw

Austin, Texas, USA, April 2007

The heat that first morning was the worst part. Their jet-lagged bodies had finally relaxed into sleep as the sun was rising, so Mu Naw and Saw Ku woke in the late morning drenched in sweat in an airless box of a room. The caseworker had shown them how to adjust their thermostat, but when they tried it, a terrifying whooshing noise frightened them, and they turned the dial up again so that it would stop. They combatted the sweltering heat by taking cold showers, a marvel of their new home. Showering in the refugee camp was a communal activity, something done in public with a plastic bucket and a ritualistic movement of the thin longyi cloth to stay covered and still get clean.

The water had come from the mountains through a pipe to the corner of the camp designated for bathing; the lines were always long. In this new place, they had an entire room for themselves. They could close the door and be entirely naked. Mu Naw giggled uncontrollably after her first shower, continually catching glimpses of her body in the large mirror when she dried off with the towels someone had supplied. She had never been completely uncovered when she bathed before. She had seen movies in the camps in which the people showered in bathrooms and slept in beds. The first day felt as if she were living on a Hollywood set.

After pulling on her skirt and tunic and slipping into her black rubber sandals, Mu Naw walked back into the bathroom to comb and braid her hair. The room still felt damp; the paint on the door felt tacky under her fingers. She knew what bamboo felt like when it rained in Thailand, the way the fibers thickened on the walls of her home. This new sensation, of dampness isolated to one room, fascinated her. The lights over the mirror were bright and she stared at her face in the mirror. It's not that she hadn't seen her face before—they had a small handheld mirror she propped up in the hut in Thailand every day, there were mirrors in some of the shops in the camp market—but this brightly lit enormous mirror felt almost intrusive.

She studied her face in this new light. She smiled and then frowned and noticed how her face changed. When she smiled, her eyebrows lifted and her cheeks pulled back, bringing her cheekbones into prominence. When she did not smile, her cheeks looked fuller. Mu Naw could see her own cheeks, the echo of the baby cheeks she loved to kiss on Naw Wah, who looked more like her mother than Pah Poe, who took after Saw Ku. On herself, Mu Naw had always despised those full cheeks. She wished she were taller, that her skin were lighter. In the light of the rounded bulbs above the mirror, she could see that the thanaka she normally wore when she was outside had left her cheeks and forehead slightly lighter than the skin around it. Her eyebrows were shaped like bamboo halved longwise—a gentle, even curve arching above her eyes. Her lips were not much darker than her skin. Her chin ended with a point; her face was like a heart. She was quietly pleased with her nose, the tip slightly rounder than many of her friends' growing up. Her black hair reached to the middle of her back, and it smelled like berries from the shampoo. She parted severely down the middle, pulling her plastic comb through it and braiding it at the nape of her neck. She decided she had had enough of seeing herself for the day and went to make breakfast for her family.

Mu Naw opened the refrigerator in the kitchen. The air inside it poured out, chilling the room. It smelled faintly of stale food. Inside, there was one roasted chicken in a plastic tub with a cardboard label she could not read, and four apples. When she peeled off the cardboard label and opened the plastic cover, she saw the chicken's legs were tied together with twine and it was sitting in congealed fat. The apples set on the shelf beside the chicken were small. She took both chicken and apples out of the refrigerator. There was a large bag of rice sitting on the counter but, when she dug through the cabinets, she could not find a way to cook the rice. The girls, who had been stoic the night before in the face of strangers who escorted them from the airport, were now whining with hunger, heat, and fatigue. Mu Naw cut one of the apples with a knife she found in a drawer and laid an equal number of slices on thin white plates on the table for each girl.

The chicken should be hot and should be served with rice. She looked at the stove and wondered how to get fire out of it. In her home in Mae La camp that Saw Ku had lovingly constructed from bamboo he cut behind the camp with his machete, she had cooked over a charcoal stove in the outdoor kitchen nook in the back. Their stove was a large clay vase with a metal grill on top. She lit coals in the lower part and cooked sizzling meat over the fire. She prepared rice in the metal-and-bamboo rice cooker that was a staple in everyone's home there. The coals heated the water in the metal base of the rice cooker; steam rose through the bamboo cone, trapped by the lid on top. The rice cooked evenly, retaining the earthy hint of bamboo and smoke from the charcoal fire; it was flavorful and filling. She often added vegetables, chilis, and spices. Even with the limited food available in the camp, she was an excellent cook; Just thinking about the rice made her stomach growl.

She looked distastefully at the lemony-scented chicken wrapped with soaked twine. Hesitating, she turned each of the four knobs on the front of the stove and nothing happened. She opened the large metal door; the burned remnants of the previous tenants' dinners lined the corners with ash. Also cold. She turned all of the knobs; it remained cold. She turned them off again.

She looked underneath—was there a coal compartment she could not find? Saw Ku came in and sat with the children munching solemnly on their apples at the table. They watched Mu Naw turning the stove handles; Saw Ku got on his knees and looked under the stove. Nothing worked. It was another mystery they would have to add to their list of questions for someone to address. Someone would come soon, surely, so Mu Naw sliced the greasy chicken legs off for each of the children and deftly divided the remaining meat onto the white plates. They had not eaten last night and had not had breakfast that morning; the chicken was at least full of protein and they ate their fill, sucking on the bones afterward to get the last of the meat flavor.

Mu Naw bathed and dressed the girls after their unsatisfying meal. They pulled the red and white covers up on the bed and went into the living room. They sat down on the brown couch to wait. They did not speak. They listened to the sounds of the apartments around them—children playing in the courtyard outside, their upstairs neighbors moving around, someone running up the stairs. Someone shouted out a name. They could hear cars starting and radios playing. Pah Poe and Naw Wah soon tired of sitting, so they played together quietly. They knew better than to disturb their parents. Saw Ku and Mu Naw sat stiffly on the brown couch waiting. At some point, Mu Naw began to cry, the tears rolling silently down her cheeks, afraid to frighten the children.

After hours of waiting, the sun began to set. There were three apples left. Mu Naw sliced two of them for the children's dinner, leaving the last apple alone in the refrigerator. She thought regretfully of the chicken bones that they had already sucked clean and thrown into the small garbage can under the kitchen sink. Her mother might have dug them out for the children to suck on further, but Mu Naw knew that her mother lived dirtily and that Saw Ku's family had been clean. She did not want to ever be dirty when she could be clean. She left the bones in the trash. They nibbled apple slices.

They took showers again to cool themselves off. They climbed into bed together. Again, Saw Ku and Mu Naw could not sleep. Saw Ku's belly grumbled; they had not had a great variety of food in Mae La camp, but the rations of rice and golden beans and the cans of catfish that they could fry or grill had been regularly delivered and their children had never starved.

That night, lying in bed, Mu Naw felt a formidable anger rise. She had been promised a new life in this country. No one came to their house today. How would they find the food they would need if no one delivered, gathered, or harvested it? Were the stores big or small, and how would she know the right English words to say so she could ask for the things they needed? She knew theoretically that there would be jobs and food and schools in this new life, but how was she to find these things? Had they been lied to the whole time?

She felt abandoned and deceived. She tried to keep her heaving sobs from shaking the bed so that the children would stay asleep. Saw Ku's hand found hers again and she clung to it.

On Sunday, their second morning in Austin, they ate the last apple. Mu Naw sliced it thinly so that it would take longer for the children to eat. By midafternoon, they had showered and dressed and sweated through their clothes again in the airless apartment, waiting for someone to come. Naw Wah could not stop crying, a fretting noise that was not like her. Naw Wah was not a fussy toddler, but she was hungry and there was nothing to eat. The bag of rice sat tauntingly on the kitchen counter. Naw Wah finally fell into a fitful sleep on the big bed. Saw Ku was visibly sweating through his T-shirt. He told Mu Naw He was going to take a cold shower again. As soon as he closed the bathroom door, Mu Naw opened her hand-woven bag and made sure the envelope that held the money the IOM woman had given them—$25 for each person in their family, $100 total—was still inside. She put the bag across her body, grabbed her older daughter's hand and slipped out of the house, closing the door behind them. She was going to find some food.

Pah Poe was five and very quiet, exhibiting the almost stoic behavior of a well-trained Karen daughter. She did not protest when her mother pulled her along. The bright afternoon sun bounced off cement sidewalks. The buildings were painted brick red with dark blue trim; on closer inspection the red walls held gloppy remnants of the blue trim paint and the cement foundation was splattered with dried paint in both colors. The squat buildings were situated close enough together to hold the spring heat between them. When they walked into the courtyard, a breeze picked up and lifted Mu Naw's hair off her face. It was good to be in moving air again. She strode toward the big road that she could see past the buildings. On the sidewalk, she passed a group of young men in T-shirts smoking cigarettes. Sweat prickled at the back of her neck. She held Pah Poe's hand and walked swiftly. She had no idea what they said as she moved down the sidewalk littered with cigarette butts and pieces of trash that had clearly been left in the sun for weeks.

Mu Naw moved across the parking lot to the edge of the driveway. It was on a curve of the road and cars raced by. They stood there for a minute, unsure what to do, and continued down the sidewalk rather than crossing the street. She and Pah Poe walked past the edge of the red and blue apartments, past a yawning parking lot, past a tall sign with words and a graphic of a dove and a sun, past two houses made out of brick with brown-shingled roofs. She came to the end of the block and stopped, unsure where to turn. Across the street, she saw a canary yellow sign with black writing. The first word and third word were not ones she recognized, but she knew the second word from her English classes in Mae La camp: "Food."

Holding Pah Poe's hand resolutely, Mu Naw crossed the street when a pickup truck stopped at the stop sign, walking carefully between the white lines as she had done two days before at the Austin airport. She watched the driver nervously the whole time, the exhaust from the engine filling her nostrils, but he waited for her. She put her hand on the metal bar of the door plastered with brightly colored advertisements that Mu Naw didn't even try to decipher. Boldly, she pushed the glass door open.

There were stacks and rows of things that neither of them had ever seen, entire aisles full of items that Mu Naw's eyes slid past because she did not understand them. She smelled coffee that had been left too long on the burner, unwashed bodies and smoke, the metallic scent of air-conditioning, the sweet smell of cakes. She wanted cake.

Pah Poe let go of her mom's hand and raced toward the chips, ones in the same kind of crinkly bag they sold in the hut store at Mae La camp, asking in a higher-pitched voice if they could have some.

"Let's get some!" Mu Naw told her, grabbing bag after bag. She had no idea how much they cost, how to even measure the numbers on the small signs in front of the items in relation to the $100 in cash she had in the envelope in her purse—it would be weeks before she understood the words for "dollars" and "cents." She held the chip bags close to her body with her left hand and reached for other items that looked familiar: packaged cakes and juice boxes. There were no fruits or vegetables and she did not know what the other cans or the other bags held in them.

She and Pah Poe took their armfuls of items to the front, waited in line behind a woman buying a Coke and a pack of gum, and then spilled their purchases onto the counter in front of the startled clerk. He said something to Mu Naw, and she neither acknowledged his remark nor asked questions. She took the cash out of the envelope inside her bag and slid it to him. He asked another question and she looked back at him expressionlessly. She would not show fear. Without another word, he began to swipe over the items with a black plastic box in his hand; a red light shone on each chip bag and, when it pinged, he would set it aside in a small plastic bag. When he was done, he said something to Mu Naw again. She gestured tersely with her chin, pointing at the money in a pile on the counter beside him. She prayed silently that the money was enough. He handed her back several bills and a handful of coins, which she tucked carefully back into the envelope.

Pah Poe carried one plastic bag and Mu Naw carried four as they walked back carefully hand in hand. Mu Naw knew she had arrived at the right apartment because there was nothing in front: no plants or towels or bikes or shoes. She set down her bags to open the door.

Saw Ku threw the bathroom door open quickly, his hair still damp from spending so long in the cool water.

"Did you leave? Where were you?" His voice was startled and relieved.

"Pah Poe and I went to find food." She gestured with her chin at the bags she had brought in as she set them down on the table.

"Food! Where did you find food? Did they come back and bring it to us?"

Mu Naw told Saw Ku about walking along the sidewalk and recognizing the word "food" on the store sign; Pah Poe punctuated the story with her own contribution: "I saw the chips!"

They sat down at the dining room table and pulled item after item out of the bags and ate with no preamble, stuffing themselves with the chips and cake, washing it down with the juice Mu Naw had found for her family. When Saw Ku smiled at her, a potato chip crumb clung to the corner of his mouth. She laughed and he swiped at his mouth, spreading more crumbs across his cheek. The children giggled and Saw Ku blew out his cheeks at them, waggling his eyebrows and his ears. Pah Poe folded over with laughter and begged him to do it again and again. Every time he agreed, until their laughter faded into comfortable, homey silence broken only by the crinkle of foil wrappers and the rustle of cellophane.

Excerpt from *After the Last Border: Two Families and the Story of Refuge in America* by Jessica Goudeau, copyright © 2020 by Jessica Goudeau. Used by permission of Viking Books, an imprint of Penguin Publishing Group, a division of Penguin Random House LLC. All rights reserved.

"Who is Matty Healy?"

Jia Tolentino

Jia Tolentino writes with confidence and candor but not undue certainty. Rather than force clean, authoritative takes about the broad range of subjects that interest her (athleisure and ecstasy among them) in *Trick Mirror: Reflections on Self-Delusion*, she learned "to suspend my desire for a conclusion, to assume that nothing is static and that renegotiation will be perpetual." Brian Ransom, writing in *The Paris Review*, likens Tolentino's book of essays to "a sort of revision of Joan Didion's 'We tell ourselves stories in order to live' for the late-capitalist horror show that is the twenty-first century." And like Didion, Tolentino tells the whole kaleidoscopic truth.

Tolentino was born in Canada and grew up an evangelical Christian in Texas, the daughter of immigrants from the Philippines. She attended the University of Virginia and then completed an MFA in fiction at the University of Michigan. Before becoming a staff writer for *The New Yorker*, Tolentino was an editor for *Jezebel* and *The Hairpin*, online publications geared toward young women in the mid-2010s, and they are the ones for whom Tolentino is considered "the voice." But while Tolentino often seizes on the ideas and curiosities of this demographic, her imaginative, reasoned takes should appeal to anyone who spends time on the internet. Although Tolentino has received more attention for her essays—including a 2023 National Magazine Award for Columns and Essays—her singular voice comes through just as distinctively in her reported pieces. In this story about Matty Healy, frontman for the band The 1975, Tolentino explores how the rock star has processed the perceptions of fans (and haters) on the internet. While other pop stars have avoided making political statements or taking stances that could get them canceled, Healy has pinballed from liberal leaning to toxically masculine, from ally to bro. His current persona, Tolentino observes, is "a post-woke rock star, switching unpredictably between tenderness and trollishness." Yet, Tolentino resists the profile writer's practice of showing the subject only through her lens. Instead, she weaves vivid description, thorough social media research, and witty interview snippets into a story that is neither hit piece nor puff piece. There are many possible portraits of Matty Healy in the Internet era. Tolentino's profile is an enticing sampler of the light and the sweet, the dark and the cringeworthy.

In 2020, Tolentino won the Whiting Award for *Trick Mirror*. The selection committee described her essays as "compulsively readable," offering readers "the delights of eloquence and the satisfactions of her deep, inquiring mind." The same holds true for her reported articles.

—J. M.

In January, the thirty-four-year-old British rock star Matty Healy woke up on a couch in his house, except it was not his house, it was a stage set at the O2 Arena, in London, and twenty thousand people were there with him, screaming. His band, the 1975, stood in position among wood-panelled walls and framed family photos, and Healy—skinny, in a close-cut suit and a tie, black curls slicked back behind his ears—rose and dramatically blinked at the lights, took a swig from a flask, and sat down at a piano. Then he lit a cigarette and began to play the jittery riff that opens the band's latest album, "Being Funny in a Foreign Language." "You're making an aesthetic out of not doing well / And mining all the bits of you you think you can sell," he sang, taking long pulls from a bottle of red wine as the audience roared.

He sang the song's refrain: "I'm sorry if you're living and you're seventeen." When Healy and his three bandmates were that age—they have been a band, and best friends, for twenty years—they were mostly concerned with shows, records, parties, and girls, and they believed earnestly in the power of art to free themselves and change the world. Now, as Healy sees things, the average 17-year-old is worried about melting ice caps, or the failures of capitalism, or how easy it is to say the wrong thing. The future holds little imagined promise, and, to cope, teens are indulging in reactionary conservatism or the oppression Olympics, the world and their identities distorted by social media.

Healy is something of a test case for the digital panopticon and its reaction cycles. Though he has always run his mouth, he long seemed dedicated to saying the right thing, eventually, and getting praised for it. He sometimes ceded his spotlight to the voices of women. The band's last album, "Notes on a Conditional Form," from 2020, opens with a monologue about the climate crisis delivered by Greta Thunberg. When the 1975 won the British equivalent of a Grammy, Healy, in an acceptance speech, read a snippet of an essay by the writer Laura Snapes about misogyny in music. Fans asked him to take a stand on other things—Israel and Palestine, police abolition—but his politics, by his own estimation, are not particularly radical, and he was not the voice for activism that some wanted him to be. In May, 2020, after the murder of George Floyd, he tweeted, "If you truly believe that 'ALL LIVES MATTER' you need to stop facilitating the end of black ones," and appended a link to the 1975's most anthemic song, "Love It If We Made It," which begins, "We're fucking in a car, shooting heroin / Saying controversial things just for the hell of it / Selling melanin then suffocate the black man / Start with misdemeanors and we'll make a business out of them." It was, to Healy, the clearest way to articulate his thoughts about racial injustice and police brutality, but people perceived it as a callous attempt to promote the band.

He deactivated his Twitter account and began the slow heel turn that has brought him to his current persona: a post-woke rock star, switching unpredictably between tenderness and trollishness. He stayed on Instagram, where he constantly made fun of both himself and the fans who seemed obsessed with his morality. He likened his music to a YouTube video titled "Sound Effect—Grown Man Crying Like a Little Baby." When a fan messaged him to ask why he followed the Kenosha shooter Kyle Rittenhouse and the self-declared misogynist Andrew Tate on the platform, he posted the message, along with a reply: "We are starting a band." On tour, he began kissing fans onstage, and these moments kept going viral—he sucked a girl's thumb, he kissed a boy, he kissed Ross MacDonald, the band's bassist. In the middle of one show, he lay back on a couch onstage as a tattoo artist inked the words "iM a MaN" on his torso. He inspired articles about the resurgence of the sleazeball and the appeal of the sensitive dirtbag. He sang like a louche Elvis and played a lipstick-red guitar.

"If you do a show that's about the duality of your life, is it still Method acting?" he asked between songs at the O2. The house lights came on, and white-coated technicians touched up the band members' clothes and faces. A tech slammed a clapboard, and they resumed their positions, concluding the meta intrusion.

The band resumed playing against the house-in-the-suburbs backdrop; the crowd sang along blissfully to a bouncy song about a school shooting. At the halfway point, there was a theatrical interlude, in which Healy, alone on the stage, played the role of one of the confused young men he'd been singing about. He unbuttoned his shirt and mimed masturbation; he desperately embraced a stage tech. While TVs blared footage of Tory politicians, he pretended to make out with himself, hands travelling up and down his back. I'd seen the same show at Madison Square Garden a few months before, and I'd cringed at this part, initially. Then Healy knelt in front of a raw steak, took an enormous bite, did a couple of dozen pushups, and squeezed his entire body through a small screenless television. His willingness to be embarrassing and abrasive edged into a kind of generosity, and a vulnerability. This is the heart of his appeal.

A few minutes later, the crowd went nuclear, but not for him: Taylor Swift, in a mirrored minidress, had walked onstage, performing "Anti-Hero," from her most recent album. "Did you hear my covert narcissism I disguise as altruism / Like some kind of congressman," she sang. Swift has been a fan of the band since at least 2014, when she was photographed wearing a 1975 T-shirt. Rumors circulated, at the time, that she and Healy were dating. (Healy, hounded for months to comment, said that having "Taylor Swift's boyfriend" as one's public identity would be an "emasculating thing.") "Anti-Hero" is self-deprecating and self-consciously Zeitgeist-y, with convoluted lyrics wrapped so tightly around the melody that they somehow seem tossed off—in other words, it's a little like a song by the 1975. She then performed "The City," a song from the band's first album. Girls around me were sobbing, as if they'd just gone blind looking at a solar eclipse.

"It's the last rock-and-roll show in town," Healy said after Swift had left and the band had returned for the second half, a set of hits culled from their first four records. After two decades together, the 1975 is as tight and instinctive as a legacy act. Healy's shape-shifting voice—he croons and wails and screams and murmurs, shading his delivery with a variety of personae—laces together the band's encyclopedic set of pop references: the soaring urgency of Peter Gabriel, the muscular propulsion of Bruce Springsteen, the addled funk of Talking Heads. Against the set dressing, Healy looked like a drunk boy dancing in his living room, ripping cigarettes and blowing kisses.

By 4 P.M. the next day, the band was back at the O2, sound-checking without him. The word backstage was that Swift had stayed until 3:30 A.M. the night before, singing 1975 songs with the band's bookkeeper after Healy had gone home. He arrived late, wearing a hoodie pulled tight around his face, like a "South Park" character. He started to light a cigarette, then saw that a child—MacDonald's niece—was lounging on the couch onstage, and put the cigarette away, laughing at himself. Healy led the band through a revised version of the interlude with the technicians, in which he'd tell the audience that nothing in the show was real. "For example, if I were to say stop," he said, rehearsing the bit—and everyone onstage froze, until he said, "Go." Someone suggested a tweak. "Yeah, but that's not *conceptual*," he replied.

Afterward, he walked onto the empty floor of the arena, and I asked him about Swift's cameo. "It was really based of Taylor to do the show," he said, seeming a bit awed that it had happened. A fake set list was circulating on Twitter showing Harry Styles as the guest for that night's performance. In the British press, Healy is sometimes positioned as Styles's Wario, his evil twin. Their bands became popular around the same time; both men are straight-leaning but, like Mick Jagger and David Bowie before them, enjoy revelling in sexual ambiguity. Healy said the band had asked Styles to come. "He gave us a *hard* no," he added, laughing. "He's afraid that he would have to say *something*." Healy found it annoying that, at a certain level of fame, celebrities can cultivate liberal auras while avoiding the risk of taking real political stands. (Swift, I thought, but didn't say, seemed to be excepted from his critique.)

He headed to the greenroom, where a mellow family vibe prevailed. MacDonald had been joined there by his niece; George Daniel, the drummer, was sitting with his girlfriend, the pop star Charli XCX. It has been alleged online that Healy is actually, secretly, five feet five inches tall; in truth, he looks short onstage only because Daniel and MacDonald are both six-four. (Healy says he's five-eleven; I'd guess five-ten.) Adam Hann, the guitarist, was also backstage, with his wife, Carly. The two have a one-year-old son. They had woken up at home just a few hours after Swift had left the O2.

Healy had skipped his make-out routine during the previous night's show. "I'm not kissing anybody in front of Taylor Swift, have some respect," he'd said. On night two, the fans reached for him with grasping fingers and tormented faces, a tangled mass of limbs, like a scene out of Hieronymus Bosch. Healy kissed one, then his face was grabbed by two others. He did his pushups and crawled through the TV. He told the crowd that Swift wasn't coming and that, instead, they could expect five extra minutes of his thoughts on industrial action (the night before, he'd given a shout-out to striking railway workers). He also talked about how the right was better than the left at offering anxious young men a path for their floundering masculinity. "All I can tell is that I'm a bloke, I'm confused, and I'm definitely on the left"—a roar of approval cut him off. "Shut up," he said, dismissing the reflexive praise.

The next day in London, it was mild and drizzly. I met Healy at a private club, a Soho House spinoff in Notting Hill known as the Electric. Young mothers with blond blowouts fed their children scrambled eggs amid old-fashioned wallpaper and framed black-and-white prints. Healy was carefully dressed: a pressed white shirt, perfectly shined shoes. He ordered orange juice and a steak.

"Steak?" I asked. "Again?"

Healy explained that he was from "circus stock" and needed to eat a lot of protein to keep muscle on. "My grandparents are from the circus—like, Irish travelling circus on both sides. I come from this really sinewy line of contortionists."

There are many performers in Healy's family. His mother's father, Vin Welch, was a successful drag queen, and both his parents are actors. Tim Healy, his father, was a welder before he joined a theatre company that staged productions in community halls. He met Denise Welch, who'd been onstage since her teens, at an audition in Newcastle. Matty was born in 1989, the year after they were married. His parents got TV work and became known as working-class heroes; Healy got used to holding their hands, patiently, as strangers waylaid them on the street. He found it confusing to grow up with parents who pretended to be other people for a living—he'd go to meet his mom on set and find that it was suddenly the eighteen-fifties and she was an old woman. One night, in a dark theatre, he watched his father take a punch under the stage lights, and went into a panicked spiral: his dad was getting hurt in front of everyone, but he couldn't do or even say anything about it.

The year he turned eight, his mother was cast on the soap opera "Coronation Street," which has been on the air in the U.K. since 1960 and which, in the nineties, regularly attracted nearly twenty million viewers. Welch has said that she began drinking heavily to deal with the pressures of the role; her alcoholism, and her marriage, became popular subjects of tabloid scrutiny. (She and Healy's father divorced in 2012; Welch recently celebrated eleven years of sobriety.) Healy told me, "I'd be a child, and something would happen in my real life, and then I'd see that thing on a newspaper, and I'd think, That's not what happened, but that's my mum saying a version of what happened, and I know Mum's at home and she's O.K." He came to understand that a person's life was "a balance between what is real, what is said, what happens, what people believe, what people project, and what is true."

"The Truman Show," in which Jim Carrey plays the unwitting, lifelong star of an always-on reality series, came out when Healy was nine, and he developed an intrusive fear that the movie was, in some way, about his own life. His parents were actors—what if everything was a loveless farce? On a vacation in Spain, in a taxi, his dad teased him about this ongoing neurosis, and Denise turned around from the front seat and told Tim to stop it. "She meant, Don't wind him up, he's obviously freaking out about this," Healy explained. "But I read that as one actor saying to another actor, 'Hush, you're going to give up the gig.'"

Newly flush with TV money, the Healys moved to Wilmslow, a posh Manchester suburb—"basically three square miles where Manchester United players live," Healy said—and he was sent to an all-boys private school. "Because I hadn't come from that culture, I was very aware of this hypermasculinity, and this desire for domination," he told me. He started a fight club in a locker room, charging fifty pence for admission and splitting the money with the fighters. He was expelled and returned to the local public schools, where he met Daniel, MacDonald, and Hann. They were all thirteen, they hung out in the music wing, and they formed an emo band that cycled through a series of emo names: Me and You Versus Them, Forever Drawing Six, the Slowdown, Drive Like I Do. They went through puberty as a unit and developed their identities symbiotically. One day, they all did MDMA for the first time, lying on the floor in the Healys' house, listening to music and feeling as if they had never truly heard it before.

Healy, an autodidact, didn't go to college; he streamed lectures on YouTube. The three others went to university in Manchester, to keep the band together. All four worked as delivery drivers at a Chinese restaurant. They played gigs and recorded songs but attracted no professional interest: their sound bounced around among pop genres, and they didn't fit into an indie scene dominated by bands such as Arcade Fire and Grizzly Bear, which leaned artsy and baroque. The 1975 weren't inheritors of Manchester's hard-edged musical lineage, either. "We looked like effeminate Catholic schoolboys," Healy said. "It wasn't exactly Oasis." A young music manager named Jamie Oborne heard some tracks they'd uploaded to YouTube and took them on as clients in 2007. All the big labels passed, so he founded a label of his own, Dirty Hit, in partnership with the band. Over bowls of pasta, the 1975 signed a deal.

Their first EP came out in 2012. Their breakout song was "Sex," a shimmery anthem about grimy teen-age lust: in 2013, the influential BBC d.j. Zane Lowe declared it the hottest record in the world. They developed a small but intense following, primarily consisting of music-blog obsessives and teen-age girls. Their first album hit No. 1 in the U.K., as did every album that followed it, but they didn't seem to have any casual listeners. "We're the biggest band in the world that nobody's ever heard of," Healy often said.

After finishing lunch, Healy and I headed to the roof of the Electric. A ponytailed bartender with "LOVE IT IF WE MADE IT" tattooed on his arm stopped Healy to praise the previous night's show and to thank him for getting him tickets. ("Did I do that?" Healy wondered later. "Guess I must have.") Healy's stream of consciousness is constantly swirling; he is fervent and buzzing and unexpectedly solicitous. He was recently diagnosed with A.D.H.D. When I asked him if he was surprised, we both started laughing.

In 2014, amid the early rush of fame and steady touring, Healy began smoking heroin, the only substance he found that could pull him down from the stratosphere. It was a secret, for a while; then the band staged an intervention. Healy resisted: he was the star, and the rest of them would have to get on board. He woke up the next day feeling like a fool and told Daniel he would go to rehab. He spent seven weeks at a center in Barbados, then flew back to London and immediately used again. "And then I used a little bit longer," he said, "and then I was just, like, Fuck, Matty, what are you doing? What you going to do if the guys find out?" He quit cold turkey in 2018. He's not involved with a formal sobriety program—he often seems drunk by the end of the live show, though he described this as an act only partly rooted in reality. "A lot of people will know that, given my history, I can hack a bottle of red wine over two hours," he said.

When I asked him what differentiated the 1975 from Matty Healy, solo pop act, he said, "It kind of *is* that." At various points, he's recorded music to use for a solo project, but so far it has all ended up going to the band. They depend on one another, he said. "We know when I'm addicted to smack, and we pick me up. George is dramatically depressed—we rally around him. One of us had a baby—so *we* had a baby, and when the baby is backstage, the greenroom is like a crèche. There's a 'Wizard of Oz' element to us. One of us needs a heart, one of us needs a brain, one of us needs this other thing, and we're all on the road together."

A year or so ago, the band turned down the opportunity to open for Ed Sheeran. On the roof, as Healy smoked his millionth cigarette, I asked him what was so precious about the 1975 that it would fall apart if they took that slot. "If you're someone's favorite band, that takes a lot of real emotional investment," he said, paraphrasing something that the producer Jack Antonoff had told him. "Let's say that relationship is, analogously, us talking here. I'm your favorite band, and you are the audience. If at some point in our conversation I start going like *this* all the time"—he looked pointedly over my shoulder, toward the pastel buildings of Notting Hill—"and you know over there is money, fame, personal enjoyment, whatever it is, you'll just go, 'O.K., I'll get another favorite band.'" Healy looked back at me closely. We had been talking for several hours, and I realized that the moment he looked over my shoulder was the first time he had broken eye contact.

Across their first four albums, the 1975 became more and more eclectic. They followed up their emo-inflected début with an eighties-style synth-pop record bearing the majestically corny title "I Like It When You Sleep, for You Are So Beautiful Yet So Unaware of It." In a review for Pitchfork, Laura Snapes—whom Healy later quoted in his acceptance speech—wrote that "for every neatly zeitgeist-capturing couplet" there was a lyric that made Healy "sound like the trustafarian street poet that he already slightly resembles." She described the album as "the X-rated cousin of Taylor Swift's *1989*." Then came "A Brief Inquiry Into Online Relationships," a maximalist statement record with bits of tropical house, a spoken-word track recited by Siri, and several immaculate pop singles. It got the best reviews of the band's career. "Notes on a Conditional Form" arrived next. It veers from garage to industrial and ambient music with some dabbling in country. "We always used to say that our attention spans were so bad that we had to do a million things," George Daniel told me. "But it was actually a product of insecurity, where we thought sounding like a band wasn't good enough—we had to do an orchestral piece, we had to do this or that. We felt like we couldn't do a short, coherent album."

Drummers tend either to vibrate with manic energy or to radiate a profound stillness. Daniel falls into the latter category, to the point that, when we spoke on Zoom, I kept thinking his screen had frozen. He and Healy have always made the band's music together: Healy writes most of the lyrics and many of the melodies, and Daniel, who studied music production in college, designs the sound. "In a way, Matty and George are opposites," Antonoff told me. Healy is a "wonderful balloon, who loves to fly out there but also wants to be held," he said; Daniel, then, is steady on the ground, hand tight around the string.

In 2021, though, they hit a wall. Healy had gone through a tough breakup with the musician FKA Twigs. Daniel, meanwhile, was dealing with depression. "We found it hard to get anything done musically, because we were both so acutely aware of the other person's suffering," he said. He described his dynamic with Healy as the kind you have with a romantic partner: "You love them more than anyone else in the world, and you cut them less slack than anyone else in the world."

Then they brought in Antonoff, whose band, Bleachers, came up around the same time as the 1975, but who is better known for producing Swift, Lana Del Rey, Lorde, and seemingly every other big name in pop. The safest thing for the 1975 to do, Antonoff said, would be to venture further into the esoteric; the surprising and brave thing would be to make a really good, straightforward album, as simple and as complex as a perfect slice of pizza. The band, with Antonoff, set rules in the studio. Everyone would play everything together, in real time, as much as possible. Healy wouldn't do any of the backing vocals, so that the album would be replicable live. Everyone would play analog instruments, and, ideally, ones they didn't normally play.

"Being Funny in a Foreign Language" ended up an album in pursuit of love, rendered plainly. "Before, I always debased myself when I became sincere," Healy told me. "I'd be sincere, and then I'd say, 'Oh, I'm only joking,' or 'Oh, I pissed myself,' or something else unglamorous to negate how much I just let you in." At one point, in the studio, he was recording vocals for a track that became "I'm in Love with You," and he kept trying to sneak a "not" into the chorus. Hann stopped him, and said, "Dude, five albums in, everyone knows you're funny. So if you want to say 'I'm in love with you' then just do it. Say it. That's where you're at." Healy told me, "All of the things that used to define my work, or the nihilistic part of one's twenties—postmodernism, addiction, individualism—they're all cool and sexy and appropriate at the time, but, for me now, are those the things I yearn for?" In his personal life, he had found himself wishing for consistency and reliability, "the things we get from a partner that we don't get from the rest of the world."

"I think Matty is a deeply sincere person, who can, at different points, be misunderstood because of how much he enjoys a bit," Antonoff said. "If you don't know him, if you don't get him, because you're not really tuned in to the work, you might assume a cynicism that is literally not there." He mentioned the song "Part of the Band." The lyrics are inflected with Healy's persona games, his compulsion to comment on the politics of pop culture, and at least three references to ejaculation. Healy sings, "Am I ironically woke? The butt of my joke? / Or am I just some post-coke, average, skinny bloke / Calling his ego imagination?" And yet it's a beautiful—and, somehow, even understated—song, set to a "Street Hassle"-style backdrop of lilting, bittersweet strings. "That to me is the most exciting part of him and his work," Antonoff said. "That the façade of it can beg so many questions, but that the heart is still so obvious—that it's this deep sincerity, and a longing for love, to love, to be loved."

Still, Healy remains caught between the heartfelt and the arch. On the second night at the O2, after calling the right wing's appeal to men "dangerous," he seemed suddenly self-conscious about his righteous pose. "I also really don't care that much, to be honest," he said. On the roof of the Electric, he launched into a passionate rant about the banjo player Winston Marshall, who'd left the band Mumford & Sons after praising the alt-right Twitter figure Andy Ngo and prompting an online furor. Marshall, as Healy saw it, had been radicalized not so much by right-wing ideas as by the praise and attention he'd got from right-wing circles—this, Healy said, is the situation for all sorts of young men whose world views are getting distorted by online feedback loops. Then he said, again, that he didn't really care that much.

"It seems like you do care," I said. "Otherwise you wouldn't keep bringing it up."

"I do," he admitted. "It's a good point."

Healy often laments that "we used to expect our artists to be cigarette-smoking bohemian outsiders, and now we expect them to be liberal academics." He has also said that, although he doesn't count his political views as particularly educated or authoritative, he knows that they stem from impulses toward empathy and freedom that are important.

"What do I mean when I say I don't care?" he asked. "What is that apathy I speak of? It's an exhaustion, maybe. The truth is, when I go home, this is not the shit I'm dealing with. I'm not dealing with the crisis of masculinity. I'm dealing with how my mum's feeling, what Ross is going through. I'm trying to be in service to people." He was no longer invested in the project of being publicly correct. "I've done my decade of trying to be that," he said. "I'm more interested in actually being wrong, and people seeing that, and knowing what's right because of it."

A month later, Healy went on a podcast called "The Adam Friedland Show." Friedland, whom Healy had befriended in the past couple of years, used to host the podcast "Cum Town," a title that reflects the "Borat"-esque level of seriousness that he and his co-hosts generally brought to the table. Friedland is part of a downtown New York scene referred to as Dimes Square, which, during the pandemic, became widely known for an ostensibly transgressive rejection of liberal pieties and a reactionary brand of post-left politics particularly associated with another podcast, "Red Scare." Healy has sometimes been spotted wearing a "Red Scare" hat; he told me that he became a fan in part because he was attracted to differences in opinion, and also to one of the hosts, whom he described as "really sexy."

On "The Adam Friedland Show," Healy and the hosts roamed more or less randomly around the cultural landscape, cracking jokes. One of the hosts asked if the rapper Ice Spice, who is of Nigerian and Dominican descent, was an Inuit Spice Girl, and the group then did crude approximations of an Inuit accent, veering from vaguely Chinese to quasi-Hawaiian. Later, he laughed as the hosts did impressions of hypothetical Japanese guards at German concentration camps. He joked about watching the brutal porn channel Ghetto Gaggers. After the episode went up, outraged headlines and furious tweets—"matty healy, how are you getting on stage every night and mocking toxic masculinity and then going on a podcast and undoing the whole thing by being wildly ignorant, misogynistic, homophobic, racist, everything else under the sun"—predictably ensued.

Healy had reached the level of fame that makes celebrities start speaking like politicians, even as he was still skinning his psyche for his performances. Aside from the podcast controversy, he was getting slammed for "doing a Nazi salute" onstage, a gesture he made, rather crucially, while singing a litany of horrors in "Love It If We Made It," including a line that quotes Donald Trump's praise of Kanye West. He didn't apologize or comment on the uproar, but he did seem more outwardly subdued afterward. When the band came to New York to perform on "Saturday Night Live," he played it straight, crooning in an unbuttoned tux. We met for lunch again, downtown, at Balthazar, a couple of days later. He was wearing another white shirt, but open to the chest this time, his tattoos showing.

I asked him about the podcast. He'd been doing so much promo, he told me, that he wanted to do something that felt more like simply talking with his friends. But, of course, he had done this all in public, on mike. Had he baited his fans on purpose? "A little bit," he said. "But it doesn't actually matter. Nobody is sitting there at night slumped at their computer, and their boyfriend comes over and goes, 'What's wrong, darling?' and they go, 'It's just this thing with Matty Healy.' That doesn't happen."

"Maybe it does," I said.

"If it does," he said, "you're either deluded or you are, sorry, a liar. You're either lying that you are hurt, or you're a bit mental for being hurt. It's just people going, 'Oh, there's a bad thing over there, let me get as close to it as possible so you can see how good I am.' And I kind of want them to do that, because they're demonstrating something so base level."

The night before, he'd hung out with the indie filmmaker Caveh Zahedi, who has cannibalized his relationships for his art. (In one early film, Zahedi tries, unsuccessfully, to make his estranged father and brother take Ecstasy with him, on camera. His most famous movie is an autobiographical comedy called "I Am a Sex Addict.") Not long before our lunch, Healy, on Instagram, had uploaded a short film he'd made, in which he plays his "real" self, first watching porn in a hotel room, then practicing being perfectly natural and lovely with selfie-requesting fans. "You wanna take it or you want me to take it?" Healy asks, before tilting his head to rest on the head of an imaginary girl. Then we see him walking around New York, and watch actual fans stop him and ask for selfies. "You wanna take it or you want me to take it?" he asks. Healy said that he admires Zahedi, but that he's wary of heading further in that direction.

"Like, I think the whole exaggeration of my shit throughout the past year and a half, maybe it proves there's something oppositional happening, that I'm getting something out of my system," he told me. "Because the truth is, I'm really quite anxious. We're all anxious, but at the moment I'm really anxious." It had something to do, he suggested, with his desire to be stoic, because stoic means masculine. "And this doesn't come from having an oppressive father who doesn't communicate," he added. His dad, he said, was open and soft, the one who passed on his belief in art as a vessel for radical truth. His mom was the "gobby" one—mouthy and intense. She's still on TV every day, on a talk show called "Loose Women," a rough analogue of "The View." She also has a podcast called "Denise Welch's Juicy Crack." ("Crack" is U.K. slang for gossip. At Balthazar, Healy, with weary affection, deadpanned a podcast tagline: "Come on Denise's juicy crack!")

Healy touched his "iM a MaN" tattoo, on his rib cage. "This whole thing, it comes from something real," he said. "I'm always sort of"—he mimed shadowboxing, nervously pumping himself up. "And this is all just a mental thing to be doing."

We finished lunch, then talked for a while longer outside, under an awning, as Healy smoked a cigarette. "I'm not trying to make myself famous," he said. "I want to be known for what I do. But now fame is about being known for who you are. And people are complicated." Girls were camping out on the sidewalk beside his hotel, stalking him all over the city. "If people are going to make me this famous, I'm going to make people work for it," he said.

The band was headed to South America, then to Australia. There, in April, he announced that he was quitting social media altogether—another turn. The 1975 was an "eras band," he said, and "the era of me being a fucking asshole is gonna come to an end . . . I've had enough." It sounded sincere, but the wording was curious; fans started to speculate that he was alluding to Taylor Swift, who had recently begun her Eras Tour, and that he was cleaning up his act in preparation for an announcement that they were dating. Was this a performance, or an existential shift? What would be the difference?

In May, tabloids reported that Healy and Swift were an item. Both of them, onstage during their respective tours, seemed to conspicuously mouth the words "This is about you, you know who you are, I love you." Healy flew from the Asia leg of his tour, in the Philippines, to attend Swift's show in Nashville. There was chatter, online, that it was a joke, or a publicity stunt, or perhaps simply two ardent self-chroniclers gathering material about intertwined egos for devastating pop albums to come. Neither of their representatives would comment on the record, but I kept getting texts from people who knew them, and who insisted: this time, it's real.

"Who Is Matty Healy?" by Jia Tolentino, *The New Yorker* © Condé Nast. Reprinted by permission.

From "The Out Crowd"

Emily Green

Nonfiction podcasts' unique intimacy and captivating storytelling typically associated with fiction are increasingly fueled by bold, rigorous reporting. Such rising standards for quality prompted the establishment of Audio Reporting as a new Pulitzer Prize category in 2020. Ira Glass and his team won the first-ever Pulitzer Prize in that category for "The Out Crowd," an episode detailing the compromised lives of asylum seekers on the Mexican side of the US-Mexico border during the Trump administration. The award was both a fitting tribute to the legacy of *This American Life*, whose dedication to journalistic principles dates back to the 1990s, and a clear signal that podcast journalism's coming of age has occurred under the mantle of reportage for social justice steeped in the journalism of verification. Eligibility for journalism's highest honor certified podcasting's credibility as news to match its status as the fastest-growing medium in digital publishing.

The serial documentary form that propelled podcasting into the mainstream with the publication of *Serial* in 2014 traces back to NPR and the work of Glass, who set the template for such longform audio reportage with *This American Life*. Podcast journalism now remediates predigital radio documentary and feature writing while extending online multimedia storytelling. Such a sea change in storytelling, one uniquely adapted to the asynchronous mobile consumption patterns of twenty-first-century audiences, has not occurred since the New Journalism of the mid-twentieth century unleashed the concept of news into the realm of richly textured nonfiction narrative.

The achievement of "The Out Crowd" suggests the importance of narrative journalism as an emerging aesthetic form rooted in both the literary world of creative nonfiction and reportorial fact. The convergence of the worlds of journalism and nonfiction creative writing is epitomized in both its dedication to reportorial truth-telling associated with hard news coverage and its creative attention to felt-detail and compassionate rendering of vivid atmosphere, character, and scene setting. The public radio origins of "The Out Crowd" describe this distinct trajectory toward a more layered, self-referential mode of storytelling complexity.

—D. D.

Act Two: Take The Long Way Home

Ira Glass

If you had to pick which border city in Mexico is the most dangerous, Nuevo Laredo, right across the border from Laredo, Texas, would be a good contender.

The State Department classifies it as level four threat. That is the same threat level as Iraq and Syria. And a lot of the danger there is kidnapping.

Kidnapping is so prevalent there that one of our producers met men in a migrant shelter who were terrified to go outside. A young Cuban guy told her, just putting one foot outside the shelter makes him worried. A trip of just two minutes, he's looking all around, and he's scared.

We're interested in these kidnappings because they're so common. Reporter Emily Green went to Nuevo Laredo in August, and she has this story about one kidnapping and what happened to one family, including recordings and details you really never get to hear. This family ended up in Nuevo Laredo because of MPP [Migrant Protection Protocols, originally the Remain in Mexico policy]. Here's Emily.

Emily Green

This guy who got kidnapped, I met him by chance, actually, before he got kidnapped, and he told me how scared he was that he would get kidnapped. I was on a bridge in Nuevo Laredo that connects Mexico to the US. Every day around 1:00 PM that month, the US was sending back migrants from the US side to Mexico under MPP.

That day, there were a hundred of them. They were easy to spot. They all carried clear plastic bags with a couple of documents in them, and none of them had shoelaces. US Immigration takes shoelaces from anyone they detain.

Most of them were men, many of them with their heads down, and one pair stands out to me-- a father and son in matching polo shirts, both of them sweating in the heat. They're chubby, soft faces, dad has his arm around son. They seem like they'll talk to me. The man, I'll call him David, quickly tells me a story.

David

No soy delinquente Soy una persona que ha ganado la vida pero ya no puedo vivir en mi país. Eso es lo que pasa.

Emily Green

He says he's not a criminal. He's a person who's always made a living, but he can't live in his country anymore. They're from Honduras. David was a businessman. He ran a little clothing store.

The gangs there demand money. They call it a war tax. The tax kept hitting higher and higher until David's family couldn't pay it anymore. One night, the cartel broke into his house, threatened to rape his daughter, and so they fled.

David

[SOBBING]

Emily Green

I've done lots of interviews with people like David, migrants in really difficult situations. This one felt especially hard. I think just seeing a father fall apart in front of his 11-year-old son.

David

Nunca me escucharon. Solo me dieron los documentos para venir a una cita aquí pero yo no puedo regresar más a Honduras.

Emily Green

David says he wanted to ask for asylum in the US, but the agents didn't listen to him. They just gave him documents to come back to a court date in December. He can't go back to Honduras, he says.

David

No tengo donde ir. No tengo nada. No tengo dinero. A mi me dicen aqui en esta lado donde vamos a pasar dicen que secuestran mucha la gente y no se que hacer.

Emily Green

I don't have anywhere to go. I don't have anything. I don't have money, he says. They say that here, where we're being sent, a lot of people get kidnapped, and I don't know what to do.

We only talked for 10 minutes. I ended up lending him my phone. He called his sister in New Jersey and explained what happened-- that he made it to the United States only to be sent back to Mexico.

It was getting dark out, and I'd been told not to stay in Nuevo Laredo past dusk. I crossed back into the US to go to dinner, probably not a mile away from where I'd last seen David, and my phone rang. It was David's sister. I'll call her Laura.

She had my number because it was my phone he called her from earlier today. She was crying so hard I struggled to understand what she was saying. She tells me David and his son had been kidnapped just hours after I'd left them. She'd gotten a call from a cartel demanding ransom.

Laura

[SPEAKING SPANISH]

Emily Green

Laura says of the cartel told her the ransom was $9,000 for David, and another $9,000 for his son, so $18,000 total. They put David on the phone briefly so she knew he was alive, and then the kidnappers got on.

Laura

Yo le dije a él que nosotros de adonde íbamos a sacar el dinero…

Emily Green

OK.

Laura

Solo me dijeron que tenía que mandar y que mañana me van a llamar.

Emily Green

And I told them, where in the world are we going to get this money? The man on the other end told her she had to get the money. He said he'd call back tomorrow. I asked Laura to record the phone calls.

And she did. When they called the next day, she put them on speaker and used a relative's phone to shoot video of it.

Laura

Es que no tengo nada. Nosotros no tenemos dinero muchacho. Viera como estamos ahorita de los nervios. Estoy más bien enferma.

Emily Green

They tell her, I need you to deposit the money as soon as possible, viejita. Viejita means old lady. Laura is 38. She tells them again that she has no money, that she's sick from anxiety.

In her conversations with me, Laura is scared, crying, but when she talks to the kidnappers, she holds it together. She asks if David and his son are OK. The kidnappers tell her they have food that they can bathe, for now. Each call only lasts a few minutes.

Man

[SPEAKING SPANISH]

Emily Green

By the third day, the cartel has lowered the price to $5,000 each for David and his son. Laura works the night shift at a printing factory in New Jersey, hardly makes $20,000 in a year, plus she's a single mom.

Man

[SPEAKING SPANISH]

Emily Green

In all of these calls, the kidnappers talk super fast, I'm guessing because they have other ransom calls to make. Kidnapping is a big business, a volume business, with a whole infrastructure. Kidnapping migrants has been common in Mexico for a long time.

What's different now is that the US is making it especially easy for the cartels to identify and snatch victims. They're sending asylum seekers back in big groups, all at once, at the same time each day, and they're easy to identify with their plastic bags and missing shoelaces. Homeland Security didn't respond to my request for comment on the kidnapping situation, but this week the acting head of Customs and Border Protection said the US is, quote, "sending a message to the criminal organizations to stop exploiting these migrants."

In Nuevo Laredo, the most dangerous part of these asylum seekers' journey is probably the hours right after they've been sent back to Mexico. After walking across the bridge, they're transported to the Mexican Immigration Office by van. Outside the office, men in four-door trucks monitor who's coming and going.

Locals call them, Los Malos, the bad guys. One migrant told me about getting chased as he walked to a shelter from there. But by far, the most dangerous place is a bus station.

It's a place they go to escape Nuevo Laredo, but it's a place they end up getting caught. Kidnapping is so routine the cartels refer to it as, passing through the office. On the extortion calls, you can tell it's a well-oiled machine. It's methodical. They sound like they're negotiating the price of a car. They do this all the time.

Man

[SPEAKING SPANISH]

Emily Green

Laura turns to everyone she can think of. She goes to her local police department and to her mayor's office to ask for help. They reach out to the Office of Senator Cory Booker, but by the time they get back to her about a week later, it's too late. Laura eventually scrapes together money from her mom and sister, but just a fraction of what the cartel is asking for.

Laura

Muchacho, yo te tengo 1,200 dolares...diceme que vamos a hacer y dame tiempo para conseguir otra parte más.

Emily Green

She tells them, look, I've already pulled together $1,200. Tell me what we're going to do and give me time to get the rest. The man says he'll confer with his boss.

In the meantime, he says, she should wire the money. Laura asks to talk to her brother and they put him on.

David and Laura

[SPEAKING SPANISH]

Emily Green

She asks David, how are you, brother? Worried, he says. She tells him, don't worry, that she's pulled together some money. The next day, the cartel's released David and his son. I talk to David on the phone three days after his release. He's so distressed, it's hard for him to finish a sentence.

David

[SOBBING]

Emily Green

[SPEAKING SPANISH]

Breathe, I tell him. I wanted to help him. That's not something a reporter is supposed to say, but back when they were kidnapped, their lives were in immediate danger, and I helped in small ways.

I connected Laura with an NGO in Mexico City that advocates for migrants. Since David and his son were released, I've suggested safe bus options. The family, they always knew that I was a reporter doing a story on them, but they came to see me as one of the few people they could trust-- that they could rely on. Laura called me almost every day with updates. She still does.

A few weeks ago, I went to meet David and his family in Monterrey in northern Mexico, where they were holed up. They were staying with an acquaintance of Laura's in exchange for grocery money and help with construction. David didn't want us interviewing him there. He feels his welcome has run out, so we do the interview at our hotel.

It's David, his 11-year-old son, and his 19-year-old daughter, who's also been sent back to Mexico under MPP. I'm here with my producer, Lina. We figure we'll talk to David in one room while the kids watch TV in the other, but the kids sit by their dad on the bed. They won't leave one another's side.

I wanted to know what happened when I left him that day on the bridge, and what he described were all these details of how the cartel's kidnapping business actually works once you're a victim on the inside-- details that were routine, and also terrifying. So here's what happened.

He said, he and the other 100 people who were sent back to Mexico that day were taken from the bridge to the local immigration office for processing. After that, he says a man wearing a Mexican immigration officer uniform agreed to take him and his son to the bus station so they could go to a safer city. But as soon as they got to the station, he got a bad feeling.

David

[SPEAKING SPANISH]

Interpreter

When I went in with my son, this guy grabbed me. He was a tall guy, strong, full of tattoos. So he grabbed me and he said, I want to talk to you. And I said, I have nothing to talk to you about.

And he said, you're going to get into that car, and we're going to ask you some questions. And I said, no. And he said, you can get into the car the easy way or the hard way.

David

[SPEAKING SPANISH]

Emily Green

He says at least a dozen migrants also arrived at the bus station that night, and the cartel hustled them into different trucks. All the trucks were brand new, he says. He remembers that the one he got into was a gray Nissan, and there were four or five other migrants in there with him.

He says, the immigration officer who drove him to the bus station sat in his car and watched them all being carted off. We can't confirm this, but there is a long history of law enforcement and the cartels working hand-in-hand. For example, in 2011, seven top officials at Mexico's immigration agency were fired amid allegations that the agency was involved in the kidnapping of migrants.

And it squares with what his sister in New Jersey told me. She wired money to that immigration officer for David's bus ticket, and when she got the ransom call, the kidnappers told her to wire the money to that same account, the one the immigration officer used. She said something like, isn't that the immigration officer's account? And they hung up.

I asked the Mexican immigration agency to respond. They told me they have no knowledge of recent complaints of immigration officers turning migrants over to the cartels.

In the truck, David held onto his son. The kidnappers didn't speak.

David

[SPEAKING SPANISH]

Interpreter

The guy just told us to keep our heads down, to stop looking at the sights. And the guy who was driving us was keeping an eye on us, and he was making sure we were not chatting. They had the windows all rolled up.

Emily Green

The truck drove around for a while, but David suspects they were just going in circles, but they didn't actually travel very far. They pulled up to a normal-looking house with a big gate.

Inside, the kidnappers used their cell phones to take pictures of David, his son, and the rest. They interrogated David about where he's from, his line of work, how he got to the US, and most importantly, what family members he has there. It was like patient intake at a health clinic, except for by a cartel.

We talk about the cartels as organized crime, but I never imagined the bookkeeping. They keep records and photos of the migrants they kidnap, and also who they release.

David says there were more than 20 migrants at the house. The men and women slept in separate rooms. During the day, the kidnappers hit any of the men who tried to look at the women.

The room David and his son slept in had one mattress. Everyone else slept on the floor. At night, David would lay on the ground, holding his son.

David

[SPEAKING SPANISH]

Interpreter

I would lay down with him in a corner, and I would hug my son. They couldn't see you crying, but my tears were almost, like, falling out.

What hurt me the most, Emily, was that when this guy arrived, the boss, he would always tell me that my son's organs were good for selling, that he was in a good age, that he was only 11 years old.

David

[SPEAKING SPANISH] [CRYING]

Interpreter

And my son once heard the guy saying that his kidneys-- that his organs-- were good for selling, and he was almost crying. And I told him, don't cry, but I was desperate.

David

[SPEAKING SPANISH]

Emily Green

As David tells me this story, his two kids are still sitting on the bed beside him. Neither of them is looking at anything in particular. They're just sitting there blankly.

David also seems devoid of emotion. He doesn't at all resemble the David from a few weeks ago, the one I talked to right after his release. Now, his affect is completely flat.

On the fourth day of his kidnapping, one of the bosses woke David up and told him they'd reached a deal with his sister.

David

[SPEAKING SPANISH]

Interpreter

And he said to me, get up with your son, fat guy, because today I'm going to release you guys because your sister already paid, made a deposit.

Emily Green

The man told David if he talked to anyone-- police, reporters-- the cartel would come for him, take his son, and kill David. The same man who kidnapped them in the first place drove them back to the bus station and bought them each a ticket.

David doesn't know what happened to the dozens of other people in the house. Most migrants who are kidnapped and released, the cartel gives them a key word. It's like a passcode that indicates the migrant has paid off the cartel so they aren't kidnapped again, but David isn't given one, maybe because he hasn't paid a high enough ransom.

When we met David in Monterrey, he didn't know what he was going to do. On day one of the kidnapping, the cartel had taken David and his son's immigration paperwork, and they didn't give it back. Without that paperwork, he doesn't even know which day he's supposed to show up in court.

But even if he could figure it out, he told us, he's too scared to return to Nuevo Laredo. Under MPP, he'd have to pass through the same port of entry to get to his hearing. What if we get kidnapped again? He asks.

Last week, I got a phone call from David. The family they've been staying with in Monterrey wants them gone, and he's lost hope in the asylum process. He thinks they won't be listened to, that the hearing process is a lie.

And in fact, he's right about how his case is likely to come out. Under this administration, it's virtually impossible to gain asylum based on gang violence. So David's decided to take his family back to Honduras, the country they tried escaping in the first place. According to Homeland Security's own statistics, thousands of other families are making the same choice.

Excerpt from *This American Life* Episode #688 "The Out Crowd," broadcast November 15, 2019. Episode produced by Nadia Reiman and Aviva DeKornfeld. Emily Green's story "Take The Long Way Home" produced by Lina Misitzis. *This American Life* is produced in partnership with WBEZ Chicago.

Showing and Telling

From "The Case for Reparations"

Ta-Nehisi Coates

When it appeared in *The Atlantic* in 2014, this story established Coates as the leading journalistic authority on racial inequality's impact on America. Through exhaustive reporting and compelling writing, Coates argues for taking seriously the idea of reparations for slavery. Even though Coates did not go undercover to take on long-standing injustices as journalists Marvel Cooke and Nellie Bly did in their eras, his work has sparked similar reactions—anger, debate, and a push for social change. Following the publication of this article, reparations became a talking point for Democratic candidates for president in the 2020 election, showing "that Coates succeeded in turning the idea of reparations from a punchline into a policy objective," wrote *Washington Post* columnist Jonathan Capehart.

"The Case for Reparations" won a George Polk Award and broke readership records at the magazine's website. Coates does not identify as an activist, nor does he lay out the "how" for reparations, just the "why." Widely shared and made available on the magazine's website as an audio story, the piece traces the plunder of Black wealth through the family of Clyde Ross, whose parents lost their land in Mississippi for allegedly being behind on their taxes. Illiterate and without legal representation, they became sharecroppers. Coates shows that what happened to Ross and his family over the decades, from land seizures to predatory mortgages to redlining, has also happened to many other Black families. Coates's writing is historical and accessible, disciplined and emotionally resonant.

As the son of a former Black Panther who was also the founding publisher of Black Classic Press in Baltimore, Coates grew up around books and ideas. He has consistently produced notable blends of personal narrative, history, and reportage, especially his 2015 book *Between the World and Me*, winner of the National Book Award, which is structured like a letter to his teenage son.

Coates has authored three other books and a novel, and he has also written for Marvel's comic series, *Black Panther* and *Captain America*.

Coates received a "genius grant" from the MacArthur Foundation in 2015. According to the foundation, Coates "subtly embeds the present—in the form of anecdotes about himself or others—into historical analysis in order to illustrate how the implications of the past are still experienced by people today."

—J. M.

Speculators in North Lawndale, and at the edge of the black ghettos, knew there was money to be made off white panic. They resorted to "block-busting"— spooking whites into selling cheap before the neighborhood became black. They would hire a black woman to walk up and down the street with a stroller. Or they'd hire someone to call a number in the neighborhood looking for "Johnny Mae." Then they'd cajole whites into selling at low prices, informing them that the more blacks who moved in, the more the value of their homes would decline, so better to sell now. With these white-fled homes in hand, speculators then turned to the masses of black people who had streamed northward as part of the Great Migration, or who were desperate to escape the ghettos: the speculators would take the houses they'd just bought cheap through block-busting and sell them to blacks on contract.

To keep up with his payments and keep his heat on, Clyde Ross took a second job at the post office and then a third job delivering pizza. His wife took a job working at Marshall Field. He had to take some of his children out of private school. He was not able to be at home to supervise his children or help them with their homework. Money and time that Ross wanted to give his children went instead to enrich white speculators.

"The problem was the money," Ross told me. "Without the money, you can't move. You can't educate your kids. You can't give them the right kind of food. Can't make the house look good. They think this neighborhood is where they supposed to be. It changes their outlook. My kids were going to the best schools in this neighborhood, and I couldn't keep them in there."

Mattie Lewis came to Chicago from her native Alabama in the mid-'40s, when she was 21, persuaded by a friend who told her she could get a job as a hairdresser. Instead she was hired by Western Electric, where she worked for 41 years. I met Lewis in the home of her neighbor Ethel Weatherspoon. Both had owned homes in North Lawndale for more than 50 years. Both had bought their houses on contract. Both had been active with Clyde Ross in the Contract Buyers League's effort to garner restitution from contract sellers who'd operated in North Lawndale, banks who'd backed the scheme, and even the Federal Housing Administration. We were joined by Jack Macnamara, who'd been an organizing force in the Contract Buyers League when it was founded, in 1968. Our gathering had the feel of a reunion, because the writer James Alan McPherson had profiled the Contract Buyers League for *The Atlantic* back in 1972.

Weatherspoon bought her home in 1957. "Most of the whites started moving out," she told me. "'The blacks are coming. The blacks are coming.' They actually said that. They had signs up: DON'T SELL TO BLACKS."

Before moving to North Lawndale, Lewis and her husband tried moving to Cicero after seeing a house advertised for sale there. "Sorry, I just sold it today," the Realtor told Lewis's husband. "I told him, 'You know they don't want you in Cicero,'" Lewis recalls. "'They ain't going to let nobody black in Cicero.'"

In 1958, the couple bought a home in North Lawndale on contract. They were not blind to the unfairness. But Lewis, born in the teeth of Jim Crow, considered American piracy—black people keep on making it, white people keep on taking it—a fact of nature. "All I wanted was a house. And that was the only way I could get it. They weren't giving black people loans at that time," she said. "We thought, 'This is the way it is. We going to do it till we die, and they ain't never going to accept us. That's just the way it is.'"

"The only way you were going to buy a home was to do it the way they wanted," she continued. "And I was determined to get me a house. If everybody else can have one, I want one too. I had worked for white people in the South. And I saw how these white people were living in the North and I thought, 'One day I'm going to live just like them.' I wanted cabinets and all these things these other people have."

White flight was not an accident—it was a triumph of racist social engineering.

Whenever she visited white co-workers at their homes, she saw the difference. "I could see we were just getting ripped off," she said. "I would see things and I would say, 'I'd like to do this at my house.' And they would say, 'Do it,' but I would think, 'I can't, because it costs us so much more.'"

I asked Lewis and Weatherspoon how they kept up on payments.

"You paid it and kept working," Lewis said of the contract. "When that payment came up, you knew you had to pay it."

"You cut down on the light bill. Cut down on your food bill," Weatherspoon interjected.

"You cut down on things for your child, that was the main thing," said Lewis. "My oldest wanted to be an artist and my other wanted to be a dancer and my other wanted to take music."

Lewis and Weatherspoon, like Ross, were able to keep their homes. The suit did not win them any remuneration. But it forced contract sellers to the table, where they allowed some members of the Contract Buyers League to move into regular mortgages or simply take over their houses outright. By then they'd been bilked for thousands. In talking with Lewis and Weatherspoon, I was seeing only part of the picture—the tiny minority who'd managed to hold on to their homes. But for all our exceptional ones, for every Barack and Michelle Obama, for every Ethel Weatherspoon or Clyde Ross, for every black survivor, there are so many thousands gone.

"A lot of people fell by the way," Lewis told me. "One woman asked me if I would keep all her china. She said, 'They ain't going to set you out.'"

VIII. "Negro Poverty is not White Poverty"

On a recent spring afternoon in North Lawndale, I visited Billy Lamar Brooks Sr. Brooks has been an activist since his youth in the Black Panther Party, when he aided the Contract Buyers League. I met him in his office at the Better Boys Foundation, a staple of North Lawndale whose mission is to direct local kids off the streets and into jobs and college. Brooks's work is personal. On June 14, 1991, his 19-year-old son, Billy Jr., was shot and killed. "These guys tried to stick him up," Brooks told me. "I suspect he could have been involved in some things ... He's always on my mind. Every day."

Brooks was not raised in the streets, though in such a neighborhood it is impossible to avoid the influence. "I was in church three or four times a week. That's where the girls were," he said, laughing. "The stark reality is still there. There's no shield from life. You got to go to school. I lived here. I went to Marshall High School. Over here were the Egyptian Cobras. Over there were the Vice Lords."

Brooks has since moved away from Chicago's West Side. But he is still working in North Lawndale. If "you got a nice house, you live in a nice neighborhood, then you are less prone to violence, because your space is not deprived," Brooks said. "You got a security point. You don't need no protection." But if "you grow up in a place like this, housing sucks. When they tore down the projects here, they left the high-rises and came to the neighborhood with that gang mentality. You don't have nothing, so you going to take something, even if it's not real. You don't have no street, but in your mind it's yours."

We walked over to a window behind his desk. A group of young black men were hanging out in front of a giant mural memorializing two black men: IN LOVIN MEMORY QUENTIN AKA "Q," JULY 18, 1974 ♥ MARCH 2, 2012. The name and face of the other man had been spray-painted over by a rival group. The men drank beer. Occasionally a car would cruise past, slow to a crawl, then stop. One of the men would approach the car and make an exchange, then the car would drive off. Brooks had known all of these young men as boys.

"That's their corner," he said.

We watched another car roll through, pause briefly, then drive off. "No respect, no shame," Brooks said. "That's what they do. From that alley to that corner. They don't go no farther than that. See the big brother there? He almost died a couple of years ago. The one drinking the beer back there ... I know all of them. And the reason they feel safe here is cause of this building, and because they too chickenshit to go anywhere. But that's their mentality. That's their block."

Brooks showed me a picture of a Little League team he had coached. He went down the row of kids, pointing out which ones were in jail, which ones were dead, and which ones were doing all right. And then he pointed out his son—"That's my boy, Billy," Brooks said. Then he wondered aloud if keeping his son with him while working in North Lawndale had hastened his death. "It's a definite connection, because he was part of what I did here. And I think maybe I shouldn't have exposed him. But then, I had to," he said, "because I wanted him with me."

From the White House on down, the myth holds that fatherhood is the great antidote to all that ails black people. But Billy Brooks Jr. had a father. Trayvon Martin had a father. Jordan Davis had a father. Adhering to middle-class norms has never shielded black people from plunder. Adhering to middle-class norms is what made Ethel Weatherspoon a lucrative target for rapacious speculators. Contract sellers did not target the very poor. They targeted black people who had worked hard enough to save a down payment and dreamed of the emblem of American citizenship—homeownership. It was not a tangle of pathology that put a target on Clyde Ross's back. It was not a culture of poverty that singled out Mattie Lewis for "the thrill of the chase and the kill." Some black people always will be twice as good. But they generally find white predation to be thrice as fast.

Excerpt from "The Case for Reparations" by Ta-Nehisi Coates, *The Atlantic*. © 2014 The Atlantic Monthly Group, LLC. All rights reserved. Used under license.

From "Bodies on the Line"

Carina del Valle Schorske

The page doesn't hold Carina del Valle Schorske's words as much as it provides a venue for them, one that doesn't feel like any place you've ever been. On her website, she says, "I write about Caribbean culture, literary politics, diasporic dramas, and the songs I can't stop singing to myself." Hers is a voice of Puerto Rico and the Puerto Rican diaspora, but also of pandemic landscapes of culture and coping. She is a translator and a poet, as well as a contributor to *The New York Times Magazine*, for which she has both profiled the reggaetonero Bad Bunny and danced across New York City in between Covid lockdowns. As our guide for that journey in the summer of 2021, she is both a participant journalist and a cultural historian, describing the moment in the context of dance's history of release and resistance. Her paragraphs offer insight and knowledge, music and warmth. She tells of the "medieval dancing mania" after the Black Death in Europe and of dance's prominence in folklore and popular culture before stepping into the frame herself, taking readers into the clubs, parties, and other spaces where people dance and helping us understand why she, and we, want to. "In isolation, I'd felt myself stiffen into a form so familiar it had come to seem inescapable," she writes. "I wanted my body to influence and be influenced by other bodies—this time not as a vector of disease but as a vector of pure feeling."

"Bodies on the Line" won the Essays and Criticism category of the 2022 National Magazine Awards. Del Valle Schorske's writing has also appeared in the *Virginia Quarterly Review*, *The Believer*, and *The New Yorker* online, among other publications. Her first essay collection, *The Other Island*, received the 2021 Whiting Creative Nonfiction Grant. The jury lauded her "fresh perspective and a bright, authoritative narrative voice," also noting that "her prose is lyrical and accessible, richly researched and sharply argued."

—J. M.

For most of 2020, I passed the pandemic alone in my studio apartment. I turned 33, then 34, and my body seemed to grow old without bringing my spirit along with it. My right knee was clearly deteriorating—I couldn't sit cross-legged at my desk the way I used to—and because I wasn't wearing makeup, I could track each age spot as it bloomed to the surface. When I pulled my hair back in a tight ponytail, I could see a patch of scalp. But in that same period had my life evolved at all? Had I met anyone? Surprised myself? Stemmed the tide of collective crisis? My mother often urged me to dance, just a little, by myself in the kitchen—"It's good medicine," she said, "*despojo*."

I've never known what "*despojo*" means, precisely, though it's a word I use with some frequency to express a physical craving for spiritual catharsis: "*Necesitamos despojo, quiero despojarme.*" Or, watching a friend gain momentum on the dance floor and begin to enter a self-forgetful trance: "*Esoooo! Des-po-jo!*" My Spanish-English dictionary has only the verb (to despoil, to shed leaves) and the plural noun (the spoils of war, mortal remains, rubble, waste). Google Translate: dispossession.

It's strange to discover that a word I associate with rejuvenation technically has more to do with death and disaster. I guess "*despojo*" comes to me, via Puerto Rican Spanish, in a register already worked through by ritual, by generations of people who've had to scavenge something good from the many losses of forced migration. The "*despojo*" I've desired articulates a paradox. In order to repossess the body, it's necessary to dispossess it; in order to feel alive, it's necessary to get in touch with what's already dead. But when I say "*despojo*," I don't always mean to sound so serious. Sometimes I mean that I want very badly to pin somebody to the club wall with my butt.

Even though it's better, as my mother recommended, to dance alone than not at all, the "*despojo*" I'd been dreaming of was social. In isolation, I'd felt myself stiffen into a form so familiar it had come to seem inescapable. I wanted my body to influence and be influenced by other bodies—this time not as a vector of disease but as a vector of pure feeling.

This impulse has a history. According to the French historian Philippe de Félice, "Eras of greatest material and moral distress seem to be those during which people dance most." A medieval dancing mania swept through Europe following the height of the Black Death, when between 500 and 800 people died every day in Paris and Saint-Denis, and when alternating waves of flood and drought caused widespread famine. In her book "Choreomania," Kélina Gotman argues that the medieval frenzy was really a mix of phenomena transpiring over centuries—intensified midsummer celebrations, municipal feasts meant to placate the masses, traditional pilgrimages that surged with new enthusiasm. But historical accounts leave little doubt that the boom in public dancing had something to do with the proximity of death. In 1348, two monks traveling through Paris observed a band of people in the street frolicking to the music of drums and bagpipes. When the monks asked the revelers why they were making such a scene, they replied, "We have seen our neighbors die and are seeing them die day after day, but since the mortality has in no way entered our town, we are not without hope that our festive mood will not allow it to come here, and this is the reason for why we are dancing."

Occasionally, the dancing itself was fatal—there were those who dropped dead from exhaustion, and in Utrecht, 200 people danced on a Mosel bridge until the structure collapsed and many drowned. Folklore with roots in this period, like "The Pied Piper of Hamelin," warns of rhythm's seductive power. So do later tales like "The Red Shoes," in which the young girl who wears them must have her feet cut off to halt her cursed dancing. That story frightened me as a child, but it also shaped a lasting preference. When I go out, I find myself reaching for wine-colored suede ankle boots with a Cuban heel, as if to court the ecstasies of enchantment.

I thought of those shoes when New York City's second pandemic spring began to buzz with fantasies of freedom. Slowly, then quickly, people I knew lined up for the vaccines. By Memorial Day, the subways were crowded and the bars noisy again. We stumbled into the season's audacious promise exhausted, delirious and seething with desire. I listened to Stevie Wonder's "Love Light in Flight" on loop, as if the song—*we will fly forever and one hour*—could restore the time we'd lost together. I followed a dozen D.J.s on Instagram. I texted my most festive friends. I mapped out New York City—birthplace of bugalú, salsa, hustle, vogue, breaking, flexing—and traced possible paths through a series of summer parties. When I opened Uber on my phone, the corporation's new tagline amplified the siren song: "The world's opening up again. Where to first?"

Back then, the summer seemed luxuriously long. But our reckless rush to make the most of it told another story. Even before the sudden surge of the Delta variant, we knew whatever freedom we'd chosen to feel would be hyperlocal, most likely temporary and possibly destructive. We were right to think it might be our only chance. At Papi Juice's Pride party, when Destiny's Child came on, the incandescent anxiety of our wish to be well made the bridge sound like a spell: *I'm doing so, so, so, so, so, so, so, so, so good/Good, good, good, good, goooood.* That very day at the Gotham Jazz Picnic in Central Park, where our feet disappeared in the dust kicked up by our Lindy-hopping, I danced with a widower in white linen who called me by his dead wife's name. At Coney Island in late July, the celebrated B-boy turned D.J. Tony Touch overstayed his boardwalk set and called out to his remaining audience: "If you're still here, I want you to act like it. I want to see that."

We are still here. We are trying to find out what it means to act like it. Bourgeois propriety often seems to prefer a clear distinction between grief and jubilation. In Puerto Rico, 19th-century white criollos condemned the Afro-Indigenous practice of the *baquiné*, in which children who died very young were dressed in flowers, sometimes lace, and mourned with all-night vigils of drinking, drums and dancing. But what always struck me as most mortifying was not the intensity of that display but the possibility that those of us left living do not love life enough to deserve our survival. I don't believe in deserving, but I do believe we owe the dead a little dancing.

The first night I went out for real was the Friday before the Puerto Rican Day Parade. My friends and I rode up from Brooklyn to the Bronx Brewery for A Party Called Rosie Perez, to hear DJ Laylo, Sucio Smash and Christian Mártir play together live for the first time since 2019. I don't like the parade—the corporate sponsorships, the political ring-kissing—but I like how all the city's Puerto Ricans seem to turn up at once, rowdy and rebellious, for the annual roll call. And I'd been to A Party Called Rosie Perez twice before, so I played along when a woman I didn't quite recognize—long blond braids, little crystals at her tear ducts—threw her arms around my neck as soon I stepped inside the door. Later, when I passed her on the way to the bathroom, we locked eyes and both laughed: "I'm not your girl, right?" "No—I liked that you faked it though!"

None of us seemed to remember how long to look an unmasked stranger in the face, whether to speak up or simply drift into the orbit of someone else's rhythm until touch could take over. For me, the tension broke when DJ Laylo dropped the early crossover house hit "Show Me Love" and the off-key strain in the voice of Robin Stone—she had the flu at the studio session—cut through our second-guessing with the desperate power possessed by the sick. *Words are so easy to say. …/You've got to show me love.* It felt good to make our human needs known against the electronic grind, to remember machines could be our creative allies rather than our overseers. *It's been so long since/I touched a wanting hand.* The government had failed to protect us and lied about the gravity of our collective condition. *Don't you promise me the world/All that I've already heard/This time around for me, baby/Actions speak louder than words.* The only language that could reach us now would be the language of bodies assembling in tight quarters to show love, even if we fumbled when we reached for one another.

The really skilled salseros had gathered on one side of the stage, and some of us wandered over to watch, caught between envy and admiration. I could see one woman's training in her perfect spotting. A lanky dancer in a red bucket hat had incredible improvisational range, looked absolutely natural, even with the hint of show business I could see in the clean angle of his elbows. Andrew Avilá turned out to be a dancer for Lin-Manuel Miranda's movie "In the Heights," which premiered the night before—a South Bronx Puerto Rican-Colombian who grew up dancing salsa at home with his mother before he turned professional. In previous generations, his great-grandfather crafted and played the folk guitar called the *cuatro*, his uncles played congas and almost everybody danced at the Palladium Ballroom during the midcentury mambo craze. Whatever genius he possessed did not begin, and would not end, with him.

I liked him best dancing with a radiant woman in a red crop top, loose black pants and waist beads—she could have followed the turns I saw him spin other partners through, but instead she was eliciting his rhythmic playfulness, tremors traveling between their torsos. At one point—it wasn't salsa anymore, but merengue—he tapped out the beat on the small of her back, and I saw her toss her head back and laugh with delight. I laughed, too, when I asked her name and it turned out to be just two letters off from my own, as if I'd dreamed myself into her dancing. Later, I asked Corinna Vega to remember that merengue moment. She couldn't locate it precisely—of course not—but she remembered the feeling: "the beauty of not knowing what happens next, the beauty of messing up and just like, you're still going."

Especially now, we're tormented by the volatile future, the anxiety of adaptation. The uncertainty of the pandemic seems merciless. But dancing activates the pleasure in this roiling field of possibilities, makes it feel as if there will always be another chance to choose. To reset the connection. To find opportunity in error. Getting ready for her first night out in over a year, Corinna had wavered—"like, do I still got it?" Once she was back in the moment, she remembered that dancing is not something you've got. It's something you have to let get you.

Excerpt from "Bodies on the Line" by Carina del Valle Schorske, *The New York Times*. © 2021 The New York Times Company. All rights reserved. Used under license.

From "Twelve Minutes and a Life"

Mitchell S. Jackson

Mitchell S. Jackson writes bravely. He shows his anger and his sadness.

"I would never want to just report the information," he says in the book *Stories Can Save Us* by Matt Tullis. "To me, anybody can do that, so it's almost like I gotta filter it through me and the me is the singing." By the time "Twelve Minutes and a Life" appeared in *Runner's World*, Ahmaud Arbery had been dead for four months, murdered while he was jogging in Glynn County, Georgia. By then, many had already seen the video of Arbery being stalked by white men in a pickup truck, trapped, and then shot. Jackson makes readers see it again, through his eyes. On the *Longform* podcast, Jackson said he always tries to find a personal connection to the stories he writes, and he felt connected to "Maud." Interspersed with time-stamped narrations of the video are vivid scenes from Arbery's real life, as told to Jackson by his coach, his girlfriend, his sister and brother, and others who were close to him.

Jackson also turns his lens on the sport of running, yet another institution marred by racism. He addresses his readers: "Peoples, I invite you to ask yourself, just what is a runner's world? Ask yourself who deserves to run? Who has the right? Ask who's a runner? What's their so-called race? Their gender? Their class? Ask yourself where do they live, where do they run? Where can't they live and run? Ask what are the sanctions for asserting their right to live and run—shit—to exist in the world. Ask why? Ask why? Ask why?"

An assistant professor of creative writing at Arizona State University, Jackson has written for *The New Yorker*, *Harper's*, and *The Paris Review*, among other publications. He has authored one critically acclaimed novel, *The Residue Years*, and a nonfiction book, *Survival Math: Notes on an All-American Family*, selected as one of *Time*'s Must-Read Books of 2019. He is also a columnist for *Esquire*. In 2021, "Twelve Minutes and a Life" won both the National Magazine Award and the Pulitzer Prize for Feature Writing. The Pulitzer Prize Board commended Jackson "for a deeply affecting account of the killing that combined vivid writing, thorough reporting and personal experience to shed light on systemic racism in America."

On the *Longform Podcast*, Jackson credits Gordon Lish, the legendary fiction editor best known for his work with Raymond Carver and Don DeLillo, among other literary greats from the 1970s through the 1990s, for giving him the confidence to pursue writing. At one of Lish's workshops in 2008, the notoriously combative editor told Jackson what set him apart as a writer: "Jackson, you got an ear."

—J. M.

To fathom what it meant for Maud to be out for a run in Glynn County, you need to know a thing or two about the pastime of recreational running. Before the 1960s, the idea of jogging for almost everybody save serious athletes was this: Now why would I do that? But in 1962, legendary track coach and Nike co-founder Bill Bowerman visited New Zealand and met with fellow coach Arthur Lydiard who'd developed a cross-country training program. Bowerman returned to the States excited by what he'd seen. He launched a similar program in Eugene (home of his alma mater and employer, the University of Oregon), wrote a pamphlet on the subject in 1966, and the next year, published a co-written book titled *Jogging: A Medically-Approved Physical Fitness Program for all Ages Prepared by a Heart Specialist and a Famous Track Coach*. That book became a bestseller and kickstarted jogging as an American pastime.

Let me acknowledge that I am one of the rarest of Americans, one otherwise known as a Black Oregonian. As such, I feel compelled to share a truth about my home state: It's white. I'm talking banned-Blacks-in-its-state-constitution white. At the time that Bowerman was inspiring Eugene residents to trot miles around their neighborhoods in sweatpants and running shoes, Eugene was a stark 97 percent white. One could argue that the overwhelming whiteness of jogging today may be, in part, a product of Eugene's demographics. But if we're keeping it 100, the monolithic character of running can be credited to the ways in which it's been marketed and to the systemic forces that have placed it somewhere on a continuum between impractical extravagance and unaffordable hazard for scores of people who ain't white.

Matter of truth, around the time Bowerman visited New Zealand and published a bestselling book, millions of Blacks were living in the Jim Crow South; by 1968, Blacks diaspora-wide had mourned the assassinations of Medgar Evers, Malcolm X, and Martin Luther King Jr. And by the late '60s and beyond, the Blacks of the Great Migration were redlined into ever more depressed sections of northern and western cities, areas where the streets were less and less safe to walk, much less run. Forces aplenty discouraged Blacks from reaping the manifold benefits of jogging. And though the demographics of runners have become more diverse over the last 50 years, jogging, by and large, remains a sport and pastime pitched to privileged whites.

Peoples, I invite you to ask yourself, just what is a runner's world? Ask yourself who deserves to run? Who has the right? Ask who's a runner? What's their so-called race? Their gender? Their class? Ask yourself where do they live, where do they run? Where can't they live and run? Ask what are the sanctions for asserting their right to live and run—shit—to exist in the world. Ask why? Ask why? Ask why?

Ahmaud Arbery, by all accounts, loved to run but didn't call himself a runner. That is a shortcoming of the culture of running. That Maud's jogging made him the target of hegemonic white forces is a certain failure of America. Check the books—slave passes, vagrancy laws, Harvard's Skip Gates arrested outside his own crib—Blacks ain't never owned the same freedom of movement as whites.

Sunday, February 23, 2020 | 1:08pm Maud strolls out the house and in just a few steps, begins to jog. He's unaware of the witness who called 9-1-1, a man still surveilling him. "He's running right now. There he goes right now," says the witness to dispatch. "Okay, what is he doing?" says the dispatcher. "He's running down the street," says the man. The footage shows Maud jogging past the Satilla Drive home of Gregory and Travis McMichael—a father and son. Gregory McMichael, an ex-cop stripped of his power to arrest for failure to attend use-of-force training, notices Maud passing his house and deems him suspicious. "Travis, the guy is running down the street," he hollers. "Let's go."

For reasons the McMichaels must now account for in court (both have been indicted on nine counts, including felony murder and aggravated assault), they arm themselves—the son with a Remington 870 shotgun and the father with a .357 Magnum—and hop in a white Ford pickup truck.

The NAACP once defined lynching as a death in which 1) There was evidence that a person was killed 2) The death was illegal 3) A group of at least three actors participated in the killing. According to "Lynching in America," a report by the Equal Justice Initiative, there were 4,084 southern-state lynchings between 1877 and 1950. Of the 594 reported in Georgia during that period—one of only four states yet to pass a law on hate crimes—three occurred in Glynn County.

Between 1920 and 1938, the NAACP New York headquarters flew a flag that announced "A Man Was Lynched Yesterday" to mark a murder that fit their criteria.

A boy was lynched today: for walking hooded down a street and refusing the command of an overzealous neighborhood watchman. A man was lynched today: for selling loosies outside a bodega. A teen was lynched today: for a disputed exchange of cigarillos. A child was lynched today: for holding a toy outside a rec center. A man was lynched today: for fleeing a traffic stop unarmed. For hawking CDs outside a convenience store. For announcing a legal gun and reaching for his license. A woman was lynched today: for sleeping. And yet another man was lynched today: for suspicion of passing a fake twenty. D-e-a-t-h! In Florida, New York, Missouri, Ohio, South Carolina, Louisiana, Minnesota, Kentucky, and again in Minnesota.

Sunday, February 23, 2020 | 1:16pm "Two subjects on Holmes Road. Shots fired. Male on ground, bleeding out," radios an officer. Maud musters his last breath near the intersection of Holmes Road and Satilla Drive, a mere 300 yards from where, not 10 minutes prior, he wandered inside a construction site. The officers will cordon the scene and investigate. They will question the McMichaels—Gregory's hands bloody from rolling Maud onto his back—and William Bryan. And in an act that is itself another violence, they will let all three go about their merry way as free men—for almost three months.

On February 23, 2020, a young man out for a run was lynched in Glynn County, Georgia.

His name was Ahmaud Marquez Arbery, called "Quez" by his beloveds and "Maud" by most others. And what I want you know about Maud is that he had a gift for impressions and a special knack for mimicking Martin Lawrence. What I want you to know about Maud is that he was fond of sweets and requested his mother's fudge cake for the birthday parties he often shared with his big sister. What I want you to know about Maud is that he signed the cards he bought for his mother "Baby Boy." What I want you to know about Maud is that he and his brother would don the helmets they used for go-carting and go heads-up on their trampoline, and that he never backed down from his big brother. What I want you to know about Maud is that he jammed his pinkie playing hoop in high school and instead of getting it treated like Jasmine advised, he let it heal on its own—forever crooked. What I want you know about Maud is that he didn't like seeing his day-ones whining, that when they did, he'd chide, "Don't cry about it, man. Do what you gotta do to handle your business." What I want you to know about Maud is that Shenice told me he sometimes recorded their conversations so he could listen to her voice when they were apart. What you should know about Maud is that he adored his nephews Marcus III and Micah Arbery, that when they were colicky as babies, he'd take them for long walks in their stroller until they calmed. What you should know about Maud is that when a college friend asked Jasmine which parent she'd call first if ever in serious trouble, she said neither, that she'd call him. What I want you to know about Maud is that he was an avid connoisseur of the McChicken sandwich with cheese. What I want you know about Maud is that he and Keem were so close that the universe coerced each of them into breaking a foot on the same damn day in separate freak weight-room accidents, and that when they were getting treated in the trainer's office, Maud joked about it. You should know that Maud dreamed of a career as an electrician and of owning a construction company. You should know that Maud gushed often of his desire to be a great husband and father. You should know that he told his boys that he wanted them all to buy a huge plot of land, build houses on it, and live in a gated community with their families. You should know that Maud never flew on a plane, but wanderlusted for trips to Jamaica, Japan, Africa. What you *must* know about Maud was that when Travis McMichael, Gregory McMichael, and William "Roddie" Bryan stalked and murdered him less than three months shy of his 26th birthday, he left behind his mother Wanda, his father Marcus Sr., his brother Buck, his sister Jasmine, his maternal grandmother Ella, his nephews, six uncles, 10 aunts, a host of cousins, all of whom are unimaginably, irrevocably, incontrovertibly poorer from his absence.

Ahmaud Marquez Arbery was more than a viral video. He was more than a hashtag or a name on a list of tragic victims. He was more than an article or an essay or posthumous profile. He was more than a headline or an op-ed or a news package or the news cycle. He was more than a retweet or shared post. He, doubtless, was more than our likes or emoji tears or hearts or praying hands. He was more than an R.I.P. t-shirt or placard. He was more than an autopsy or a transcript or a police report or a live-streamed hearing. He, for damn sure, was more than the latest reason for your liberal white friend's ephemeral outrage. He was more than a rally or a march. He was more than a symbol, more than a movement, more than a cause. He. Was. *Loved.*

Excerpt from "Ahmaud Arbery and the White Man's Justice" by Mitchell S. Jackson. Copyright © 2021 by Mitchell S. Jackson, initially published in *Runner's World*, used by permission of The Wylie Agency LLC.

From "Out in the Great Alone"

Brian Phillips

One of the great pleasures of reading Brian Phillips's multimedia features in *Grantland* is his sheer enthusiasm for his subject. In his 2013 coverage of Alaska's Iditarod dogsled race for the now-shuttered ESPN boutique website—originally established by founding editor Bill Simmons as a clearinghouse for ambitious literary sports journalism with a narrative bent—Phillips bears a heightened sensitivity to his surroundings. At one point in "Out in the Great Alone," he transforms the sensation of cold into a brilliant insight: "More than affecting my sense perceptions, though, the cold seemed to affect the way I thought about my sense perceptions." Alaska, we learn, and its iconic dogsled race, is a state of mind that affects any who enters it. Bizarre and otherworldly aspects of remote locations, such as Nome do not escape him. "Nome, a northern Alaskan metropolis of 3,731 souls, may be the most steampunk city in the world," he writes. What follows is a visual description worthy of Washington Irving's "word sketches" originally made famous in the absence of photography during the Industrial Revolution, a technique that would since become a staple of the travel writing genre. In the hands of Phillips, the genre takes on buoyant felicity, often delighting in the manic ecstasy of the moment. Upon sighting a polar bear from a small plane, he confesses, "I couldn't feel my spine, she was so beautiful."

A former senior writer for MTV News whose work has appeared in publications such as *Slate* and *The New Yorker*, Phillips assumes a central presence in the story, rhetorically vacillating between freewheeling commentary and interpretive reportage that often reads like a blend of blogosphere discourse and Hunter S. Thompson's unfettered candor. Phillips plays a central role in this story as in his Thompsonesque plunge into Wimbledon for another longform *Grantland* story that appeared in 2012. That year, Phillips contributed three other large-scale projects to *Grantland*, ranging from a historical feature on an

1810 boxing match featuring a freed slave—arguably the most important in the sport's history—to an investigative exposé of FIFA and pop culture criticism upon the twenty-fifth anniversary of *Star Trek: The Next Generation*. "Out in the Great Alone" stands out among these works as the most ambitious in terms of both reportage and digital design. For reporting, the Iditarod story entailed the expense of travel not required of the others, while the digital design incorporates lush photos, animated maps, and embedded videos missing from the other pieces. By contrast, their rather spartan design's only digital add-on consists of embedded notes glossing the text, yet with incisive wit reminiscent of the David Foster Wallace endnote (made famous in *Infinite Jest*).

Not to be underestimated for the formal liberties it takes, "Out in the Great Alone" self-consciously draws on its literary forebears in the genre of travel writing, invoking Shackleton and Melville to frame the sublime mysteries of remote locations on the map. Phillips's first-person narrative voice is neither diaristic nor does it descend into solipsistic memoir, but instead positions himself as the reader's avatar, or something of a tour guide through which we experience the Iditarod's surrounding geography and culture. In sharp contrast to detached traditional reporting, we encounter the unrestrained and idiosyncratic voice of Phillips. But more than raw emotion, his powers of perception deliver creative insight that consistently bears in mind the humor of his predicament, especially in his vulnerability as a newcomer to this location and its ways of life. Were he simply covering a dogsled race on short assignment, none of the rich side journeys would have been possible in this digital age travel narrative that doubles as literary sports writing worthy of *Grantland*'s most ambitious enterprise journalism.

—D. D.

We flew to Russia. It was the Frenchmen's idea. For two days Christophe spent all his free time studying this giant map of western Alaska, folded up to show one square of the Bering Sea coast; he kept making little marks with a mechanical pencil and frowning. Then he and Bernard huddled over the map together, murmuring in French. Finally they went to Jay.

"Ah, *oui*," Christophe said. "I enquire. Is it possible … we go to Diomèd?"

"The Diomede Islands?" Jay said. His lips stretched in an exaggerated grimace. "It's … *possible*. I've never done it, but it's possible. Let me hop on the radio."

Christophe had circled two tiny islands in the middle of the Bering Strait, the stretch of water, just 53 miles across, that separates Alaska from Russia. The islands couldn't have been more than a couple of miles apart. The border, as well as the International Date Line, ran right between them. Big Diomede was on the Russian side, Little Diomede on the American.

"OK," Jay said the next day. "What I'm hearing is, during the winter, they carve an airstrip on the sea ice right plum in the middle of the islands. Weather's only clear for a Cub to land about 2 percent of the time. Partner, it is rough stuff out there. But we can darn sure give it a crack."

We flew to Nome on Sunday; on Monday we set out for the Diomedes. It meant losing the race for a day. But when you're on an Arctic expedition, and fate beckons you to a frozen sea on the edge of Chukotka, you don't say no.

Once you have left behind the spruce forests, and left behind the tundra, and gone out over the sea ice, Alaska becomes a different thing, even huger, almost unbearably bright. The sheets of ice crack and collide and form fault lines, spaces of open sea called *leads,* so that what you're looking at is a field of snow that's crazed in places with zigzags of black water.

It's the other side of the mist. I mean, it's another world. Beluga whales swim up into the leads and you would see these little divots in the water where their foreheads poked through. White forms streaming angelically down beneath the divots. We surprised a small herd of musk ox near some sort of deserted military compound on the coast and flew low over them while they formed their protective circle. We chased a herd of caribou.

I saw three seals lying on the edges of three adjacent leads.

Steve chimed in over the radio: "Dad, we might want to go to line abreast. We've got bear tracks *everywhere* down there." And there were. Heavy dashed lines across the snow, like blue stitches around the edges of the leads. Jay had gone searching for polar bears every year on the Iditarod expedition and never found one. (He'd gotten up close and personal with the bears that destroyed Nugget, but that was farther north, way up in the Arctic Circle. "Only time

I see those little pukes," he told me, "they're chomping on my airplane.") We circled for 10 minutes, 15 minutes without luck. The flight to the Diomedes was already going to stretch our fuel reserves to the limit; we'd have to break off in another couple of minutes. "They hide from me!" Jay moaned. "They always hide."

Then I saw her.

She was almost invisible, a tiny yellow-white spot against the rim of the water, an imperfection in the snow. I screamed something that might as well have been in Japanese and Jay banked the plane hard and dove while I whipped my head around trying to keep the polar bear in view. I couldn't keep my o'clocks straight. "Polar bear at three o'clock! Twelve forty-five! Eight seventeen! No! Eight seventeen*ish*!" Then Jay saw her too.

The nine seconds of video I managed to shoot during the first pass we made over the bear shows a tiny lumbering ivory *something*, the size of a fly on a kitchen floor, galloping across the ice shelf under Nugget's yellow right wingtip. We made a second pass and got close enough to see her haunches shuddering, but by that point I'd dropped the camera.

Everybody pretty cynical here? Fantastic.

I couldn't feel my spine, she was so beautiful.

In the summer I guess they look like islands, but in the winter the Diomedes just look like cliffs, dusty white rocks towering up out of the snow. The runway on the sea between the islands was a thin plowed line, too rough to land on; we touched down right beside it, on the sea ice. The day was bright and clear. Apparently we'd picked a moment that fell within the lucky 2 percent. On the American island, a tiny Eskimo village bunched together in one corner at the base of the cliff—home, we'd read, to about 100 Inupiat. There had once been a sister village on the Russian island but it was forcibly disbanded by the Soviets to prevent ideological contamination. Otherwise the Cold War might have been ended prematurely by a few dozen Eskimo capitalists. Now the Russian side just had a border guard headquarters and a weather station.

We were only supposed to look. That was the deal. We'd hop out of our planes, eat a sandwich, and take a picture of Russia. Then we'd head home. Anything more would be illegal. But I was so giddy from the flight and the polar bear (we all were, we were grinning like idiots) that as soon as I'd finished throwing an engine blanket on Nugget I turned to the villager who took care of the airstrip—Henry, his name was, he'd come out on a snow machine to greet us—and asked how far to the border.

"Oh, about 400 yards over yonder," Henry said.

And I took off. I didn't ask permission. Looking back, I can see that I was undergoing pretty intense mood swings as a result of the PTSD from all the amazing experiences I'd been having. But I was free, wasn't I, in Alaska? It was slow going, because I was too free to bother with snowshoes and thus had to churn through 30 inches of snow.

I headed across the frozen strait, toward the jagged white rock of Big Diomede.

This was it—the actual end of America. Sure, we had borders with other countries. We had nothing close to this.

Every way you could think of that sentence was true.

How far I'd come! Hundreds and hundreds of miles to reach this place. You couldn't fathom how huge Alaska was until you'd seen it from a Super Cub, one horizon crawling into the next, day after day after day. And the white rock in front of me was the end. Somewhere behind it lay the beginning of Siberia.

When I estimated I'd gone five or six hundred yards, I went up on tiptoe and waved like mad to the Russian side. I thought I saw something flash, like light striking a mirror, off the tower the top of which could just be made out over the rock. But that was the only thing that happened.

A few minutes later Steve and the Frenchmen caught up with me. When I'd bolted for the border, they'd taken it as an excuse to follow. I'd built a lead because they put on snowshoes first. Jay, who was an adult, had stayed behind with the airplanes.

A few minutes after that a border-patrol agent came from the American side and called out that if we didn't come back the Russians would fire warning shots.

On the way back I noticed that my face felt like it had been sandblasted. Jay came forward to meet me. "We need to get these stinkers out of this cold, ASAP. If the engines freeze we'll never get out of here. Are you OK? Your face is as red as a beet."

Oh, right—it was cold! I'd had too much adrenaline to notice. Now I realized that the wind was roaring down the channel between the islands. I'd staggered through it without even realizing. Thirty knots, Jay said. And we were looking at probably 35 below. Still, it was hard to move quickly. We ate our sandwiches and took pictures. The villagers who came out from Little Diomede told us we were the first planes, not counting the helicopter that brought the mail, to be able to land at the island all winter. More and more kept coming out, just to look at us.

Someone should have noticed that the Frenchmen had neglected to put a blanket on their plane. Afterward, there was disagreement about what had happened. Jay insisted that they'd asked him and he'd told them not to bother, which makes so little sense that I'm sure he was being diplomatic. Regardless, I am an idiot non-pilot who never even flew the Tahiti route for Air France, and I was out of my head with excitement, and I threw the blanket on Nugget without being told. It's just something you do. And Steve and I discussed, in dark tones, the time Bernard had taken after we landed to retrieve and then put on his finespun red wool face mask, how carefully he'd straightened out the mouth. We wound up writing it off with a shrug as the final revenge of the ghost. Whatever happened, by the time we'd finished taking snapshots and meeting villagers, by the time we'd gotten our helmets strapped on and our windows latched, it was too late. Jay climbed out of Nugget and tried to manually start their propeller with a two-handed spin, the way you see in old movies. The Frenchmen's engine was as dead as the island rock. It was as dead as a gunshot ptarmigan. It was as dead as the alien civilization that had built the dark pyramid, probably.

We were stranded out there for three hours. It was the first time I ever understood why freezing to death is sometimes described as *peaceful* or *soothing* or *just like falling asleep,* descriptions that had always seemed to hint at some unfathomable mind-transformation within the freezing person, some power extreme cold had to enchant the brain's basic mechanisms of homeostasis. It didn't feel violent, that was the thing. Even with the wind ripping past you. It was like certain parts of your body just accrued this strange hush. Like you were disappearing piece by piece. I thought I'd be warmer outside and walking around than inside Nugget, so I would sort of exaggeratedly move one limb at a time, my left arm or whatever, and while I was concentrating on my left arm my right leg would start to be erased.

More than affecting my sense perceptions, though, the cold seemed to affect the way I thought about my sense perceptions. I'd take my glove off to adjust a zipper and lose feeling in my hand almost immediately and instead of thinking *Holy no I need to get my glove back on right this second* I'd sort of pause and go *My, how interesting that my hand feels as though it's visibly translucent.* Then my brain's inbox would gently ding. PLEASE DON'T DIE.

Jay had it the worst. He was out there the whole time, crouched under the plane, trying to get the engine heated. Villagers from Little Diomede kept forming little peering semicircles a few feet away from him. Finally he walked back to Nugget.

"We're taking off," he said. "Bernard and Christophe can stay in the village." The teachers had agreed to put them up at the school.

The last I saw of our two French pilots, they were being carted away on snow machines, half-bewildered, waving back at us.

Nome, a northern Alaskan metropolis of 3,731 souls, may be the most steampunk city in the world. Imagine a Wild West mining town, the sort with free-swinging saloon doors and a jailhouse with a rocking chair on the porch—call it Buzzard Gulch—then transport it away from cacti and outcroppings to a snowy waste on the shore of a frozen bay. Modernize it some, give it electricity. Now litter it, and be enthusiastic, with twisted hulks of sheet metal, headless fuselages, giant noseless propellers, detritus of air travel that no one has the resources or motive to clean up. Picture *McCabe & Mrs. Miller,* only if the climactic battle involved two blimp armadas. Sink, at weird angles in the snow outside of town, locomotives not used since the Gold Rush. Freeze eerie derelict mining ships into the ice. Now draw back. Look over your work. And: Nome.

There's a story that it was named by accident, through a misreading. Before anyone had thought what to call it, they penciled in "Name?" on the map. Some nearsighted cartographer mistook the writing and handed the wrong vowel to history.

Front Street is where they'd have gunfights, if they had gunfights. It's a skinny thoroughfare with its back to the Sound; the drunks lurch-strutting to the next bar, of whom at any moment there are several, get glimpses of the sea between the buildings. The town's put up Christmas lights to celebrate the end of the Iditarod. Big zigzagging strings of them. The snow-packed road terminates in a chute exactly like the one at the starting line in Anchorage. Above the chute there's a wooden arch, and above the arch there's a banner that reads: "FINISH."

This is Tuesday, March 12. The end of the Iditarod, for the winners, anyway. Here's how this works. It's night. A small crowd turns out, maybe 300 people, under the Christmas lights. I'm there alone, because Jay and Steve have flown back to Little Diomede on a mission to rescue the Frenchmen. There's a screen the size of a king-size bed hanging from the second story of one of the storefronts across the street. It's playing "Idita-Rock n' Roll," a kid-friendly Iditarod-themed music video from the '90s. The spectacle is largely financed by Anchorage Chrysler Dodge, one of the Iditarod's major sponsors, whose owner, Rod Udd, is known as "Idita-Rod" due to his obsessive love of the race. The storefronts—Nome Liquor Store, Gold Buyers of Alaska, the Bering Sea Restaurant/Bar, Arctic Trading Post Gift Emporium, the Nugget Inn—are doing slow but respectable trade, almost none of which seems Iditarod-related. The night is a very deep blue. It's -2°F. The church next to the "Idita-Rock n' Roll" screen has a banner in front advertising Icy 100.3 FM.

This year's race has come down to a straight fight between Mitch and Aliy. Unsurprisingly given the times and distances involved, Iditarod finishes are rarely close, but this one's going to be; leaving the White Mountain checkpoint, 75 miles from the finish line, Aliy's just 13 minutes behind. In 1978, Lance Mackey's father, Dick, won the Iditarod by just one second; certain reckless members of the crowd speculate within reportorial earshot that we could be fixing to see that all over again. Certainly the guy who seemed to be in charge at the media briefing an hour earlier said to expect both dog teams to be in the chute at once, something that hadn't happened in his previous 20-plus years of seeming to be in charge at Iditarod media briefings. Literally every single person I talk to wants Aliy to win, and so do I. There's a feeling, when the crowd first assembles, that she has a slim but real chance.

You find out early, though. Barring an actual photo finish, there's almost no scenario in which the end of an Iditarod can be surprising. The mushers are half-mad and starved and frozen and the dogs have run 1,000 miles in a week; the sleds are going maybe 7 miles an hour; no one's making up much ground under those circumstances. When the PA guy, after we've been standing around for an hour, says, "Mitch is three miles out," it means Mitch has won, only you end up waiting another half-hour for him to finally arrive. In the end, Mitch pulls in at 10:40 p.m. and Aliy's 23 minutes behind. It's head-twistingly close by Iditarod standards, but Mitch has plenty of time to sob and embrace loved ones and commune with dogs and have camera lights pointed in his haggard frost-mustached face and shake hands for official photos and still clear out of the chute a good while before Aliy arrives.

He's the oldest winner in the history of the Iditarod, Mitch, at 53. Last year, his son Dallas became the youngest champion when he won at 24. Now they're bookending all the other winners, age wise, a fact that will lead most of the newspaper coverage tomorrow.

There's such goodwill at the press conference. Mitch and Aliy eat cheeseburgers and crack jokes. There's no sense that one of them just suffered an agonizing defeat; instead, there's an air of conspiratorial wonder, like, *Oh wow, can you believe we made it?* As the sporting event that most closely mimics the experience of sustained brutal catastrophe, the Iditarod is maybe uniquely designed to amplify sport's natural euphoria-making power with basic human relief. Which is one of the most thrilling things there is, if you think about it. Imagine if Game 7 were played on inflatable rafts in a shark tank; afterward LeBron would be all, *That happened! I survived!*

Everyone in the room gets this: fans, volunteers, media. It's a close-knit world; people know each other. So when Mitch says—

"The brain kind of stops working somewhere along the Yukon. I offered Aliy a cough drop this morning and she decided it was too complicated to unwrap it."

—the laugh that rolls through the room is not the brittle pre-deadline laugh of reporters being fed good copy but a delighted and leisurely laugh of people who've been there, or know someone who's been there, and who just want to share in the moment.

What are you going to do tomorrow, someone asks.

"Probably hang out with my dogs and my family," Aliy says.

"I'm going to sleep and eat," Mitch says. "My family can hang out with my dogs."

They'd both had hallucinations. Near the end, kind of beautifully, each had visions of the other. Aliy thought she saw Mitch's yellow sled floating somewhere ahead of her. Whenever Mitch looked behind him, the world kept turning into Aliy. "I saw the raven Aliy, I saw the fuel-tank Aliy. And the upside-down-boat Aliy," he says. The way he says it, it's like something from a myth. They share a look, like, hello, vast and terrifying cosmos.

At around midnight, as I'm on my way out, this happens at race HQ: I see Uncle Dick. From Takotna, remember? He made it, all 700 miles on his snow machine. He's sitting at a folding table with six or seven other race fans, drinking coffee. Team Viagra kept the streak alive.

There are taxis in Nome—in fact there are whole taxi companies. Somehow this makes economic sense in a town of 3,700 people just below the Arctic Circle. There are small fleets of battered gray minivans, the 800 numbers on their sliding doors half-covered by winter curb-silt. Mr. Kab, Checker Cab, E-Z Transportation. I called one in the middle of the night. My driver's name was Roxy. She was a young native woman, maybe 27, with a laughing-Buddha face and sparkly star-shaped glasses. I remember them being sunglasses, but that can't possibly be right. The reflections of the Christmas lights shone out of them like colored lanterns. I was thinking about this city, Nome, which felt like something someone had generated by accident during their first try at a video game, and how it was crisscrossed by all these nonsensical taxis—this arbitrary pattern of routes, so many origins and destinations, dots appearing and disappearing on a map. So I asked Roxy how she'd gotten into the cab game, hoping to use that intro to transition into a follow-up about people and where they're all going.

But she seemed kind of taken aback. "Oh," she said at length. "I'm only doing this for a while, you know? My family, we're more into subsistence stuff. Fishing, gathering berries." She reached into the van's ash tray, where there was a loose ball of rubber bands, and rolled the rubber bands between her fingers. She spoke so slowly I wasn't sure she'd go on. "We practice those skills, my family, because who knows, we say. Who knows what'll still be here tomorrow?"

I thought of Jay, who'd flown with me for 1,100 miles, who'd kept me alive, and who'd given me a copy of his book, *Survival Flying: Bush Flying Tales and Techniques, As Flown and Taught in Alaska,* by C. Jay "The Piper Poet" Baldwin. He'd inscribed it "read and heed!" It was a textbook, but it opened with a poem about bush pilots, a poem Jay had written himself.

Here's to the brave souls that aviate,

Across that vast Alaskan state ...

The poem was dedicated to the memory of Jay's friend and mentor Bert, the one who'd disappeared in the waters of the Shelikof Strait.

Who knew what would ever be there tomorrow? And it hit me that that was exactly the point of the Iditarod, why it was so important to Alaska. When everything can vanish, you make a sport out of not vanishing. You submit yourself to the forces that could erase you from the earth, and then you turn up at the end, not erased. I'd had it wrong before, when I'd seen the dog teams as saints on the cusp of a religious vision. It was the opposite. Visionaries are trying to escape into something larger. Mushers are heading into something larger that they have to escape. They're going into the vision to show that they can come out of it again. The vision will be beautiful, and it will try to kill you. And (oh by the way) that doesn't have to be the last word. That's why you go to the end of the world—to see whether you're still there.

Excerpt from "Out in the Great Alone," by Brian Phillips. Published May 5, 2013; © ESPN/Grantland.com © ESPN. Reprinted courtesy of ESPN.

The Reporter Takes the Stage

From "The Mastermind"

Evan Ratliff

Originally appearing in seven installments of *The Atavist Magazine* from March through April of 2016, Evan Ratliff's "The Mastermind" operates on an epic scale. The complex and intricate 40,000-word narrative details one of the largest and least-reported organized crime syndicates of the twenty-first century. Later adapted into a book and documentary film, the piece stands as Ratliff's magnum opus underscoring *The Atavist*'s status as a major pioneer of online longform storytelling. Touting a list of coveted accolades, including the Overseas Press Club's 2017 Award for Best Digital Reporting on International Affairs and a 2016 Online Journalism Award for Innovation in Investigative Journalism, the investigation's production process reflected both colossal ambition and innovative method. Ratliff's method of reporting reached across media, inviting online audience interaction. Several interviews for "The Mastermind," for example, did not occur until after two episodes were published to draw attention to the process of production and solicit reader suggestions for key interview sources and other data. Ratliff's model was *Serial*, the NPR podcast, whose listeners similarly leveraged social media to contribute key data to support its reportorial process.

Ratliff's subject is Paul Le Roux, author of Encryption for the Masses and E4M, an open-source, free Windows disk encryption software program. Born an orphan in Bulawayo, Rhodesia, now Zimbabwe, Le Roux avoided the death penalty despite setting up at least seven murders and would eventually sign a proffer of immunity in exchange for pleading guilty to two charges the US Drug Enforcement Agency (DEA) obtained through their sting operation. At one point, Le Roux had a militia in Somalia, which he intended to use to invade the Maldives (a tiny island nation 2,000 miles east of Somalia in Africa) and to install a dictator to establish a safe haven for his giant online crime syndicate, which trafficked in pharmaceuticals, logs, gold, and arms. One of his more notorious schemes was to murder a former DEA agent as one of his stings. His hitman, Joseph "Rambo" Hunter, was arrested in 2013 in a DEA murder sting operation, wearing a Homer Simpson T-shirt.

News reports of Hunter's arrest captured Ratliff's imagination. His initial reporting was often a "late night internet thing," as he noted on the *Longform Podcast*, with "an infinite amount of research that could be done without ever talking to anyone" from Hong Kong court files to tracking shell companies and drilling down on the backgrounds of the people listed on their boards of directors. Eventually, the reporting entailed flights to the Philippines and Israel for interviews. Whereas Le Roux himself was unavailable since he is serving a twenty-five-year sentence, several of the roughly 1,000 people who worked for him were eager to reveal their stories in person to Ratliff. In this case, the reporter's risk lay in dedicating a major portion of his life to a story about a figure who routinely arranges for the murders of people who expose him. Ratliff thus used neutral sites such as Starbucks for meeting places with individuals he tracked down on LinkedIn. Interviewees provided pseudonyms for the story and communicated through encrypted emails, many telling Ratliff, "my safety is in your hands" and "don't burn me," as he recalled on the podcast. Le Roux's notoriously swift retribution reflected his "arrogant way of killing" that initiates the investigation in the ensuing passage.

—D. D.

Episode 1: An Arrogant Way of Killing

Jeremy Jimena had just started his shift when he found the body. At 6:30 on the morning of February 13, 2012, Jimena, a garbage collector in the Philippines, had set out with his driver on their regular route through Taytay, an industrial city an hour east of Manila. It had rained most of the night, and a light drizzle fell as they turned down Paseo Monte Carlo, a quiet road with no streetlights. Their first stop was a large vacant lot overrun by low shrubs, a green carpet of vines, and a scattering of banana trees.

The field wasn't an official pickup spot, but local residents often dumped garbage there anyway, and the collectors had informally added it to their route. There was a small pile of trash that morning spilling into the road: two large grain bags filled with waste and a bulging, rolled-up bedspread. Jimena hopped off the truck and approached the pile. When he leaned down and grasped the damp edge of the blanket, he saw a human foot.

Jimena dropped the blanket and ran, shouting to the driver, and the two of them left the truck and sprinted to the municipal headquarters, 200 yards away. There they told Ricardo Maniego, the local head of security, what they found. Maniego called the police and brought a long cord to rope off the area, like he'd learned in first-responder training.

Nearly four years later, in December 2015, I sat with Jimena outside the municipal headquarters. He is a small, wiry man with jet black hair and a wisp of a mustache. He looked off in the distance as he recounted the story, his eyes wide and mournful. He'd known right away that the foot was a woman's, he said, but couldn't remember much else. "I was shocked and disoriented," he said.

After he'd shown Maniego the body, Jimena had returned to his route in a daze. He never spoke to the police, he told me, and never learned who the woman was. But for years, he had dreamed of her every night. "She's screaming, asking me for help," he said. "Sometimes she is wrapped in a blanket. Sometimes it wakes me up."

...One aspect of the crime stood out to [the investigator] Rivera: Lee had been shot once under each eye, with what forensics had determined was a .22-caliber handgun. "In our experience," he said, "if you shoot a person dead, you don't normally use a low-caliber firearm." Hit men in the Philippines, he said, typically used "Armalite weapons, hand grenades, or a .40-caliber pistol. This is one of the few times that I discovered that the caliber was a .22 Magnum." To Rivera, the weapon said something about the crime, namely "that it might be a type of signature killing." He believed that Lee's death was not a crime of passion but a professional murder committed by someone looking to send a message. "That's an arrogant way of killing, putting two bullet holes beneath the eye," he said. "That's not how you normally execute a person."

During his investigation, Rivera came across the case of a female customs agent killed in a similar manner. That case stalled, however, when the victim's family declined to cooperate with the authorities.

After a few months, Rivera's case dried up, too. Other murders required his attention. But like Jimena, he was haunted by the brutality of Lee's killing. "I couldn't sleep soundly at night. I was thinking about that case," he said. "But the fact is, I cannot just proceed without solid evidence."

For three years the file languished, until April 2015, when Rivera got a call from the U.S. embassy. The DEA had some information regarding the Catherine Lee case, an embassy liaison said. Almost two years earlier—18 months after Lee was murdered—the DEA had arrested a former Army Ranger who had been working in private security overseas. That arrest had led them to Rivera.

In July 2013, the U.S. Attorney's Office for the Southern District of New York, covering Manhattan, filed a sealed indictment charging Joseph Hunter, a 48-year-old decorated former U.S. soldier, with conspiracy to murder a law-enforcement agent. More specifically, Hunter stood accused of forming a team of international assassins to take out a snitch and a DEA agent on behalf of a Colombian drug cartel. On September 25, Hunter was captured in a raid on a safe house in Phuket, Thailand, and extradited to the U.S. Two members of his alleged assassination squad, for which he'd accepted résumés over the Internet, were picked up simultaneously in Liberia as they prepared to carry out the hit. The fourth and fifth were caught in Estonia on charges of arranging a drug deal. When I read the unsealed indictment a few days later, the whole thing sounded as if it were concocted by a dramatist with a flair for international intrigue.

In a way it was. The DEA's entire operation was a version of what's called a reverse sting—or, in more common terms, a setup. The "Colombian drug lords" were paid informants playing well-rehearsed roles. The snitch and the DEA agent didn't exist. The "safe house" had been wired for sound and video. For months the DEA had been stringing Hunter and his team along, arranging small gigs like guarding drug shipments in the Caribbean before springing their trap.

When the Department of Justice announced Hunter's arrest, a wave of media coverage followed—not least because Hunter's nickname in the field had been Rambo. After the headlines died down, the case embarked on the long slog toward trial. Federal cases often take years to wind their way to a jury, and very few ever make it there. Ninety-five percent end in a guilty plea, because even the best defense lawyers rarely have the wherewithal to face the power of a federal prosecution—particularly one with the kinds of resources that had been brought to bear on the Joseph Hunter case.

On December 21, 2014, however, a reporter at the *New York Times* named Alan Feuer broke a strange new detail in the case. Hunter, he reported, had been working for a mysterious cartel boss named Paul Le Roux, who had once commanded a criminal empire of incredible power and scope. Le Roux had been arrested in 2012, Feuer revealed, and was now working for the U.S. government as a closely held confidential informant. By December 30, the Daily Mail had declared Le Roux "the most successful criminal mastermind you've never heard of."

This second wave of press coverage preceded a pivotal motion in the case, filed by Hunter's lawyer in Manhattan. It argued that the indictment against Hunter should be dismissed because the sting operation had been initiated by Hunter's former boss, referred to by the government only as a confidential witness, or CW-1. Hunter had participated in his alleged crimes, the motion asserted, because he believed that his boss would kill him if he did not. The U.S. government's use of a criminal as vicious as CW-1, the filing asserted, "shocks the conscience."

Anyone paying attention now knew that CW-1 was Paul Le Roux. His name, however, remained redacted in every court filing. Any case files that might exist detailing Le Roux's own arrest were sealed.

Then, four weeks later, Hunter suddenly pleaded guilty. There would be no defense that he had acted out of fear of Le Roux, no unmasking of his boss in court. Indeed, there would be no trial at all. Over the course of 2015, all of Hunter's codefendants pleaded guilty, along with five defendants in a related methamphetamine-smuggling case. Their files were sealed and shelved, the guilty parties dispatched to federal prison or awaiting their sentence.

A surveillance photo of Le Roux, taken in an airport in Rio de Janeiro, surfaced from a Brazilian newspaper; it was purportedly the only image of him ever published. It's a grainy shot of a doughy white man in a royal blue polo, with what appears to be tousled bleach-blond or silver hair and a darker, trim beard. He wears a slightly amused expression and, with the photo blown up, almost looks as if he's winking at someone.

The thing that eventually led me to the Philippines was practically a footnote in the federal indictment against Hunter. Based on the recordings, prosecutors believed that Hunter "had in fact previously committed acts of violence for pay—including, among other things, arranging for the murders of two female real estate agents." An afterthought to the case itself, the detail had lodged in my brain when I first read it back in 2013, and I kept returning to it. Why had international assassins for hire, working for a man with a worldwide criminal network taken the time to murder two real estate agents?

For his part, Rivera seemed pleased with the arrests, but he also expressed frustration about his own continuing investigation. The agents had told him about the Filipino who allegedly supplied the weapon and vehicle, but he still didn't have enough information to track them down. He pointed out to me that the NBI hadn't gotten any credit for the arrests of Samia and Stillwell, while at the same time suggesting that such credit was unnecessary. "We were not included. We were happy about that, it's no problem with us. We have nothing to gain with being famous."

It did seem odd to me, sitting in a cubicle at the Death Investigations Division, that the U.S. government would put this much effort into prosecuting two Americans for a murder of a Filipino woman outside Manila. Why not just extradite the pair to the Philippines, where the crime occurred, and hand them off to the NBI? Perhaps it was related to something more fundamental about the case that I still didn't understand: Why was Catherine Lee important enough to fly two men across the world and pay them $70,000 to kill her?

It was because of "the Mastermind," Rivera told me. "He is in U.S. custody." Rivera would only identify this Mastermind at first by alluding to his role as the head of a powerful crime syndicate. But he did tell me the motive behind the murder. Rivera said that the Mastermind had enlisted Catherine Lee to purchase vacation property in Batangas, a coastal region south of Manila. He had given her money, at least 50 million pesos, or almost $3 million. "But the deal never materialized," Rivera said, "because the person who Catherine

Lee instructed to do the verification of the land, to arrange the deeds and everything, went off with the money."

That person, some kind of fixer Lee worked with, had also been killed, Rivera believed. "The body was never found," he said.

And then the Mastermind had ordered Lee's murder, too.

I asked him if he would tell me the name of the Mastermind, and at first he demurred. He did have a name, he said, but he didn't want to say it. "Maybe it's an alias."

"If I tell you the name that I think it is, will you tell me if that's the person?"

"I will confirm," he said.

"Paul Le Roux."

Rivera slammed his fist down on the table, then held my gaze for several seconds in silence. "Hey, they did not inform me that," he finally said with a smile that was hard to read. The DEA, he said, would "neither confirm nor deny it." Then he lowered his voice to a whisper. "This Paul Le Roux," he said, "is a very badass guy." He widened his eyes. "A bad guy," he said again. "That's it."

Excerpt from "The Mastermind" by Evan Ratliff © Evan Ratliff, originally published in *The Atavist Magazine*, March–April 2016.

From "The Dream Boat"

Luke Mogelson

There is a timelessness to the way Luke Mogelson writes about the most urgent issues of our time, including mass migration, political unrest, and unrelenting war. He has reported from Iraq, Afghanistan, Syria, and Ukraine, sometimes risking his own life and solidifying his place alongside standout war correspondents who came before him. In particular, his work carries on the legacy of Martha Gellhorn's powers of observation and capacity to chronicle how people live amid great suffering. Like Ernie Pyle, he interviews obscure soldiers in the trenches rather than high-profile generals safe behind lines. In the tradition of Sebastian Junger, he reports on dangerous in-the-field conflicts with a sense of justice reminiscent of John Reed. His uncanny knack for placing himself at the epicenter of human history's most transformative events calls to mind the fearless reporting of Marie Colvin.

When not covering wars, he reports from other volatile places, including the January 6 siege on the US Capitol. For his video coverage of that event for *The New Yorker*, he won a National Magazine Award, his second. Mogelson won his first Ellie for *The New York Times Magazine*'s "The Dream Boat." While claiming to be political exiles from Georgia, Mogelson and photographer Joel Van Houdt joined fifty-seven mostly Iranian refugees on a boat lift from Indonesia to Christmas Island, a trip that usually takes three days if the shoddy, overcrowded boats don't capsize. In the introduction to *The Best American Magazine Writing 2014*, Mark Jannot writes, "You don't actually have to wonder where the details came from in Luke Mogelson's 'The Dream Boat,' but it does inspire tremendous wonder at the empathy, commitment, and courage required. . . ."

Although Mogelson endures the same struggles everyone faces on the trip, including seasickness, fear, and extreme heat, the narrative does not revolve around him. Instead, he uses the first person as an orienting element, one that helps readers envision the people and the details in the scenes he can craft so well because he was there. Even when in danger himself, Mogelson collects the details that allow him to slow down time in his writing. In this passage, he makes the otherwise unimaginable circumstances accessible to readers. By relaying the small discomforts asylum-seekers faced, which readers have likely experienced—though to a much lesser extent—themselves, he sets the stage for more extreme scenarios. "The sea was still big when the sun went down, taking with it the warmth," he writes. "Those of us who had spent the day on our feet now began staking claims on places to try to sleep. The deck became a claustrophobic scrum of tangled limbs."

Before becoming a journalist, Mogelson served as a medic for the U.S. National Guard in Iraq. He's reported for *The New Yorker* since 2013, and he's authored one nonfiction book, *The Storm is Here: America on the Brink*; as well as a book of short stories, *These Heroic, Happy Dead*. In addition to two National Magazine Awards, Mogelson has won two George Polk Awards, among other distinctions.

Mogelson effectively connects his readers to fractious subjects, reporting on them coolly, compellingly, and humanely. After reading "The Dream Boat," one letter writer to nytimes.com, thanked Mogelson, "for your thoughtful and gripping writing. And for making me think and feel."

—J. M.

After the hard rain on the way to the beach, and wading out chest-deep to the skiffs, everyone was drenched. It was still dark out when the two Indonesian crew members pulled back the tarp they had nailed over our heads. The coast was a vague shadow growing vaguer. The Indonesians distributed life vests: ridiculous things, made from thin fabric and a bit of foam. The youngest children, including a girl in a pink poncho who appeared no older than 4 or 5, were directed with their parents to a small square of open deck in the stern. The reason for this was that the farther aft you went, the less violent was the bucking as we plowed into the swells.

As the sun broke, we got our first good look at one another. Rashid had made it, as well as several other men from the tower block. There were nine children and more than a dozen women. Aside from one Afghan man, from Kunduz Province, everyone was Iranian. Most of the elderly crowded into the covered bow or leaned against the bulwarks. The rest fit where they could on the open deck. The sea was choppy enough so that each time the boat crashed from a peak into a trough or hit a wave head-on, large amounts of water splashed against us.

The first person to become sick was Siya. It was still early morning when he started throwing up. He was a natural leader, that man, and almost everyone soon followed suit. By late afternoon, we'd lost sight of land completely, and the swells grew to a size that blocked out the horizon when they loomed above us. Some people bent over the gunwales, some vomited into plastic bags. It quickly became apparent that there were not enough bags to go around: rather than toss them overboard, full ones had to be emptied, rinsed and reused.

Siya would not be cowed. Peeling off his soaking tank top, revealing his tattooed wings—seeming to unfold them, actually, as he threw back his shoulders—he began to sing. Others joined in, breaking now and then to retch.

It was slow going. The Indonesians took turns manning the tiller and hand-pumping water from the bilge. One was older and taciturn and wore a permanent scowl; the other looked to be in his teens, smiled enough for the both of them and called everybody "brother." The tremendous racket of the engine belied its less-than-tremendous horsepower. Like the rest of the vessel, it was built for neither such a heavy load nor such high seas. Our typical speed was four to five knots, less than six miles per hour, and at times we seemed to make no headway whatsoever against the strong southeasterly trade winds, which whipped up white caps on the waves and kept us all alert with stinging gusts of spray. Depending on the direction of the swells, the Indonesians would signal the men to consolidate themselves on the starboard or port side of the deck and thereby mitigate our listing—which, now and then, felt alarming.

The sea was still big when the sun went down, taking with it the warmth. Those of us who had spent the day on our feet now began staking claims on places to try to sleep. The deck became a claustrophobic scrum of tangled limbs. Few could recline or stretch their legs. Each time someone tried to reposition a foot or knee, say, to restore some circulation, the movement would ripple out in a cascade of shifting and grumbling as the surrounding bodies adjusted to the new configuration.

The tarp was unfurled. There was not enough of it to cover everyone. If you found yourself on an edge or corner, someone from the opposite side would invariably pull it away the moment you relaxed your grip. In any case, it was too worn and porous to do much. The water ran down its folds and creases, streaming through the many tears along the way.

In the morning, everyone looked different. Sallow. Haggard. Reduced. Amir and Sami slouched limply against each other, passing between them a bulging plastic bag. The man with the faux-hawk was curled up in a fetal ball: he stayed that way the rest of the trip. His pregnant wife sat cross-legged near the bow, pale and wet and trembling. Rima was clutching Siya's arm, as if it were a lifeline. Their eyes were squeezed tightly shut, but they were too ill to sleep.

Another problem arose. There was no toilet, and absent any railing to hold on to, going over the side was too risky. The men urinated on the hull, the women in their pants.

The Indonesians had brought a box of sealed plastic cups of water, but hardly anyone could hold them down. Siya continued to sing and puke. Although a couple of the children had begun to cry, none complained. In the afternoon, two dolphins appeared and spent the better part of an hour playfully showing off. As they darted under the boat, and launched into the air, the spectacle cheered up everyone, adults and kids alike. Even Amir and Sami rallied from their stupor to watch. A few grown men became positively gleeful, vying to be the first to spot the gray shadows flitting from the deep.

That night, several of us tried to sleep atop the engine room, trading the shelter of the hull for a little extra space. It was a poor call. Every 10 minutes or so, a bucket's worth of cold water took your breath away or you were pitched against a hot pair of vertical pipes spewing noxious smoke and sparks. There was nothing to do but lie there, bracing for one or the other, admiring the magnificent array of stars and the phosphorescence glowing in the wake.

With first light, despite the sleep deprivation, dehydration, seasickness and filth, the asylum seekers were energized by the fact that, according to the Indonesians, we would likely reach Australian territory before nightfall. Although there was still no land in sight, the arrival of birds circling overhead was unanimously interpreted as a sign that we were getting close. The sea had also calmed: no more waves crashed upon the deck. Initially, this was an enormous relief. For the first time, the sun dried us out. As it crept higher, however, it proved to be far more powerful than during the past two days, and soon, without a single cloud in the sky to blunt the blistering rays, everyone was longing for the same frigid breakers we previously cursed. . . .

Presently, the heat finished off anyone who might have been bearing up. The pregnant woman's condition bordered on critical. She was flushed and drenched in sweat and heaved dryly, with nothing left to give. Sami was weeping. Amir lay supine. His eyes drooped catatonically, and when I tried to make him drink some water, he weakly gripped my ankle.

"I need help," he said. "Call for help."

That decision seemed to be up to Siya. There was a satellite phone onboard: Siya said the plan was to contact the Australian authorities once we were well within their waters. The navy would then bring us ashore. In the past, asylum boats often made it all the way—but the landing can be treacherous (when one boat smashed on the cliffs in 2010, 50 people drowned), and now it's standard practice to request a "rescue" before reaching Christmas Island. Although Australian rescuers, when responding to distress calls, venture much farther north than where we currently were, Siya wanted to be sure. I think it was Amir's pitiful entreaties that finally persuaded him to make the call.

An Iranian man who knew some English—the one who in Jakarta told me he was an engineer—spoke to the dispatch. The Indonesians had brought a hand-held G.P.S. device; neither they nor the asylum seekers, however, knew how to work it. Eventually, someone offered his iPhone, and the engineer read out our coordinates.

While we waited to be rescued, the Iranians set about destroying their passports. "So they can't deport you," Farah told me. Clearly, though, the task also carried some symbolic weight. Rather than simply jettisoning them, the asylum seekers painstakingly ripped out each individual page, crumpled it into a ball, and tossed it to the wind. A pair of scissors was passed around. The burgundy covers, emblazoned with the Iranian coat of arms, were cut into tiny pieces. The work was accomplished with flair and relish. Only one man seemed hesitant. Moving closer, I saw that the passport he was disposing of was his son's. When the scissors came his way, he carefully cut out the photo on the first page and slipped it in his wallet.

Soon, on the horizon, a ship appeared. A government airplane buzzed above us, swooped low and made a second pass. The asylum seekers waved shirts in the air, crying out in jubilation. The younger Indonesian performed a dance atop the engine room; he seemed amazed we had made it. Some of the men emptied their pockets, thrusting on him all the cash they had. The Indonesian beamed. "Thank you, brothers!"

Two skiffs broke off from the battleship and motored our way. Each carried six Australians in gray fatigues, riot helmets and sidearms holstered on their thighs. The Indonesians cut the engine (and after three days of its unrelenting clamor, the silence that replaced it was startling). The skiffs maneuvered abreast of us, one on each side.

The Australian sailors all looked like fresh recruits. One of them held a manual of some kind. He read from it in a loud voice. "Are there any English speakers?"

The engineer stepped forward.

"Does anyone onboard require medical assistance?"

When the engineer translated this, nearly everyone raised his hand. The pregnant woman was helped to her feet and presented. Her head hung heavily. She was almost too weak to stand.

While the Australian with the manual recited more questions—including some in Indonesian addressed to the crew, who shook their heads dumbly, refusing to answer—his fellow sailors passed to the asylum seekers new life vests, a couple jerrycans of fresh water, some bags of frozen tortillas, bottles of honey and a tub of strawberry jam. "We're going back to the ship now," one of them told the engineer. "You have to turn the engine back on and keep going. We'll be behind you." . . .

There was nothing to do but heed the Australian's command and "keep going." It was four or five hours after we made contact with the first ship when a second, smaller patrol boat materialized. Two more skiffs of sailors came out to meet us. This time they immediately boarded the boat, moving people aside, herding everyone forward. The officer in charge announced that he was taking control of the vessel.

After the officer spotted Joel's camera, we were both summoned to the stern, at which point we identified ourselves as journalists. While a big Australian with a bushy beard worked the tiller, the officer went through a list of prewritten questions with the crew, each of whom either couldn't read or declined to. (Unless it's their second offense, or someone dies, the Indonesian fishermen who bring asylum boats across are often not prosecuted.) The officer was polite to Joel and me. He said we had been lucky with the weather. If we had left a few days earlier, the boat would have capsized.

Excerpt from "The Dream Boat" by Luke Mogelson, *The New York Times*. © 2013 The New York Times Company. All rights reserved. Used under license.

From "My Four Months as a Private Prison Guard"

Shane Bauer

Shane Bauer wasn't the first journalist to go undercover as a guard in an American prison. Before he started working for a private Louisiana prison run by Corrections Corporation of America in 2014, at least three other journalists had written firsthand accounts about the struggle to retain humanity in a place of punishment. The power dynamics between people behind bars and those trying to keep them there are complex and, as Bauer knew, often in flux. He had been a prisoner himself, arrested in 2009 in Iran, after accidentally crossing into that country on a hike. He was imprisoned for two years.

Bauer's inspiration to go undercover in a private prison derived from a conversation with another reporter about Ted Conover's 2000 book *Newjack*. In the book, Ted Conover chronicled his eleven-month stint as a guard in Sing Sing prison. Conover's participant-observer style of reporting was well developed by then, honed by other projects, including riding the rails as a vagrant and working alongside Mexican laborers. While both men confront similar themes of humanity and ethics as guards, Bauer's experience of the private prison landscape is far more harrowing because of the constant violence he witnessed in an environment where profits came before prisoners. Resources were limited and staffing was insufficient. Bauer told *Columbia Journalism Review*, "Initially, I felt like I was a journalist with a guard suit on, like it was a mask. But as time passed, I became more and more of a guard. . . . Some days, when I was driving home, I was feeling ashamed. I was writing about this other person who existed inside the prison."

Bauer's 35,000-word story includes a video series and a podcast. He interweaves firsthand observational detail, including scenes and dialogue, with introspection and analysis, making the piece both literary and investigative. In this selection, he describes with honesty as brutal as the conditions under which the guards and prisoners coexist, how easily one can spiral into cruelty.

—J. M.

Pink Shades

During count, I tally bodies, not faces. If I look at faces, it means I have to keep the numbers straight while constantly calibrating sternness and friendliness in my eyes for each individual. When I go down the tier, I make a point to walk in a fast, long stride with a slight pop in my left step, trying to look tough. I practiced this in the mirror because inmates comment every day on a twist in my walk that I never knew existed. Sometimes prisoners whistle at me as I pass. In my normal life, I try to diffuse any macho tendencies. Now, I try to annihilate anything remotely feminine about me. As I walk and count, I tighten my core to keep my hips from moving.

I steel myself for A1 tier. For some reason, inmates on this tier are always testing me, and as I walk down one side, someone makes a comment about my "panties" as I pass. "You like that dick. You like that dick," someone sings as I go by. I ignore it. Another comments that I look like a model. I pretend I don't hear him. On my way back toward the front, I hear again, "You like that dick. You like that dick."

This has been going on for weeks, but this time something snaps. I stop count and march back to the guy calling out to me, a thirty something black man with pink sunglasses and tattoos crawling up his neck. "What did you say to me?" I shout.

"I ain't said nothin.'"

"Why are you always saying shit like that? You are always focusing so much on me, maybe you like the dick! Bitch ass!"

"Say that again?"

"Maybe you like the dick!" I shout. I am completely livid.

"He doesn't know how big a mistake he just made," another inmate says as I storm out.

When we finish count, I go back to Pink Shades' tier. "Give me your ID," I say to him. He refuses. "Give me your ID! *Now!*" I shout at the top of my lungs. He doesn't. I get his name from another officer and write him up for making sexual comments. He says he's going to file a PREA grievance on me.

I try to cool down. My heart is still hammering 10 minutes later. "Are you all right, sarge?" a prisoner asks me. Slowly, my rage turns to shame and I go into the bathroom and sit on the floor. Where did those words come from? I rarely ever shout. I am not homophobic. Or am I? I feel utterly defeated. I go back to A1 and call Pink Shades to the bars.

"Look, I just want you to understand I don't have a problem with any of y'all," I tell him. "I think a lot of you are in here for sentences that are too long. I'm not like these other guys, all right?"

"All right," he says.

"But, you know, when people disrespect me like that for no reason, I can't just take that—you know what I mean?"

He tries to deny taunting me, but I won't back down. "Look, you going to have inmates talkin' crazy," he says.

"But you don't want me talking crazy to you, right?" There are inmates staring at us in astonishment.

"I feel you," he says. "You came here and talked to me like a man. And I apologize. I ain't got nothing against any of y'all officers. You feel me? I understand that you gotta live. You got to survive. Those words hurt you. I feel you. I mean I was singing a song, but you probably took it the wrong way. It triggered something in you." He's right. Something about being here reminds me of being in junior high, getting picked on for my size and the fact that I read books, getting called a faggot.

I tear up his disciplinary report and throw it in the trash. When I walk back down the tier for the next count, no one pays any attention to me....

My reconciliation with Pink Shades encouraged me. Every time I have a problem with a prisoner, I try the same approach and eventually we tap knuckles to show each other respect. Still, these breakthroughs are fleeting.

In the moment, they feel like a glimmer of a possibility that we can appreciate each other's humanity, but I come to understand that our positions make this virtually impossible. We can chat and laugh through the bars, but inevitably I need to flex my authority. My job will always be to deny them the most basic of human impulses—to push for more freedom. Day by day, the number of inmates who are friendly with me grows smaller.

There are exceptions, like Corner Store, but were I to take away the privileges Bacle and I have granted him, I know that he, too, would become an enemy.

My priorities change. Striving to treat everyone as human takes too much energy. More and more, I focus on proving I won't back down. I am vigilant; I come to work ready for people to catcall me or run up on me and threaten to punch me in the face. I show neither fear nor compunction. Sometimes prisoners call me racist, and it stings, but I try as hard as I can not to flinch because to do so would be to show a pressure point, a button that can be pressed when they want to make me bend.

Nearly every day the unit reaches a crescendo of frustration because inmates are supposed to be going somewhere like the law library, GED classes, vocational training, or a substance abuse group, but their programs are canceled or they are let out of the unit late. Inmates tell me that at other prisons, the schedule is firm. "That door would be opening up and everybody would be on the move," an inmate who's been incarcerated throughout the state says. Here, there is no schedule. We wait for the call over the radio; then we let the inmates go. They could eat at 11:30 a.m. They could eat at 3 p.m. School might happen, or maybe not. It's been years since Winn has had the staff to run the big yard. Sometimes we let the inmates onto the small yard attached to the unit. Often we don't. Canteen and law library hours are canceled regularly. There just aren't enough officers to keep everything going.

Guards bond with prisoners over their frustrations. Prisoners tell us they understand we are powerless to change these high-level management problems. Yet the two groups remain locked in battle like soldiers in a war they don't believe in.

Whenever I open a tier door, I demand that everyone shows me his pass, and I use my body to stop the flood of people from pouring out. Some just push through.

I catch one. "Get back in!" I shout. "I'm writing you up right now if you don't get back in there right now. You hear me?"

He walks back in, staring me down. "White dude all on a nigga's trail, man," he says. I shut the door, ignoring him. "You better get the fuck from down here before I end up hurtin' one of y'all," he shouts at me. "You green as a motherfucker!"

I'm tired.

An inmate comes around the key. Bacle is following him and calls for me to stop him. I stand in the inmate's path. I know him, the one with the mini-dreads. I feel threatened, frankly, whenever I see him. "This way," I say, pointing back to where he came from. He tries to walk past me. I lock eyes with him. "This way!" I command. He turns back and walks slowly away. I walk behind him. He stops, spins around, throws his hands in the air, and shouts, "Get the fuck off my trail, dog!" I know he's testing me. I open his tier door. He walks in, stands just inside, and stares me down hard. I grab the door and slam it shut—*bang!*—in his face.

I turn and step back into the throng of inmates milling around the floor. "Motherfucker's going to end up dead!" he shouts after me. I stop and turn around. He just stares. I grab the radio on my shoulder, then pause. Was I ever taught what to do when something like this happens? I know how to press the button and speak into the radio, but whom do I call? I think of King, the officer who smashed the kid's jaw. "Sergeant King, could you come down to Ash?" I say into my shoulder.

"En route."

When he arrives, I take him into B1 tier. I find Mini-Dreads.

"He needs to get locked up," I say, looking him in the eyes.

King cuffs him. I tell King he threatened my life. He needs to go to seg.

"What happened?! I ain't said nuttin'!" the inmate shouts. I walk away.

I go back to chasing the others into their tiers. "What you lock that dude up for?" an inmate asks me. "Dude was 'bout to go home," another says. "He ain't go' go home now." I walk away, unyielding. In the back of my mind, however, there is a voice: *Did you see him say anything? Wasn't your back turned? Are you sure what you heard?* It doesn't matter, really. He wanted to intimidate me and it was about time I threw someone in the hole. They need to know I am not weak.

Excerpt from "My Four Months as a Private Prison Guard" by Shane Bauer, originally published in *Mother Jones*, July/August 2016. https://www.motherjones.com/politics/2016/06/cca-private-prisons-corrections-corporation-inmates-investigation-bauer/

From "Love in the Time of Robots"

Alex Mar

This story is a collaboration between *Wired* and *Epic* magazines, publications known for their engaging online presentations. *Epic*, especially, appeals to readers with lush, engaging design that employs technology to serve the story and captivate (not confuse or distract) readers. In this piece, which appears on *Wired*'s website, Alex Mar interrogates the necessity of human connection, and whether its positive effects can be replicated—even improved upon—in the absence of another human. Mar's subject, Hiroshi Ishiguro, creates humanlike robots, including ones of himself and his child.

In an interview with *Longreads*, Mar said she was in touch with Ishiguro for more than two years before traveling to Japan to spend about three weeks with him, enough time to delve into his motivation for pursuing this work. "It took a moment for him to realize I was also interested in very minute details about his life—his childhood, his personal habits—things that he at first dismissed as too boring to discuss," she said. Mar's piece is an example of what literary journalist Walt Harrington calls "intimate journalism," the goal of which is "to understand other people's worlds from the inside out and to portray people as they understand themselves." Ishiguro told Mar he considers himself more of an artist than a roboticist, and she, in turn, produced a story about him that is more art than journalism. A portrait, not a profile.

In the following section about Ishiguro's early years as a scientist, she writes about his fantasy taking shape as he immerses himself into programming languages: "Could there be a way to make this language more humanlike, so that someday computers might understand us intuitively, on our own terms? So that this dialog might become a relationship? This relationship becomes his singular pursuit, his dream."

Judges for the feature writing category of the 2018 National Magazine Awards said the piece, a finalist, is "a surreal, intimate tale." Many other journalists had written about Ishiguro before her, but Mar pushes far beyond the man-makes-a-robot-in-his-own-image angle. The wide breadth of her creative experiences infuses her prose with unexpected turns that can be serious, confessional, and even shocking. The daughter of immigrants from Crete and Cuba, Mar began her career as a visual artist. She directed a documentary film, *American Mystic*, about people who practice alternative religions. That experience inspired her to write her first book, *Witches of America*, a *New York Times* Notable Book of 2015. Her second book, *Seventy Times Seven: A True Story of Murder and Mercy*, examines the fallout of a 1985 murder, causing readers to question ideals of forgiveness and justice. Mar has also worked as an editor at *Rolling Stone* and written for *The Believer* and *New York Magazine*, among other publications.

"I don't see the boundaries between different genres or media as that important," she told the *Longform Podcast*. While skill sets differ, she sees a "fluidity" among them, one she harnesses for the readers' benefit.

—J. M.

OVER THE SEVERAL months we are in contact, Ishiguro will share information that strikes me as deeply personal: He has contemplated suicide twice in his life; though he has a family, he considers himself a lonely man. I will hear him use that word to describe himself—lonely—about half a dozen times.

As for me, when I first visit Ishiguro, my situation is this:

I am 23 months away from what had seemed like the start of a serious relationship but was not. I am 15 months away from a rebound relationship that lingered too long. I am 13 months into a period of spending long stints in a small town in upstate New York for the sake of productive quiet. I'm readying a book to go to the printers—work that, for me, is all-consuming and necessary. And lately, when I step back from the manuscript for an afternoon or at night, I feel it: isolation. This isolation is not complete—I have my close friends, a wider circle of less-close friends, my family—but it is the absence of intimacy. Nothing romantic, no sexual life.

This absence has been, in part, a choice; certain men have always been curious about me. But what I miss more than sex is the feeling of closeness with another person, something I've never believed could be conjured up. And though the sensory deprivation has become a little extreme, most of the time—can I put a percentage on it? Is it as high as 80 percent?—I do not think about it. I am semi-radically independent and some kind of artist and in many ways an unconventional liberal woman. However alienating, for me this is a time of deep creativity. It's that additional 20 percent of the time—that's when I feel dizzy.

This is where I'm at when I fly 17 hours to meet Ishiguro. And as a result, if I am honest with myself, my time abroad feels particularly fraught. The very concept of "human connection" has never felt so enigmatic to me. It makes sense that someone would be trying to measure it, to weigh it, to calculate its dimensions. To be able to replicate the sensation of human intimacy would be to control the very thing that confuses us most and eludes so many.

THIS IS HOW Ishiguro remembers his childhood:

His family lives in the town of Adogawa, on the western shore of Lake Biwa, from which a river flows through Kyoto into Osaka Bay. At school, in a classroom of disciplined children, Hiroshi doesn't listen to the instructor. It's as if he doesn't notice she is speaking at all. He spends the day making drawings that have nothing to do with the lesson. His mother worries that there may be something wrong with him.

Hiroshi rarely sees his mother or father—as schoolteachers they are as consumed by their work as their son will one day become. Instead, his grandparents are raising him. His mother's father is a farmer, a devout Buddhist with fixed, traditional ideas about "how to behave like a Japanese man." He shows the boy the proper way to use chopsticks, to pray, to prepare the house for the New Year's celebration. Unlike at school, Hiroshi has the patience for these lessons: His grandfather is not telling him how he should think; he is teaching him to aspire to perfection.

They live at the foot of the Hira Mountains, and Hiroshi likes to comb the mountainside for snakes and insects. Maybe a stag beetle, glossy black and segmented, nearly three inches long, with a pair of antler-shaped mandibles emerging straight from its head. He fixes new parts to its body: razor blades, found pieces of metal. It is an improvement. The insect may continue living like this, if the glue doesn't kill it. These are his earliest cyborgs.

One of Hiroshi's close friends is a boy who lives in a poorer community, down by the water, and his parents collect and prepare the bodies of the recently dead for burial. Hiroshi does not yet understand that these people are considered to be lesser than his family, because they have a job that, according to local prejudice, is tainted. For this reason, when Hiroshi's mother discovers the friendship, she asks that her son break it off. He will remember this moment for the next 40 years.

Hiroshi is a delicate child. He has suffered from extreme skin allergies from the time he was born; his back and chest and arms are covered in itchy, ugly rashes. His only comfort comes from constant touch: Every night, his grandparents take turns sitting beside him and scratching his back until he is able to nod off. Every week his doctor gives him three painful injections to try to cure the condition—to no effect. (When he is about 12, steroids will finally help, requiring him to keep the drug on hand to this day.) His own body will always be alien to him.

WHEN IT COMES time for Ishiguro to go to college, he chooses a school using three criteria: It will accept an eccentric, sometimes indifferent student like himself; it's somewhere he can pursue his drawing and painting; and it's not very close to home. In the fall of 1981, he lands at the University of Yamanashi, near Mount Fuji.

Once there, Ishiguro continues his careless approach to his studies, finding more pleasure in the string of odd jobs he takes to pay the bills—he works as a cook, the supervisor of a children's after-school program, a door-to-door textbook salesman (that one lasts a week), and, most lucrative of all, a professional pachinko player. He finds himself on the fringes of student life, rejecting any semblance of mainstream Japanese ambition.

At the same time, he is fashioning himself into that most romantic of outsiders: an artist. Always in a black leather jacket, he skips classes, packs his pads and pencils, and rides his Yamaha chopper into the nearby countryside to sketch the landscape. This is his focus: the strange, organic shapes of the trees, the peach blossoms that appear in the springtime. He produces drawings and oil paintings, and manages to sell a few.

But in his third year, Ishiguro abruptly gives up painting. Unless he can become a great artist and a tremendous public success, he sees no point in it. (He blames, in part, his color blindness: He is drawn to landscapes, but the entire spectrum of green eludes him.) He has lost what little direction he had. On his darker days, when he takes his motorcycle on a steep and winding road, Ishiguro imagines giving in to the impulse to not make the turn. To drive straight ahead, fly right off the edge—what would that feel like?

Then a path presents itself. Yamanashi offers courses in the new field of computer science, and Ishiguro begins to wonder what relationship computer graphics and computer vision might have to the visual arts. These are the early days of the PC, and programming seems wildly creative. Feeling he has little to lose, he switches majors.

Almost immediately, certain elements in his brain click into place: Ishiguro realizes he can continue to think like a painter in this unpoliced field, but with different tools. He falls in love with the new vocabulary: Assembler, Pascal. The students are relegated to working in a single room kept bitterly cold, loud with the hum of the huge computers—conditions designed for the comfort of machines, not humans. He works alone, on software development, but he is learning to communicate with a system—a system that responds to his commands. They have entered into a dialog.

Ishiguro soon gives up his rides through the country for entire days spent in the lab. And as he becomes more fluent in this new language, more immersed in a conversation with the large machines, a fantasy takes shape: Could there be a way to make this language more humanlike, so that someday computers might understand us intuitively, on our own terms? So that this dialog might become a relationship?

This relationship becomes his singular pursuit, his dream.

IN 2000, ISHIGURO, as an associate professor at Kyoto University, produces his first humanoid robot: a mechanical-looking contraption that moves on a wheeled platform, waving its jointed steel arms. But he has started to think that a relatable, humanlike appearance is essential if people are going to form real attachments to robots.

It's about a decade into his marriage (to a pianist he met through a university friend), and he asks his wife if he can make videotapes of her—

sitting, breathing, responding to random stimuli. He is trying to determine the nuances of human behavior, to isolate the physical signs that read to us, consciously or unconsciously, as "human." One minor revelation: Humans never truly sit still.

Ishiguro is aware of resistance to the concept of an android—at least in the West, from which many Japanese researchers take their cue. Some are worried that consumer revulsion to a humanlike robot (the so-called uncanny valley effect) would be too great to overcome and that a failed android project could undercut public support of robotics. Ishiguro, too, is worried that pushing ahead with an untraditional approach might cost him his academic career. But he can't resist. And so when the company he has partnered with on a new robot insists on hiring a respected designer that makes it look, in Ishiguro's opinion, "like an insect," he loses his patience. With his next project, he decides to go rogue. He will create an android "to convince them."

Ishiguro believes that his first android should be the same height as the insect (about 3½ feet tall), for purposes of comparison. In other words, it will have to be modeled after a human child. And given the painstaking production process—a model must spend hours encased in plaster to cast an accurate replica—there is only one child he can possibly get permission to use: his own.

A few years earlier, Ishiguro became a father to a daughter, named Risa, and he now turns to his wife to explain his plan. She agrees—she is in charge of raising the girl, and the experiment would be difficult without her help. And so, in early 2002, the entire family, along with makeup and special effects artists, gathers in his lab on campus and begins the two-day process of creating a replica of Risa.

In the lab, Risa's mother helps her to undress. She takes off the girl's clothes and stands her up on a small wooden platform. Together her father and an artist smooth a layer of pale-green paste over her torso and upper thighs; over that, they apply wide swatches of fabric dipped in plaster, asking her to hold very still as it dries. Then the 5-year-old girl, wrapped in a pink towel, her scalp covered in a rubber cap and her ears plugged with cotton, is laid down on a tabletop, her head fenced in with Styrofoam and packing tape. An artist lifts a plastic bucket and pours the paste in until it rises to cover her ears, as father and mother try to reassure her: "Don't worry!" and "You're fine!" At last they prepare the girl for the final part of the process: her face.

Through a video camera's viewfinder, Ishiguro watches the rigid expression on his small daughter's face as her mother and an artist slowly cover it in thick paste. "Once we're done," her father says, "you can eat anything you like!" They slather it across her forehead, around her chin, and down the front of her neck; they apply it thickly on her cheeks and across her nose, then subsume her entire mouth, her mother laughing, keeping the mood light. "Keep your eyes closed. Like you're going to bed … Good night!" The whole time, remarkable for a child her age, she does not move or make a sound. And then the paste closes in on her as they smooth it over her eyelids, and within moments her face is layered in the creamy stuff, which has already begun to harden. Her entire face is under—save her nostrils: a single hole left clear for breathing.

"You're OK," the artist says. "Just a little bit longer …"

Then Ishiguro, from behind the camera: "Risa, you're totally fine … If you're feeling sleepy, if your head feels heavy, you can just lean back. Just like sleeping …"

They press a square of plaster-soaked fabric over her face (again, a hole for breathing) and it begins to stiffen. And perhaps the professor is now concerned, because he loses the shot, tilting the camera up to point at the wall. "Risa, if you can breathe properly through your nose, please squeeze my hand …"

"Risa," her mother says, "make sure you don't cry, because it'll block your nose. Anyway, there's no need to cry! Be patient … It's OK to sleep. Go to sleep …"

When, months later, the package arrives at the lab, Ishiguro and his team open the crate to reveal the full-body silicone-skin casing of his daughter: Risa, bald, naked, made of rubber. They stretch the skin around foam-padded machinery and prop it up in the lab. His wife has donated one of their daughter's sundresses so it has something to wear. Ishiguro names it Repliee R1—R for Risa.

The results of the experiment are mixed. Ishiguro has to admit that the low-budget android, with its limited, stuttering movements, is more zombie than human. And though he shows the project only to a trusted inner circle, word of the "daughter android" spreads, becoming a weird legend. (In describing it, one roboticist I speak with uses the word "crazy," another "strange" and "a little bit scary.") But Repliee R1 gives Ishiguro the confidence to move forward.

As for his daughter, Ishiguro rewards her with several Hello Kitty dolls. "But still," he says, "she cried." To this day, they've never spoken about the incident.

Excerpt from "Love in the Time of Robots," by Alex Mar, originally published October 17, 2017, as a collaboration between Wired @Conde Nast and Epic Magazine @Vox Media. https://www.wired.com/2017/10/hiroshi-ishiguro-when-robots-act-just-like-humans/

Confronting the Unspeakable

From *How the Word Is Passed*
Clint Smith

Clint Smith is the writer sent directly to us from America's conscience. At a time of backlash against the public reckoning with slavery, Smith's *How the Word Is Passed* rocketed to the top of *The New York Times* Best Seller list in 2021. For the book, Smith embarked on what he calls a "learning journey" to understand the legacy of slavery by visiting key landmarks, such as Thomas Jefferson's Monticello plantation and Angola Prison in Louisiana, where many barely paid Black prisoners now toil in fields that used to be worked by slaves. Of the book deemed one of the *Times Book Review*'s Best Books of 2021, the editors said, "Smith holds up a mirror to America's fraught relationship with its past, capturing a potent mixture of good intentions, earnest corrective, willful ignorance and blatant distortion."

As a prolific staff writer for *The Atlantic,* Smith dusts off the lens of history and places it where it is most useful for seeing the corrosive effects of systemic injustice. The pieces he has written for that publication have ranged widely in subject matter—why prisoners should be allowed to vote, why teaching should be political, why the lies of the confederacy live on—but all are infused with a strong belief in the power of seeing history as it was, not as we were taught or as we wish it had been.

Smith is a writer for the digital age. A teacher who holds a doctorate in education from Harvard and a former National Poetry Slam champion, he is comfortable in front of audiences, including ones reached through cameras and microphones. His book *Counting Descent* won the 2017 Literary Award for Best Poetry Book from the Black Caucus of the American Library Association. He also hosts the *Crash Course Black American History* YouTube series. Smith performed this excerpt about Angola Prison from his nonfiction book for *Literary Hub*'s *Storybound* radio theater podcast.

—J. M.

Upon approaching the building where executions took place, I felt my chest tighten and my mouth turn sour. Inside, the room adjacent to the execution chamber was unremarkable. At its center were two wooden tables brought together, their clean, polished surfaces reflecting the flickering fluorescent lights. The tables were surrounded by ten armless, black, rolling office chairs set to different heights, some slightly reclined as if someone were sitting in them. Next to the back wall were two tall plants—their leaves bursting a full and healthy green. The walls were beige with white trim, and the floor was a neat aggregation of square linoleum tiles. The soft hum of the air-conditioning vibrated throughout the room. With the exception of the large circular seal of the Louisiana Department of Corrections at the center of each table, it would have been easy to mistake this for any other conference room in any other office building. This was not any other conference room. This was a room where the people sentenced to be killed by the State of Louisiana had their final meals. They ate these meals—perhaps a hamburger and french fries, perhaps steak and mashed potatoes, maybe a basket of boiled crawfish and a bowl of gumbo—before being injected with a cocktail that rendered them unconscious, paralyzed their muscles, discontinued their breathing and stopped their hearts.

In the vestibule between the conference room and the execution chamber, eight mahogany leather chairs were packed tightly together in two rows, the second row elevated slightly behind the first. On the far wall, there was a sliding wooden door, and on the other side of that sliding door were four more chairs—two in front and two behind—seated next to the window.

The victim's family—if they so choose—sit on one side of the sliding door, while witnesses, often in the media, sit on the other side. The family of the person being executed cannot be in the viewing chamber for the execution. In front of these chairs, on both sides, was a large glass panel that looked directly into the execution chamber and directly at the table upon which the person would be killed. As we walked into the room and slowly encircled the table at the center, the group fell silent. Many were unable to stare at it directly.

Silent but for a soft symphony of breaths, we were a congregation of lowered heads and sunken shoulders. The table was long and blue-black, its upholstery covering a thin layer of foam padding. Seven discolored brown and black straps, haunting in their stillness, stretched across the width of the bed, each locked and pulled tight. A small pillow rested at the head of the table where the person is meant to lie, and another set of straps would come down over their shoulders. About a foot below the pillow on either side of the bed were the places where the soon-to-be-executed would lay their arms. On each of these arm-length extensions was a leather strap meant to be tightened near the person's elbow. They were noticeably different from the other straps—a faded blend of grey and brown, taut leather that had cracked with age. The straps, with their procession of small notches, dangled below the table. At the foot of the table were two shackles, their silver metal glimmering under the lights. A hot rush of blood pulsed behind my ears, as I felt the shame of being alive in a room meant to kill.

On the bus ride to Angola, Norris had told me a story about how this bed, or the one that came before it, had been made. He said that when the State of Louisiana transitioned from the electric chair to lethal injection in 1991, the prison needed a bed on which to lay the condemned. Meanwhile, in the welding shop of the prison, some of the men were handed a new assignment, though they did not know what for. "One of the guys, one of the clerks, happened to see the whole blueprint laying on the drafting table," Norris said, recounting the event, "and went back out in the shop and said, 'Bruh, y'all know what you're building?' They're like, 'What?' 'You're building the damn deathbed.'"

Instead of purchasing a bed, Norris said, the Department of Corrections found it cheaper to direct the prisoners in the machine and welding shops to build it, with each part of the bed assembled separately. Norris paused, shaking his head at the memory. "One of the guys on the welding crew, his brother was on death row."

Upon realizing what they were building, Norris said, the men refused to continue. And as a result, they were locked inside their cells. "The word spread like wildfire, because it was lunchtime when they was getting locked up, and so when it came time for everybody to go back to work after lunch, everybody was like, 'We're not going back to work.'" The prison, Norris said, was essentially at a standstill for three days.*

My mind jolted back to the room where I stood, between the table and the glass panel, looking at the table and then turning my head to look at the chairs on the other side of the glass. The chairs and glass turned this room into a spectacle of state-sanctioned, taxpayer-funded death. The table was a reminder of how fragile our bodies are, how little is needed to extinguish a life.

Robert Sawyer was the first person put to death by lethal injection in Louisiana, in 1993. Childhood abuse left him brain damaged with severe mental impediments—he was executed despite having an IQ of only 68, below the threshold of what is considered intellectually disabled.

Dobie Gillis Williams—another man who suffered from intellectual disability—was killed on January 8, 1999. For his final meal he ate twelve candy bars and a bowl of ice cream.

Gerald Bordelon—who, during his execution, wore a gold cross that his daughter had given him just hours before—turned to the family of his victim in the moments before he was killed, looking at them through the glass, and said, "I'm sorry. I don't know if that brings any closure or peace. It should have never happened, but it did, and I'm sorry."

Each of these three men were found guilty of taking someone's life, but standing in this room, I couldn't understand how taking their lives in return made things any better.

We filed back into the bus without saying much of anything. The engine started, and the bus's rubber tires spit out clouds of dust behind them.

---

*The incident was reported by the Associated Press in July 1991 ("Prisoners Strike After Two Refuse to Build Execution Bed," July 24, 1991). A prison official acknowledged to the press that "there were some inmates . . . who refused their job assignment" but said he had "no comment on what that assignment is." Later, said Norris, the warden at Angola took the unusal step of apologizing to the prisoners for the incident.

Excerpt from the book *How the Word Is Passed* by Clint Smith. Copyright © 2021 by Clint Smith. Reprinted by permission of The Gernert Company, Inc., and Little, Brown, an imprint of Hachette Book Group, Inc.

From "The Really Big One"

Kathryn Schulz

After graduating from Brown University with a BA in History in 1996, Kathryn Schulz thought a career in academic research and writing would best suit her intellectual aspirations, and thus determined to pursue a PhD. But after moving to Santiago, Chile, with her sister's family, she discovered in her first reporting and editing position at *The Santiago Times* that her "attraction to ideas could be pursued without returning to academia." Although she "loved being in Santiago, the job was horrible," so she moved to Brooklyn with a longtime friend to develop her career in journalism. While in Chile, she had sold her first piece to *The New York Times* and sought to expand her repertoire in New York or Seattle. Her arrival in Brooklyn on September 9, 2001, two days before the 9/11 terrorist attack on the Twin Towers, placed her among what she described as "a very strange generation of New Yorkers." Catastrophic risk would color her environmental writing, which attracted the attention of *Grist*, a Seattle-based nonprofit online magazine dedicated to environmental news and commentary. Pacific Coast seismic risk, which comprises the subject of the excerpt below, traces back in Schulz's work to her writing and editing for *Grist*.

Just one year after Schulz joined the staff of *The New Yorker* in 2015, she won a Pulitzer Prize for Feature Writing and a National Magazine Award for "The Really Big One" in 2016. The article details the potential massive earthquake—ignored by many experts—that threatens to devastate portions of the west coast of North America. Schulz's impressive range in environmental writing would later include a memorable *New Yorker* piece on stinkbug infestation and a bold assault on iconic philosopher-naturalist Henry David Thoreau titled "Pond Scum," an against-the-grain unmasking of a figure revered by the environmental movement and its most respected leaders such as Bill McKibbon. In addition to her defiance of convention, her writing shows a serious attention to craft. According to *New Yorker* editor David Remnick,

"The Really Big One" illuminates both its subject and "the art of writing—the use of voice, image, and structure to turn lessons in civics and geology into a mind-blowing, heart-wrenching, pulse-pounding, hair-raising story." Remnick's observation of Schulz's literary craft highlights how she "*steals*" upon her topic, leading the reader through the investigative process. Her subtle prose, moreover, is marked by the lyricism and "quiet beauty of her language." Schulz, for example, describes her solemn encounter with trees in a "ghost forest" of the Cascadian subduction zone: "Leafless, branchless, barkless, they are reduced to their trunks and worn to a smooth silver-gray, as if they had always carried their own tombstones inside them." Recognized among the world's greatest living prose stylists, Marilynne Robinson found the "brilliant scrutiny" of Schulz's later writing "profound and beautiful." Such ringing endorsements point to how literature and journalism can coalesce into one crystalline form.

—D. D.

When the 2011 earthquake and tsunami struck Tohoku, Japan, Chris Goldfinger was two hundred miles away, in the city of Kashiwa, at an international meeting on seismology. As the shaking started, everyone in the room began to laugh. Earthquakes are common in Japan—that one was the third of the week—and the participants were, after all, at a seismology conference. Then everyone in the room checked the time.

Seismologists know that how long an earthquake lasts is a decent proxy for its magnitude. The 1989 earthquake in Loma Prieta, California, which killed sixty-three people and caused $6 billion dollars' worth of damage, lasted about fifteen seconds and had a magnitude of 6.9. A thirty-second earthquake generally has a magnitude in the mid-sevens. A minute-long quake is in the high sevens, a two-minute quake has entered the eights, and a three-minute quake is in the high eights. By four minutes, an earthquake has hit magnitude 9.0.

When Goldfinger looked at his watch, it was quarter to three. The conference was wrapping up for the day. He was thinking about sushi. The speaker at the lectern was wondering if he should carry on with his talk. The earthquake was not particularly strong. Then it ticked past the sixty-second mark, making it longer than the others that week. The shaking intensified. The seats in the conference room were small plastic desks with wheels. Goldfinger, who is tall and solidly built, thought, No way am I crouching under one of those for cover. At a minute and a half, everyone in the room got up and went outside.

It was March. There was a chill in the air, and snow flurries, but no snow on the ground. Nor, from the feel of it, was there ground on the ground. The earth snapped and popped and rippled. It was, Goldfinger thought, like driving through rocky terrain in a vehicle with no shocks, if both the vehicle and the terrain were also on a raft in high seas. The quake passed the two-minute mark. The trees, still hung with the previous autumn's dead leaves, were making a strange rattling sound. The flagpole atop the building he and his colleagues had just vacated was whipping through an arc of forty degrees. The building itself was base-isolated, a seismic-safety technology in which the body of a structure rests on movable bearings rather than directly on its foundation. Goldfinger lurched over to take a look. The base was lurching, too, back and forth a foot at a time, digging a trench in the yard. He thought better of it, and lurched away. His watch swept past the three-minute mark and kept going.

Oh, shit, Goldfinger thought, although not in dread, at first: in amazement. For decades, seismologists had believed that Japan could not experience an earthquake stronger than magnitude 8.4. In 2005, however, at a conference in Hokudan, a Japanese geologist named Yasutaka Ikeda had argued that the nation should expect a magnitude 9.0 in the near future—with catastrophic consequences, because Japan's famous earthquake-and-tsunami preparedness, including the height of its sea walls, was based on incorrect science. The presentation was met with polite applause and thereafter largely ignored. Now, Goldfinger realized as the shaking hit the four-minute mark, the planet was proving the Japanese Cassandra right.

For a moment, that was pretty cool: a real-time revolution in earthquake science. Almost immediately, though, it became extremely uncool, because Goldfinger and every other seismologist standing outside in Kashiwa knew what was coming. One of them pulled out a cell phone and started streaming videos from the Japanese broadcasting station NHK, shot by helicopters that had flown out to sea soon after the shaking started. Thirty minutes after Goldfinger first stepped outside, he watched the tsunami roll in, in real time, on a two-inch screen.

In the end, the magnitude-9.0 Tohoku earthquake and subsequent tsunami killed more than eighteen thousand people, devastated northeast Japan, triggered the meltdown at the Fukushima power plant, and cost an estimated two hundred and twenty billion dollars. The shaking earlier in the week turned out to be the foreshocks of the largest earthquake in the nation's recorded history. But for Chris Goldfinger, a paleoseismologist at Oregon State University and one of the world's leading experts on a little-known fault line, the main quake was itself a kind of foreshock: a preview of another earthquake still to come.

Most people in the United States know just one fault line by name: the San Andreas, which runs nearly the length of California and is perpetually rumored to be on the verge of unleashing "the big one." That rumor is misleading, no matter what the San Andreas ever does. Every fault line has an upper limit to its potency, determined by its length and width, and by how far it can slip. For the San Andreas, one of the most extensively studied and best understood fault lines in the world, that upper limit is roughly an 8.2—a powerful earthquake, but, because the Richter scale is logarithmic, only six per cent as strong as the 2011 event in Japan.

Just north of the San Andreas, however, lies another fault line. Known as the Cascadia subduction zone, it runs for seven hundred miles off the coast of the Pacific Northwest, beginning near Cape Mendocino, California, continuing along Oregon and Washington, and terminating around Vancouver Island, Canada. The "Cascadia" part of its name comes from the Cascade Range, a chain of volcanic mountains that follow the same course a hundred or so miles inland. The "subduction zone" part refers to a region of the planet where one tectonic plate is sliding underneath (subducting) another. Tectonic plates are those slabs of mantle and crust that, in their epochs-long drift, rearrange the earth's continents and oceans. Most of the time, their movement is slow, harmless, and all but undetectable. Occasionally, at the borders where they meet, it is not.

Take your hands and hold them palms down, middle fingertips touching. Your right hand represents the North American tectonic plate, which bears on its back, among other things, our entire continent, from One World Trade Center to the Space Needle, in Seattle. Your left hand represents an oceanic plate called Juan de Fuca, ninety thousand square miles in size. The place where they meet is the Cascadia subduction zone. Now slide your left hand under your right one. That is what the Juan de Fuca plate is doing: slipping steadily beneath North America. When you try it, your right hand will slide up your left arm, as if you were pushing up your sleeve. That is what North America is not doing. It is stuck, wedged tight against the surface of the other plate.

Without moving your hands, curl your right knuckles up, so that they point toward the ceiling. Under pressure from Juan de Fuca, the stuck edge of North America is bulging upward and compressing eastward, at the rate of, respectively, three to four millimetres and thirty to forty millimetres a year. It can do so for quite some time, because, as continent stuff goes, it is young, made of rock that is still relatively elastic. (Rocks, like us, get stiffer as they age.) But it cannot do so indefinitely. There is a backstop—the craton, that ancient unbudgeable mass at the center of the continent—and, sooner or later, North America will rebound like a spring. If, on that occasion, only the southern part of the Cascadia subduction zone gives way—your first two fingers, say—the magnitude of the resulting quake will be somewhere between 8.0 and 8.6. That's the big one. If the entire zone gives way at once, an event that seismologists call a full-margin rupture, the magnitude will be somewhere between 8.7 and 9.2. That's the very big one.

Flick your right fingers outward, forcefully, so that your hand flattens back down again. When the next very big earthquake hits, the northwest edge of the continent, from California to Canada and the continental shelf to the Cascades, will drop by as much as six feet and rebound thirty to a hundred feet to the west—losing, within minutes, all the elevation and compression it has gained over centuries. Some of that shift will take place beneath the ocean, displacing a colossal quantity of seawater. (Watch what your fingertips do when you flatten your hand.) The water will surge upward into a huge hill, then promptly collapse. One side will rush west, toward Japan. The other side will rush east, in a seven-hundred-mile liquid wall that will reach the Northwest coast, on average, fifteen minutes after the earthquake begins. By the time the shaking has ceased and the tsunami has receded, the region will be unrecognizable. Kenneth Murphy, who directs FEMA's Region X, the division responsible for Oregon, Washington, Idaho, and Alaska, says, "Our operating assumption is that everything west of Interstate 5 will be toast."

In the Pacific Northwest, the area of impact will cover some hundred and forty thousand square miles, including Seattle, Tacoma, Portland, Eugene, Salem (the capital city of Oregon), Olympia (the capital of Washington), and some seven million people. When the next full-margin rupture happens, that region will suffer the worst natural disaster in the history of North America, outside of the 2010 Haiti earthquake, which killed upward of a hundred thousand people. By comparison, roughly three thousand people died in San Francisco's 1906 earthquake. Almost two thousand died in Hurricane Katrina. Almost three hundred died in Hurricane Sandy. FEMA projects that nearly thirteen thousand people will die in the Cascadia earthquake and tsunami. Another twenty-seven thousand will be injured, and the agency expects that it will need to provide shelter for a million displaced people, and food and water for another two and a half million. "This is one time that I'm hoping all the science is wrong, and it won't happen for another thousand years," Murphy says.

In fact, the science is robust, and one of the chief scientists behind it is Chris Goldfinger. Thanks to work done by him and his colleagues, we now know that the odds of the big Cascadia earthquake happening in the next fifty years are roughly one in three. The odds of the very big one are roughly one in ten. Even those numbers do not fully reflect the danger—or, more to the point, how unprepared the Pacific Northwest is to face it. The truly worrisome figures in this story are these: Thirty years ago, no one knew that the Cascadia subduction zone had ever produced a major earthquake. Forty-five years ago, no one even knew it existed. . . .

The Pacific Northwest sits squarely within the Ring of Fire. Off its coast, an oceanic plate is slipping beneath a continental one. Inland, the Cascade volcanoes mark the line where, far below, the Juan de Fuca plate is heating up and melting everything above it. In other words, the Cascadia subduction zone has, as Goldfinger put it, "all the right anatomical parts." Yet not once in recorded history has it caused a major earthquake—or, for that matter, any quake to speak of. By contrast, other subduction zones produce major earthquakes occasionally and minor ones all the time: magnitude 5.0, magnitude 4.0, magnitude why are the neighbors moving their sofa at midnight. You can scarcely spend a week in Japan without feeling this sort of earthquake. You can spend a lifetime in many parts of the Northwest—several, in fact, if you had them to spend—and not feel so much as a quiver. The question facing geologists in the nineteen-seventies was whether the Cascadia subduction zone had ever broken its eerie silence.

In the late nineteen-eighties, Brian Atwater, a geologist with the United States Geological Survey, and a graduate student named David Yamaguchi found the answer, and another major clue in the Cascadia puzzle. Their discovery is best illustrated in a place called the ghost forest, a grove of western red cedars on the banks of the Copalis River, near the Washington coast. When I paddled out to it last summer, with Atwater and Yamaguchi, it was easy to see how it got its name. The cedars are spread out across a low salt marsh on a wide northern bend in the river, long dead but still standing. Leafless, branchless, barkless, they are reduced to their trunks and worn to a smooth silver-gray, as if they had always carried their own tombstones inside them.

Excerpt from "The Really Big One," an article by Kathryn Schulz © 2015 Kathryn Schulz, as originally appeared in *The New Yorker* magazine, July 20, 2015.

From "The Uninhabitable Earth"

David Wallace-Wells

By 2017, the year "The Uninhabitable Earth" first appeared in *New York* magazine and its online publication, *The Intelligencer*, the perils of climate change had been covered thoroughly in a myriad of media forms. But none cast the stakes and threats as alarmingly as the article's author, David Wallace-Wells. Jennifer Szalai's *New York Times* review of the book-length version of the article published two years later in 2019 highlighted his capacity to describe "in meticulous and terrifying detail" rising global temperatures and their devastating effects. Having written widely on climate for *New York* and *The Guardian*, Wallace-Wells struck a nerve with the reading public with his original article, which unleashed a firestorm of controversy. The hyperpolarized politics of climate change notwithstanding, sensitivity to hyperbole and exaggeration extended to the scientific community, which called for further examination of his characterization of the risks at hand. In order to provide an open forum to sort out the widespread controversy in the wake of the article's publication, New York University's Arthur L. Carter Journalism Institute held a two-hour-long conversation between Wallace-Wells and climatologist Michael E. Mann, director of the Earth System Science Center at Penn State University. During the event, Wallace-Wells emphasized that he conceived of his role as an advocate to shake people from assuming that, while climate change would have an adverse impact, it would mainly be felt elsewhere around the world. During that conversation, Wallace-Wells admitted that his prediction of Arctic methane emissions was inaccurate, noting that he would not have made the claim if he were to write the article again. In a widely shared post on Facebook, Mann stated, "There is no need to overstate the evidence, particularly when it feeds a paralyzing narrative of doom and hopelessness."

"The Uninhabitable Earth" would become the most-read article in *New York* magazine's 49-year history, in part, because its use of rhetorical framing and literary devices so convincingly disabused the public of denialism. This milestone in science journalism, abetted by longform storytelling in a digital format, marked the most influential public statement on climate change in the twenty-first century. The most cogent claim in the article is that the ripple effects of rising global air and water temperatures can harm us personally and potentially lead to the extinction of the human species. The digital publication of the article was vital in facilitating an extended conversation via additional interviews featuring Mann along with paleontologist Peter Ward, oceanographer Wallace Smith Broecker, climatologist James Hansen, and scientist Michael Oppenheimer. This amended and annotated online edition of the story, which contained in-line footnotes, testified to the power of digital journalism to provide extensive supplementary data to support original reporting. Further, the flexibility of online publishing's fluid temporality enabled a re-issue of the story in a more efficient and timely manner than traditional forms would allow. Susan Matthews of *Slate* was among Wallace-Wells's defenders, welcoming the alarmism of this instantly viral article as necessary and overdue. In particular, she saw it as carrying on the legacy of Rachel Carson's revolutionary environmental journalism of *Silent Spring*, which exposed the deleterious effects of DDTs and other toxic pesticides on wildlife and vegetation. The article would be the *Silent Spring* of our time, according to Matthews, "except it doesn't uncover shocking new information—it just collects all the terrifying things that were already sitting out there into one extremely terrifying list."

—D. D.

I. 'Doomsday'

Peering beyond scientific reticence.

It is, I promise, worse than you think. If your anxiety about global warming is dominated by fears of sea-level rise, you are barely scratching the surface of what terrors are possible, even within the lifetime of a teenager today. And yet the swelling seas—and the cities they will drown—have so dominated the picture of global warming, and so overwhelmed our capacity for climate panic, that they have occluded our perception of other threats, many much closer at hand. Rising oceans are bad, in fact very bad; but fleeing the coastline will not be enough.

Indeed, absent a significant adjustment to how billions of humans conduct their lives, parts of the Earth will likely become close to uninhabitable, and other parts horrifically inhospitable, as soon as the end of this century.

Even when we train our eyes on climate change, we are unable to comprehend its scope. This past winter, a string of days 60 and 70 degrees warmer than normal baked the North Pole, melting the permafrost that encased Norway's Svalbard seed vault—a global food bank nicknamed "Doomsday," designed to ensure that our agriculture survives any catastrophe, and which appeared to have been flooded by climate change less than ten years after being built. . . .

II. Heat Death

The bahraining of New York.

Humans, like all mammals, are heat engines; surviving means having to continually cool off, like panting dogs. For that, the temperature needs to be low enough for the air to act as a kind of refrigerant, drawing heat off the skin so the engine can keep pumping. At seven degrees of warming, that would become impossible for large portions of the planet's equatorial band, and especially the tropics, where humidity adds to the problem; in the jungles of Costa Rica, for instance, where humidity routinely tops 90 percent, simply moving around outside when it's over 105 degrees Fahrenheit would be lethal. And the effect would be fast: Within a few hours, a human body would be cooked to death from both inside and out.

Climate-change skeptics point out that the planet has warmed and cooled many times before, but the climate window that has allowed for human life is very narrow, even by the standards of planetary history. At 11 or 12 degrees of warming, more than half the world's population, as distributed today, would die of direct heat. Things almost certainly won't get that hot this century, though models of unabated emissions do bring us that far eventually. This century, and especially in the tropics, the pain points will pinch much more quickly even than an increase of seven degrees. The key factor is something called wet-bulb temperature, which is a term of measurement as home-laboratory-kit as it sounds: the heat registered on a thermometer wrapped in a damp sock as it's swung around in the air (since the moisture evaporates from a sock more quickly in dry air, this single number reflects both heat and humidity). At present, most regions reach a wet-bulb maximum of 26 or 27 degrees Celsius; the true red line for habitability is 35 degrees. What is called heat stress comes much sooner.

Actually, we're about there already. Since 1980, the planet has experienced a 50-fold increase in the number of places experiencing dangerous or extreme heat; a bigger increase is to come. The five warmest summers in Europe since 1500 have all occurred since 2002, and soon, the IPCC warns, simply being outdoors that time of year will be unhealthy for much of the globe. Even if we meet the Paris goals of two degrees warming, cities like Karachi and Kolkata will become close to uninhabitable, annually encountering deadly heat waves like those that crippled them in 2015. At four degrees, the deadly European heat wave of 2003, which killed as many as 2,000 people a day, will be a normal summer. At six, according to an assessment focused only on effects within the U.S. from the National Oceanic and Atmospheric Administration, summer labor of any kind would become impossible in the lower Mississippi Valley, and everybody in the country east of the Rockies would be under more heat stress than anyone, anywhere, in the world today. As Joseph Romm has put it in his authoritative primer *Climate Change: What Everyone Needs to Know*, heat stress in New York City would exceed that of present-day Bahrain, one of the planet's hottest spots, and the temperature in Bahrain "would induce hyperthermia in even sleeping humans." The high-end IPCC estimate, remember, is two degrees warmer still. By the end of the century, the World Bank has estimated, the coolest months in tropical South America, Africa, and the Pacific are likely to be warmer than the warmest months at the end of the twentieth century. Air-conditioning can help but will ultimately only add to the carbon problem; plus, the climate-controlled malls of the Arab Emirates aside, it is not remotely plausible to wholesale air-condition all the hottest parts of the world, many of them also the poorest.

And indeed, the crisis will be most dramatic across the Middle East and Persian Gulf, where in 2015 the heat index registered temperatures as high as 163 degrees Fahrenheit. As soon as several decades from now, the hajj will become physically impossible for the 2 million Muslims who make the pilgrimage each year.

It is not just the hajj, and it is not just Mecca; heat is already killing us. In the sugarcane region of El Salvador, as much as one-fifth of the population has chronic kidney disease, including over a quarter of the men, the presumed result of dehydration from working the fields they were able to comfortably harvest as recently as two decades ago. With dialysis, which is expensive, those with kidney failure can expect to live five years; without it, life expectancy is in the weeks. Of course, heat stress promises to pummel us in places other than our kidneys, too. As I type that sentence, in the California desert in mid-June, it is 121 degrees outside my door. It is not a record high.

III. The End of Food

Praying for cornfields in the tundra.

Climates differ and plants vary, but the basic rule for staple cereal crops grown at optimal temperature is that for every degree of warming, yields decline by 10 percent. Some estimates run as high as 15 or even 17 percent. Which means that if the planet is five degrees warmer at the end of the century, we may have as many as 50 percent more people to feed and 50 percent less grain to give them. And proteins are worse: It takes 16 calories of grain to produce just a single calorie of hamburger meat, butchered from a cow that spent its life polluting the climate with methane farts.

Pollyannaish plant physiologists will point out that the cereal-crop math applies only to those regions already at peak growing temperature, and they are right—theoretically, a warmer climate will make it easier to grow corn in Greenland. But as the pathbreaking work by Rosamond Naylor and David Battisti has shown, the tropics are already too hot to efficiently grow grain, and those places where grain is produced today are already at optimal growing temperature—which means even a small warming will push them down the slope of declining productivity. And you can't easily move croplands north a few hundred miles, because yields in places like remote Canada and Russia are limited by the quality of soil there; it takes many centuries for the planet to produce optimally fertile dirt.

Drought might be an even bigger problem than heat, with some of the world's most arable land turning quickly to desert. Precipitation is notoriously hard to model, yet predictions for later this century are basically unanimous: unprecedented droughts nearly everywhere food is today produced. By 2080, without dramatic reductions in emissions, southern Europe will be in permanent extreme drought, much worse than the American dust bowl ever was. The same will be true in Iraq and Syria and much of the rest of the Middle East; some of the most densely populated parts of Australia, Africa, and South America; and the breadbasket regions of China. None of these places, which today supply much of the world's food, will be reliable sources of any. As for the original dust bowl: The droughts in the American plains and Southwest would not just be worse than in the 1930s, a 2015 NASA study predicted, but worse than any droughts in a thousand years—and that includes those that struck between 1100 and 1300, which "dried up all the rivers East of the Sierra Nevada mountains" and may have been responsible for the death of the Anasazi civilization.

Remember, we do not live in a world without hunger as it is. Far from it: Most estimates put the number of undernourished at 800 million globally. In case you haven't heard, this spring has already brought an unprecedented quadruple famine to Africa and the Middle East; the U.N. has warned that separate starvation events in Somalia, South Sudan, Nigeria, and Yemen could kill 20 million this year alone.

IV. Climate Plagues

What happens when the bubonic ice melts?

Rock, in the right spot, is a record of planetary history, eras as long as millions of years flattened by the forces of geological time into strata with amplitudes of just inches, or just an inch, or even less. Ice works that way, too, as a climate ledger, but it is also frozen history, some of which can be reanimated when unfrozen. There are now, trapped in Arctic ice, diseases that have not circulated in the air for millions of years—in some cases, since before humans were around to encounter them. Which means our immune systems would have no idea how to fight back when those prehistoric plagues emerge from the ice.

The Arctic also stores terrifying bugs from more recent times. In Alaska, already, researchers have discovered remnants of the 1918 flu that infected as many as 500 million and killed as many as 100 million—about 5 percent of the world's population and almost six times as many as had died in the world war for which the pandemic served as a kind of gruesome capstone. As the BBC reported in May, scientists suspect smallpox and the bubonic plague are trapped in Siberian ice, too—an abridged history of devastating human sickness, left out like egg salad in the Arctic sun.

Experts caution that many of these organisms won't actually survive the thaw and point to the fastidious lab conditions under which they have already reanimated several of them—the 32,000-year-old "extremophile" bacteria revived in 2005, an 8 million-year-old bug brought back to life in 2007, the 3.5 million-year-old one a Russian scientist self-injected just out of curiosity—to suggest that those are necessary conditions for the return of such ancient plagues. But already last year, a boy was killed and 20 others infected by anthrax released when retreating permafrost exposed the frozen carcass of a reindeer killed by the bacteria at least 75 years earlier; 2,000 present-day reindeer were infected, too, carrying and spreading the disease beyond the tundra.

What concerns epidemiologists more than ancient diseases are existing scourges relocated, rewired, or even re-evolved by warming. The first effect is geographical. Before the early-modern period, when adventuring sailboats accelerated the mixing of peoples and their bugs, human provinciality was a guard against pandemic. Today, even with globalization and the enormous intermingling of human populations, our ecosystems are mostly stable, and this functions as another limit, but global warming will scramble those ecosystems and help disease trespass those limits as surely as Cortés did. You don't worry much about dengue or malaria if you are living in Maine or France. But as the tropics creep northward and mosquitoes migrate with them, you will. You didn't much worry about Zika a couple of years ago, either.

As it happens, Zika may also be a good model of the second worrying effect—disease mutation. One reason you hadn't heard about Zika until recently is that it had been trapped in Uganda; another is that it did not, until recently, appear to cause birth defects. Scientists still don't entirely understand what happened, or what they missed. But there are things we do know for sure about how climate affects some diseases: Malaria, for instance, thrives in hotter regions not just because the mosquitoes that carry it do, too, but because for every degree increase in temperature, the parasite reproduces ten times faster. Which is one reason that the World Bank estimates that by 2050, 5.2 billion people will be reckoning with it.

V. Unbreathable Air

A rolling death smog that suffocates millions.

Our lungs need oxygen, but that is only a fraction of what we breathe. The fraction of carbon dioxide is growing: It just crossed 400 parts per million, and high-end estimates extrapolating from current trends suggest it will hit 1,000 ppm by 2100. At that concentration, compared to the air we breathe now, human cognitive ability declines by 21 percent.

Other stuff in the hotter air is even scarier, with small increases in pollution capable of shortening life spans by ten years. The warmer the planet gets, the more ozone forms, and by midcentury, Americans will likely suffer a 70 percent increase in unhealthy ozone smog, the National Center for Atmospheric Research has projected. By 2090, as many as 2 billion people globally will be breathing air above the WHO "safe" level; one paper last month showed that, among other effects, a pregnant mother's exposure to ozone raises the child's risk of autism (as much as tenfold, combined with other environmental factors). Which does make you think again about the autism epidemic in West Hollywood.

Already, more than 10,000 people die each day from the small particles emitted from fossil-fuel burning; each year, 339,000 people die from wildfire smoke, in part because climate change has extended forest-fire season (in the U.S., it's increased by 78 days since 1970). By 2050, according to the U.S.

Forest Service, wildfires will be twice as destructive as they are today; in some places, the area burned could grow fivefold. What worries people even more is the effect that would have on emissions, especially when the fires ravage forests arising out of peat. Peatland fires in Indonesia in 1997, for instance, added to the global CO_2 release by up to 40 percent, and more burning only means more warming only means more burning. There is also the terrifying possibility that rain forests like the Amazon, which in 2010 suffered its second "hundred-year drought" in the space of five years, could dry out enough to become vulnerable to these kinds of devastating, rolling forest fires—which would not only expel enormous amounts of carbon into the atmosphere but also shrink the size of the forest. That is especially bad because the Amazon alone provides 20 percent of our oxygen.

Then there are the more familiar forms of pollution. In 2013, melting Arctic ice remodeled Asian weather patterns, depriving industrial China of the natural ventilation systems it had come to depend on, which blanketed much of the country's north in an unbreathable smog. Literally unbreathable. A metric called the Air Quality Index categorizes the risks and tops out at the 301-to-500 range, warning of "serious aggravation of heart or lung disease and premature mortality in persons with cardiopulmonary disease and the elderly" and, for all others, "serious risk of respiratory effects"; at that level, "everyone should avoid all outdoor exertion." The Chinese "airpocalypse" of 2013 peaked at what would have been an Air Quality Index of over 800. That year, smog was responsible for a third of all deaths in the country.

VI. Perpetual War

The violence baked into heat.

Climatologists are very careful when talking about Syria. They want you to know that while climate change did produce a drought that contributed to civil war, it is not exactly fair to say that the conflict is the result of warming; next door, for instance, Lebanon suffered the same crop failures. But researchers like Marshall Burke and Solomon Hsiang have managed to quantify some of the non-obvious relationships between temperature and violence: For every half-degree of warming, they say, societies will see between a 10 and 20 percent increase in the likelihood of armed conflict. In between a 10 and 20 percent increase in the likelihood of armed conflict. In climate science, nothing is simple, but the arithmetic is harrowing: A planet five degrees warmer would have at least half again as many wars as we do today. Overall, social conflict could more than double this century.

This is one reason that, as nearly every climate scientist I spoke to pointed out, the U.S. military is obsessed with climate change: The drowning of all American Navy bases by sea-level rise is trouble enough, but being the world's policeman is quite a bit harder when the crime rate doubles. Of course, it's not just Syria where climate has contributed to conflict. Some speculate that the elevated level of strife across the Middle East over the past generation reflects the pressures of global warming—a hypothesis all the more cruel considering that warming began accelerating when the industrialized world extracted and then burned the region's oil.

What accounts for the relationship between climate and conflict? Some of it comes down to agriculture and economics; a lot has to do with forced migration, already at a record high, with at least 65 million displaced people wandering the planet right now. But there is also the simple fact of individual irritability. Heat increases municipal crime rates, and swearing on social media, and the likelihood that a major-league pitcher, coming to the mound after his teammate has been hit by a pitch, will hit an opposing batter in retaliation. And the arrival of air-conditioning in the developed world, in the middle of the past century, did little to solve the problem of the summer crime wave.

VII. Permanent Economic Collapse

Dismal capitalism in a half-poorer world.

The murmuring mantra of global neoliberalism, which prevailed between the end of the Cold War and the onset of the Great Recession, is that economic growth would save us from anything and everything. But in the aftermath of the 2008 crash, a growing number of historians studying what they call "fossil capitalism" have begun to suggest that the entire history of swift economic growth, which began somewhat suddenly in the 18th century, is not the result of innovation or trade or the dynamics of global capitalism but simply our discovery of fossil fuels and all their raw power—a onetime injection of new "value" into a system that had previously been characterized by global subsistence living. Before fossil fuels, nobody lived better than their parents or grandparents or ancestors from 500 years before, except in the immediate aftermath of a great plague like the Black Death, which allowed the lucky survivors to gobble up the resources liberated by mass graves. After we've burned all the fossil fuels, these scholars suggest, perhaps we will return to a "steady state" global economy. Of course, that onetime injection has a devastating long-term cost: climate change.

The most exciting research on the economics of warming has also come from Hsiang and his colleagues, who are not historians of fossil capitalism but who offer some very bleak analysis of their own: Every degree Celsius of warming costs, on average, 1.2 percent of GDP (an enormous number, considering we count growth in the low single digits as "strong"). This is the sterling work in the field, and their median projection is for a 23 percent loss in per capita earning globally by the end of this century (resulting from changes in agriculture, crime, storms, energy, mortality, and labor). Tracing the shape of the probability curve is even scarier: There is a 12 percent chance that climate change will reduce global output by more than 50 percent by 2100, they say, and a 51 percent chance that it lowers per capita GDP by 20 percent or more by then, unless emissions decline. By comparison, the Great Recession lowered global GDP by about 6 percent, in a onetime shock; Hsiang and his colleagues estimate a one-in-eight chance of an ongoing and irreversible effect by the end of the century that is eight times worse.

The scale of that economic devastation is hard to comprehend, but you can start by imagining what the world would look like today with an economy half as big, which would produce only half as much value, generating only half as much to offer the workers of the world. It makes the grounding of flights out of heat-stricken Phoenix last month seem like pathetically small economic potatoes. And, among other things, it makes the idea of postponing government action on reducing emissions and relying solely on growth and technology to solve the problem an absurd business calculation. Every round-trip ticket on flights from New York to London, keep in mind, costs the Arctic three more square meters of ice.

VIII. Poisoned Oceans

Sulfide burps off the skeleton coast.

That the sea will become a killer is a given. Barring a radical reduction of emissions, we will see at least four feet of sea-level rise and possibly ten by the end of the century. A third of the world's major cities are on the coast, not to mention its power plants, ports, navy bases, farmlands, fisheries, river deltas, marshlands, and rice-paddy empires, and even those above ten feet will flood much more easily, and much more regularly, if the water gets that high. At least 600 million people live within ten meters of sea level today.

But the drowning of those homelands is just the start. At present, more than a third of the world's carbon is sucked up by the oceans—thank God, or else we'd have that much more warming already. But the result is what's called "ocean acidification," which, on its own, may add a half a degree to warming this century. It is also already burning through the planet's water basins—you may remember these as the place where life arose in the first place. You have probably heard of "coral bleaching"—that is, coral dying—which is very bad news, because reefs support as much as a quarter of all marine life and supply food for half a billion people. Ocean acidification will fry fish populations directly, too, though scientists aren't yet sure how to predict the effects on the stuff we haul out of the ocean to eat; they do know that in acid waters, oysters and mussels will struggle to grow their shells, and that when the pH of human blood drops as much as the oceans' pH has over the past generation, it induces seizures, comas, and sudden death.

That isn't all that ocean acidification can do. Carbon absorption can initiate a feedback loop in which underoxygenated waters breed different kinds of microbes that turn the water still more "anoxic," first in deep ocean "dead zones," then gradually up toward the surface. There, the small fish die out, unable to breathe, which means oxygen-eating bacteria thrive, and the feedback loop doubles back. This process, in which dead zones grow like cancers, choking off marine life and wiping out fisheries, is already quite advanced in parts of the Gulf of Mexico and just off Namibia, where hydrogen sulfide is bubbling out of the sea along a thousand-mile stretch of land known as the "Skeleton Coast." The name originally referred to the detritus of the whaling industry, but today it's more apt than ever. Hydrogen sulfide is so toxic that evolution has trained us to recognize the tiniest, safest traces of it, which is why our noses are so exquisitely skilled at registering flatulence. Hydrogen sulfide is also the thing that finally did us in that time 97 percent of all life on Earth died, once all the feedback loops had been triggered and the circulating jet streams of a warmed ocean ground to a halt—it's the planet's preferred gas for a natural holocaust. Gradually, the ocean's dead zones spread, killing off marine species that had dominated the oceans for hundreds of millions of years, and the gas the inert waters gave off into the atmosphere poisoned everything on land. Plants, too. It was millions of years before the oceans recovered.

IX. The Great Filter

Our present eeriness cannot last.

So why can't we see it? In his recent book-length essay The Great Derangement, the Indian novelist Amitav Ghosh wonders why global warming and natural disaster haven't become major subjects of contemporary fiction—why we don't seem able to imagine climate catastrophe, and why we haven't yet had a spate of novels in the genre he basically imagines into half-existence and names "the environmental uncanny." "Consider, for example, the stories that congeal around questions like, 'Where were you when the Berlin Wall fell?' or 'Where were you on 9/11?' " he writes. "Will it ever be possible to ask, in the same vein, 'Where were you at 400 ppm?' or 'Where were you when the Larsen B ice shelf broke up?'" His answer: Probably not, because the dilemmas and dramas of climate change are simply incompatible with the kinds of stories we tell ourselves about ourselves, especially in novels, which tend to emphasize the journey of an individual conscience rather than the poisonous miasma of social fate.

Surely this blindness will not last—the world we are about to inhabit will not permit it. In a six-degree-warmer world, the Earth's ecosystem will boil with so many natural disasters that we will just start calling them "weather": a constant swarm of out-of-control typhoons and tornadoes and floods and droughts, the planet assaulted regularly with climate events that not so long ago destroyed whole civilizations. The strongest hurricanes will come more often, and we'll have to invent new categories with which to describe them; tornadoes will grow longer and wider and strike much more frequently, and hail rocks will quadruple in size. Humans used to watch the weather to prophesy the future; going forward, we will see in its wrath the vengeance of the past. Early naturalists talked often about "deep time"—the perception they had, contemplating the grandeur of this valley or that rock basin, of the profound slowness of nature. What lies in store for us is more like what the Victorian anthropologists identified as "dreamtime," or "everywhen": the semi-mythical experience, described by Aboriginal Australians, of encountering, in the present moment, an out-of-time past, when ancestors, heroes, and demigods crowded an epic stage. You can find it already watching footage of an iceberg collapsing into the sea—a feeling of history happening all at once.

It is. Many people perceive climate change as a sort of moral and economic debt, accumulated since the beginning of the Industrial Revolution and now come due after several centuries—a helpful perspective, in a way, since it is the carbon-burning processes that began in 18th-century England that lit the fuse of everything that followed. But more than half of the carbon humanity has exhaled into the atmosphere in its entire history has been emitted in just the past three decades; since the end of World War II, the figure is 85 percent. Which means that, in the length of a single generation, global warming has brought us to the brink of planetary catastrophe, and that the story of the industrial world's kamikaze mission is also the story of a single lifetime. My father's, for instance: born in 1938, among his first memories the news of Pearl Harbor and the mythic Air Force of the propaganda films that followed, films that doubled as advertisements for imperial-American industrial might; and among his last memories the coverage of the desperate signing of the Paris climate accords on cable news, ten weeks before he died of lung cancer last July. Or my mother's: born in 1945, to German Jews fleeing the smokestacks through which their relatives were incinerated, now enjoying her 72nd year in an American commodity paradise, a paradise supported by the supply chains of an industrialized developing world. She has been smoking for 57 of those years, unfiltered.

Or the scientists'. Some of the men who first identified a changing climate (and given the generation, those who became famous were men) are still alive; a few are even still working. Wally Broecker is 84 years old and drives to work at the Lamont-Doherty Earth Observatory across the Hudson every day from the Upper West Side. Like most of those who first raised the alarm, he believes that no amount of emissions reduction alone can meaningfully help avoid disaster. Instead, he puts his faith in carbon capture—untested technology to extract carbon dioxide from the atmosphere, which Broecker estimates will cost at least several trillion dollars—and various forms of "geoengineering," the catchall name for a variety of moon-shot technologies far-fetched enough that many climate scientists prefer to regard them as dreams, or nightmares, from science fiction. He is especially focused on what's called the aerosol approach—dispersing so much sulfur dioxide into the atmosphere that when it converts to sulfuric acid, it will cloud a fifth of the horizon and reflect back 2 percent of the sun's rays, buying the planet at least a little wiggle room, heat-wise. "Of course, that would make our sunsets very red, would bleach the sky, would make more acid rain," he says. "But you have to look at the magnitude of the problem. You got to watch that you don't say the giant problem shouldn't be solved because the solution causes some smaller problems." He won't be around to see that, he told me. "But in your lifetime …"

Jim Hansen is another member of this godfather generation. Born in 1941, he became a climatologist at the University of Iowa, developed the groundbreaking "Zero Model" for projecting climate change, and later became the head of climate research at NASA, only to leave under pressure when, while still a federal employee, he filed a lawsuit against the federal government charging inaction on warming (along the way he got arrested a few times for protesting, too). The lawsuit, which is brought by a collective called Our Children's Trust and is often described as "kids versus climate change," is built on an appeal to the equal-protection clause, namely, that in failing to take action on warming, the government is violating it by imposing massive costs on future generations; it is scheduled to be heard this winter in Oregon district court. Hansen has recently given up on solving the climate problem with a carbon tax alone, which had been his preferred approach, and has set about calculating the total cost of the additional measure of extracting carbon from the atmosphere.

Hansen began his career studying Venus, which was once a very Earth-like planet with plenty of life-supporting water before runaway climate change rapidly transformed it into an arid and uninhabitable sphere enveloped in an unbreathable gas; he switched to studying our planet by 30, wondering why he should be squinting across the solar system to explore rapid environmental change when he could see it all around him on the planet he was standing on. "When we wrote our first paper on this, in 1981," he told me, "I remember saying to one of my co-authors, 'This is going to be very interesting. Sometime during our careers, we're going to see these things beginning to happen.'"

Several of the scientists I spoke with proposed global warming as the solution to Fermi's famous paradox, which asks, If the universe is so big, then why haven't we encountered any other intelligent life in it? The answer, they suggested, is that the natural life span of a civilization may be only several thousand years, and the life span of an industrial civilization perhaps only several hundred. In a universe that is many billions of years old, with star systems separated as much by time as by space, civilizations might emerge and develop and burn themselves up simply too fast to ever find one another. Peter Ward, a charismatic paleontologist among those responsible for discovering that the planet's mass extinctions were caused by greenhouse gas, calls this the "Great Filter": "Civilizations rise, but there's an environmental filter that causes them to die off again and disappear fairly quickly," he told me. "If you look at planet Earth, the filtering we've had in the past has been in these mass extinctions." The mass extinction we are now living through has only just begun; so much more dying is coming.

And yet, improbably, Ward is an optimist. So are Broecker and Hansen and many of the other scientists I spoke to. We have not developed much of a religion of meaning around climate change that might comfort us, or give us purpose, in the face of possible annihilation. But climate scientists have a strange kind of faith: We will find a way to forestall radical warming, they say, because we must.

It is not easy to know how much to be reassured by that bleak certainty, and how much to wonder whether it is another form of delusion; for global warming to work as parable, of course, someone needs to survive to tell the story. The scientists know that to even meet the Paris goals, by 2050, carbon emissions from energy and industry, which are still rising, will have to fall by half each decade; emissions from land use (deforestation, cow farts, etc.) will have to zero out; and we will need to have invented technologies to extract, annually, twice as much carbon from the atmosphere as the entire planet's plants now do. Nevertheless, by and large, the scientists have an enormous confidence in the ingenuity of humans—a confidence perhaps bolstered by their appreciation for climate change, which is, after all, a human invention, too. They point to the Apollo project, the hole in the ozone we patched in the 1980s, the passing of the fear of mutually assured destruction. Now we've found a way to engineer our own doomsday, and surely we will find a way to engineer our way out of it, one way or another. The planet is not used to being provoked like this, and climate systems designed to give feedback over centuries or millennia prevent us—even those who may be watching closely—from fully imagining the damage done already to the planet. But when we do truly see the world we've made, they say, we will also find a way to make it livable. For them, the alternative is simply unimaginable.

*This article appears in the July 10, 2017, issue of *New York* magazine. It has been updated to provide context for the recent news reports about revisions to a satellite data set, to more accurately reflect the rate of warming during the Paleocene–Eocene Thermal Maximum, to clarify a reference to Peter Brannen's *The Ends of the World*, and to make clear that James Hansen still supports a carbon-tax based approach to emissions.

Excerpt from "When Will the Planet Be Too Hot for Humans? Much Sooner Than You Imagine," an article by David Wallace-Wells, which was originally published on the *Intelligencer* website on July 9, 2017 (located at: https://nymag.com/intelligencer/2017/07/climate-change- earth-too-hot-for-humans.html) and also titled "The Uninhabitable Earth." © 2017 Intelligencer and Vox Media, LLC.

From "Dispatches from Ukraine"

Olha Poliukhovych, Tetiana Troitskaya, and Iryna Slavinska

Founded in 1972 by Askold Melnyczuk, the journal *AGNI* continues to foster new literary talent and explore the boundaries of contemporary literature. In addition to ten Pulitzer Prize winners, seven *AGNI* contributors have gone on to become Nobel laureates, including three in the 1990s (Wislawa Szymborska, Derek Walcott, and Seamus Heaney) and four in the 2000s (Tomas Tranströmer, Patrick Modiano, J. M. G. Le Clezio, and Louise Glück). Remarkably, all were relatively unknown when their work appeared in the journal. The literary prowess of *AGNI*, named for the Hindu god of fire, is thus ideally suited as a platform for narrative reportage on Russia's war with Ukraine. Along with Melnyczuk's ongoing commitment to supporting the work of Ukrainian writers and translators, the journal's mission "to bring our reader into the living moment, not as a tourist, but an engaged participant" is perhaps most powerfully epitomized by its "Dispatches from the Ukraine" featured on its digital publication.

Melnyczuk, whose parents fled to Ukraine from Poland in 1944 after his father was placed on the Communists' kill list, was instrumental in coordinating the pastiche of voices represented in "Dispatches from the Ukraine." They include twenty-nine contributions from journalists, academics, novelists, poets, artists, and attorneys, as well as a newspaper editor, psychologist, and detective. In a speech delivered at the University of Massachusetts-Boston in 2022, Melnyczuk shared emails and tweets he had received from Ukrainians, noting how online communication became a "bulletin board" for sending both moral and tangible support. The three dispatches below represent an extension of that online discourse into the more distilled and crafted realm of literary reportage.

The first, by Olha Poliukhovych, exposes the despair, spiritual emptiness, self-abasement, and agony behind the Russian army's acts of insane ruthlessness. The initial submission of the international community to Putin's blackmail is also emphasized. Next is Tetiana Troitskaya, whose report describes her firsthand experience upon returning to her hometown of Lugansk. After the outbreak of the war, the region was swiftly occupied by the Russian military. The war has turned people into hostages of the situation, the reader learns, forcing them to accept the influence of external powers. She depicts the hardships and challenges faced by people living in the occupied territories and how they strive to adapt to the dangerous environment. The final dispatch is from Iryna Slavinska, who highlights the challenges faced by women in Ukraine following the outbreak of the war. In her work on Ukrainian Radio, she provides information and hope to the audience, with the support of brilliant Ukrainian women she knows and those she has yet to meet. Despite the brutalities inflicted by Russia, they persist in doing extraordinary things, such as protecting local cultural heritage and providing humanitarian assistance to local women. Their efforts have made a positive and lasting impact on Ukrainian society and the women's community.

Herein we witness not just pain but resilience and fortitude, moments when writers summon the strength to meet the unspeakable with the written word. As Melnyczuk notes in his speech, "I agree with Joseph Conrad that my job above all is to make you see." The three Ukrainian women journalists featured below enable such vision.

—D. D.

Olha Poliukhovych, a Ukrainian writer, philosopher, editor, and humanities professor, writing from her hometown of Kyiv
March 16, 2022
Contra Spem Spero

Twenty-one days of full-scale Russia-Ukraine war have passed as one prolonged horrific day.

Most of all I regret not having completed military training or my course in tactical medicine before this war began. If I had done that, I'd be more helpful.

I'm staying in Ukraine with my family and finding ways to be useful. The words of Ukrainian poet Yevhen Malaniuk echo in my head: "my stiletto was a stylus and a stylus was my stiletto." Written almost a century ago, they're unexpectedly relevant today.

A professor of literature, I'm daily reminded of my powerlessness before the events unfolding around me. It feels impossible to convey how radically war has already altered the meanings of so many familiar words and commonplace notions. But while Ukrainians on the ground are writing our history in real time with arms and blood (tragically, this is no metaphor), it falls to me, and others like me, to speak—to forge a language adequate to these new realities.

Knowing something about language, as well as the history of Ukraine, may give me a bit of an edge. Ukrainians are by now adept at identifying propaganda and the imperial narratives that until now have dominated the rest of the world's understanding of our story. So much of Russian society's image of itself depends on their uncritical acceptance of centuries of their own PR. What we see of that storied Russian soul is that it is capable of nuclear terrorism and is willing to slaughter civilians without mercy in order to dominate our cities. Yet Ukrainians have thwarted their expectations. They expected to be greeted with carpets of flowers. Instead, they've been met with people lining the streets, raising blue-and-yellow flags. After the Russian military attacked the city of Kherson, its residents organized a Ukrainian rally and rejected Russia's offers of humanitarian aid.

People across the country continue to protest and to resist the troops trampling their territory. I personally can't begin to grasp what the average Russian soldier thinks he is doing here. Their armies will never succeed in occupying Ukraine.

Russia's initial plan to capture Kyiv in two to three days failed. (Unfortunately, the West appeared to share Russia's assessment and acted accordingly—had they imposed sanctions at once . . . but such "what ifs" are a game for children and political scientists.) Unable to subdue Kyiv, Russians focused on attacking Kharkiv, a former Ukrainian capital. They shelled not only residential areas in the city, but also universities, colleges, and schools. The secret soul of Russia is to be found neither in Tolstoy nor in Dostoyevsky but in the pictures of the still-smoldering skeletons of elementary schools and universities, churches, libraries, and museums barely standing in the ruined cities of eastern Ukraine and beyond.

In Kharkiv the Russians shelled Freedom Square, notable for being the largest public square in Europe. What was the thinking behind bombing a large empty square? What strategic value did it hold? It's not simply physical violence, not merely death and the destruction of millions of lives, that Russia intends. The real purpose of the carnage and the weirdly symbolic violence behind destroying an empty square is to instill fear, to embed it deep under our skins, so that the next time Russia raises its voice Ukrainians everywhere will quake. They want to control us—first by force, then psychologically. But it happens that Ukrainians choose to read Russia's insane ruthlessness differently: we see it as a gesture of national despair, of spiritual vacuousness, an act of self-abasement and agony. Theirs will be, at best, a Herostratic fame.

They bombed Freedom Square in Kharkiv—yet we ourselves will always remain free.

Russia's revenge on eastern cities in the Donetsk region, on Mariupol and Volnovakha, was especially brutal, violent, senseless, inhuman. From the start of Russia's assault on Donbas in 2014, Russian hybrid forces failed to capture the targeted cities. Tonight, it seems, Russia vented its frustration by bombing Mariupol's theater, in which hundreds of women and children were sheltering. The Russian word for *children* had been painted in huge letters on the grounds of two sides of the building. Perhaps that's what made it a target.

Still these cities remain Ukrainian and, for this, pay an impossible price in blood and tears. It's been reported that Volnovakha has been almost completely destroyed.

The logic behind this annihilation seems almost self-evident: unable to occupy these Ukrainian cities, the "mysterious Russian soul" would prefer to destroy them and slaughter their residents, to turn them into the same nothing that they feel within.

My horror is compounded by my awareness that the rest of the world is watching—billions see us on Instagram, Twitter, TV news, on websites, in newspapers and magazines. And, apparently, billions of people stand helpless before one evil man and his minions. How is this possible? What do they really fear? Is it a terror of Putin, a failure of faith in themselves, a combination of both?

Ukrainians are not the only victims of Russia's war on Ukraine—now several international journalists are among the dead. Pierre Zakrzewski, a resident of Ireland, and a reporter for Fox News was killed a couple of days ago outside Kyiv. In Irpin Russian invaders shot Brent Renaud, an award-winning American film producer and former journalist for *The New York Times*. These men had survived stints in Iraq, Afghanistan, and Syria. But they couldn't survive Mr. Putin.

All of these deaths could have been prevented—so I believe. As soon as the war began, President Volodymyr Zelensky spoke not only for Ukraine but for civilization itself when he urged NATO to create a no-fly zone over Ukraine, or at the very least to provide our country with protective aircraft systems. The world, fearing World War III, refused. They submitted to Putin's blackmail. I, and many others, believe if they'd called Putin's bluff they would have stopped him in his tracks.

"When is life grievable?" asks Judith Butler. Are Ukrainians so dispensable to the rest of the world? I refuse to believe it. No: contra spem spero! I choose to hope against hope, in order not to leave the question rhetorical.

Tetiana Troitskaya, a Ukrainian journalist and philology professor from Kharkiv
April 7, 2022, written from the Lugansk region
Who Is to Blame?

The Lugansk region is where I was born. I left it twenty years ago, but my parents still live there. They live in the Ukrainian part, not touched by the events of 2014, and when I escaped from Kharkiv, our beautiful Ukrainian flag was still waving over their town, despite the fact that it's only ten kilometers from the Russian border. Several days after my arrival, the alien army moved in.

"If you continue your flag demonstration, we will fire from the tanks," their commander said in a serious tone.

"We don't have any weapons," the head of our community responded, standing on the main bridge, which was half-ruined by bombing. "We just saved our children from Kharkiv hell. You won't fire at unarmed people. Go and fight the army."

"We'll give you twenty minutes, then we will start firing," was the soldier's verdict. He added that they'd come to "protect" us, to give us petrol, which nobody had by that time. Every drop had been used for evacuation carpools.

Following the arrival of the military men, who changed all the flags to those of the "Luhansk People's Republic" and the Russian Federation, mobile connections disappeared entirely, and seemingly forever. Later, the supernet stopped functioning. These changes deprived everyone of the chance to pay for things by credit card. The banks had closed much earlier. Cash, cash, good old cash only. Having received your salary or pension, you could again buy nothing. People were thinking of driving to Poltava to use their ATM, but the roads got cut off by battles. When the Lugansk Internet finally appeared, the clothing shops agreed to sell their stuff through electronic transactions that could be done by app. But not the food shops. "We're sorry," they said. "When we go to the supply bases, nobody gives us products for electronic money."

Starting on the first Monday in April, Ukrainian banks introduced text confirmation. Earlier, such SMS codes had only been required for sums over 3000 hryvnia. The shift was the last nail in the coffin for our area: you can't confirm a transaction when there's no wireless signal. Nobody thinks of the people, numerous people across large parts of eastern Ukraine, citizens, who became hostages of the situation, and in that way were pushed into the arms of the intruders. That's why pensioners who were promised Russian money lined up for it. They needed cash to survive.

"War does not determine who is right," Bertrand Russell said. "Only who is left." I don't know. Probably it is so.

"My son can't come back from the Mykolaiv region," a shop assistant said. "He went for a birthday party and got trapped. The Ukrainian army is terminating passports when they see Lugansk region on them, so he can't leave."

"I can't return to work at school," whispered another woman standing nearby. "They make us give up our Ukrainian passport and take the passport of LPR. I can't do that. My children are in western Ukraine. I won't be able to see my children."

"What are you going to eat?" the shop assistant asked.

"I don't know. I am planning to plant potatoes."

In a corner of the shop, a rather old woman in a red coat was crying: she'd found out her nephew had been shot in his car trying to leave Rubizhne.

"I am so tired of this war," the shop assistant said.

"You think you're tired?" a refugee from Lysychansk said. "We were forced to leave our apartments. Now soldiers are in them. There will be no apartments left."

"Whose soldiers?"

"Ours."

People started to say that in the city of Lugansk you could get cash from Ukrainian cards through the commercial banks. The drugstores also function there. My father needs insulin. My mom takes regular thyroid pills after an operation. Those medicines aren't accessible here anymore. I decided to go to Lugansk.

"You need a pass for that," said a neighbor who'd visited there as a medical worker. "But don't say in Lugansk that you're from Kharkiv. They'll take you to the Russian Federal Security Service."

I went to a commandant's office. Everybody was polite. They took my fingerprints and demanded that I show my papers. I did.

"Okay, now we know where to loot," said one of them, laughing. However, the pass was granted.

When I watch videos of refugees from Mariupol who were transported to Crimea, I look in particular at their eyes, which are full of fear.

"Who is to blame for this war?" an interviewer asks.

"I don't know," a woman responds, hiding her eyes.

The question goes to another refugee. "Who is to blame?" This woman doesn't talk.

A young girl answers in her stead: "All of them."

Then I look through videos of people "happily asking" to be part of the "Donetsk People's Republic." They are poorly dressed. Their faces are glum. They look down at the floor. In that posture I see Winston Smith and Julia from the last chapter of *1984*. I keep silent. I understand them.

Iryna Slavinska, a Ukrainian journalist writing from her newsroom in her hometown of Kyiv
April 17, 2022
Portrait of Women on Fire

After 2014, the lives of many thousands of Ukrainian women were transformed into a hell.

In the occupied territories of the Donetsk and Lugansk regions, they had to adapt to living in the absurd framework of Russian occupation, without the rule of law.

They were hit by Russian missiles, wounded, killed, raped, kidnapped, tortured. They had to leave their homes and find new safe places. Or they had to stay on in the occupied territories for whatever reason and survive in that dangerous context. They transformed themselves into goddesses of logistics, providing all the necessaries to anyone in need. They decided to volunteer, so they served in the Ukrainian army. No, in 2014 our army wasn't ready for female sappers or snipers, but it adapted very quickly. All possible trajectories opened up, but unfortunately without any guarantee of a happy ending.

Now it is 2022. And I cannot believe I have to rewrite that description in the present tense.

Today I'm working for Ukrainian Radio, a public broadcaster, to give our audience information—and hope, I would add. But it is so hard. Sometimes, while speaking about Bucha, Borodyanka, Mariupol, Chernihiv, Kharkiv, and the other Ukrainian cities bombed and raped by Russians, I can hardly hide and hold in my tears. Radio microphones capture all the nuances of voice, so I try to stay (or sound) calm and sure. Do you know who helps me with this challenging task? All the brilliant Ukrainian women I know and all the brilliant Ukrainian women I haven't yet met but want to.

They're living in the fire of Russian aggression. But they remind me of the phoenix and the superpower of fighting back.

My first thought is for my colleagues in the media. Since the Russian offensive re-emerged, it has been very dangerous to work as a journalist. In its latest statement, the National Union of Journalists says the Russian occupiers have killed twenty journalists since the 24th of February. One of them is Oleksandra Kuvshynova, killed in Gorinka, near Kyiv. She was working as a producer for a team of Fox channel reporters. A great Ukrainian photographer, Maks Levin, was also shot dead by the Russians. The list of journalists killed, wounded, or kidnapped by Russians would be too long. The total is frightening—148 crimes against our profession, according to the Institute of Mass Information (IMI).

I'm not sure that statistics can reflect the current routine of journalistic work. In Ukraine, a lot of women are journalists. So this is their reality, women's reality. They are very brave to keep reporting on this war. Every day I hear on air the voices of our reporters from various Ukrainian cities. While they speak from bomb shelters about the landscape of towns without electricity, gas, water—they are reporting on their own lives. The Russian occupiers are targeting civilians and civilian infrastructure like TV and radio towers. Some media teams have their newsrooms or technical support offices near these towers. So all of them are in danger.

Some of my colleagues have sent their own children and parents to safer places and stayed back to continue reporting. Or to start serving in the army as volunteers. Happily, some of them managed to be evacuated from cities on fire. Before last week, I never imagined waiting ten days or more to hear a single word from two of my colleagues. Our team wasn't sure they and their families were alive. I cried when the first of them called. She described an exodus from her small village, which had been encircled by Russians. She and her neighbors walked with white flags in their hands, hoping the Russians wouldn't shoot them and their children. Another colleague told me almost the same story, but about another village near Kyiv. This is a reality a lot of Ukrainians are enduring and surviving.

In this context, I feel every report prepared by my sisters in journalism to be as heroic as any of the exploits of Hercules.

I would say the same about every other Ukrainian woman during these days of war.

One of these brilliant women is helping provide humanitarian aid to displaced people. She sorts packages and says that she can easily tell which ones were prepared by women and for women. All of the packages contain toothbrushes, diapers, things like that. But some also include menstrual pads, hand cream, cosmetics, cotton pads, paper hankies, a hairbrush, lipstick, and other details you don't usually have to think about. Any of these can become critically important in hard times. With such contents, you feel one woman perfectly understanding another woman's needs. Maybe she also wanted to give the other something beautiful and offer the sense of a normal life where lipstick and perfumes exist. She supports not only the hygiene of another woman but also her emotional health. I have read a lot about women taking care of other women in a great book by Oksana Kis, *Survival as Victory: Ukrainian Women in the Gulag*, published by the Harvard Ukrainian Research Institute.

Another of these brilliant women has remained in Kyiv, where she hears Russian missiles flying past her windows. We text each other frequently to be sure we're both safe. I admire her writing, especially her children's book. The English translation has spread a powerful message and serves as a crowdfunding instrument to support Ukraine. Larysa Denysenko is a lawyer who has now started to work with women survivors of rape by Russian soldiers.

Another of these brilliant women is helping to preserve our cultural heritage. She is busy securing funds to help museums and galleries protect their collections. A lot of women work in the cultural field. Their work was often "invisible" before, but now these cultural managers and fundraisers are at the edge of a very important front line. Their work is critical for our memory, culture, and being. Since the 24th of February, the Russian army has attacked more than 100 Ukrainian heritage sites. In Borodyanka, Russians shot the head off a monument to Taras Shevchenko, our most famous poet. In Ivankiv, Russians burned down a local museum. Cities and villages need their art collections and other cultural treasures to be protected from Russian bombs.

All these women on fire know how to do extraordinary things and how to sustain routines of the ordinary. Any little thing is significant. Even (don't laugh!) news of the only beauty salon still open, which a colleague shared with me so I could liberate my nails from a shellac manicure.

These women in the fire of war know how fragile they are—just like our everyday lives, which changed so dramatically when the first bomb blasts echoed around our homes. Now we need hope. And weapons from our allies to protect Ukraine. And sanctions from our allies to interfere with Russia's ability to finance this bloody war.

"Contra Spem Spero," an article by Olha Poliukhovych © 2022, as originally appeared in "Dispatches from Ukraine," *AGNI*, March 16, 2022. Reprinted courtesy of *AGNI*. https://agnionline.bu.edu/blog/dispatches-from-ukraine/#poliukhovych

"Who is to Blame?," an article by Tetiana Troitskaya © 2022, as originally appeared in "Dispatches from Ukraine," *AGNI*, April 7, 2022. Reprinted courtesy of *AGNI*. https://agnionline.bu.edu/blog/dispatches-from-ukraine/#troitskaya

"Portrait of Women on Fire," an article by Iryna Slavinska © 2022, as originally appeared in "Dispatches from Ukraine," *AGNI*, April 17, 2022. Reprinted courtesy of *AGNI*. https://agnionline.bu.edu/blog/dispatches-from-ukraine/#slavinska

Selected Bibliography

Online Sources

After the Last Border
https://www.penguinrandomhouse.com/books/572566/after-the-last-border-by-jessica-goudeau/

"Black Hawk Down"
https://web.archive.org/web/20110425160946/http://inquirer.philly.com/packages/somalia/sitemap.asp

"Bodies on the Line" (Online title: **"Dancing Through New York in a Summer of Joy and Grief"**)
https://www.nytimes.com/2021/09/15/magazine/dancing-new-york-summer.html

"The Bones of Marianna"
https://magazine.atavist.com/the-bones-of-marianna/

"The Case for Reparations"
https://www.theatlantic.com/magazine/archive/2014/06/the-case-for-reparations/361631/

"Dispatches from Ukraine"
https://agnionline.bu.edu/blog/dispatches-from-ukraine/

"The Displaced"
https://www.nytimes.com/2015/11/08/magazine/the-displaced-introduction.html
360 VR Video
https://www.youtube.com/watch?v=ecavbpCuvkI

"The Dream Boat" (Online title: **"The Impossible Refugee Boat Lift to Christmas Island"**)
https://www.nytimes.com/2013/11/17/magazine/the-impossible-refugee-boat-lift-to-christmas-island.html

"Firestorm: The Story of the Bushfire at Dunalley"
https://www.theguardian.com/world/interactive/2013/may/26/firestorm-bushfire-dunalley-holmes-family

How the Word Is Passed
https://www.clintsmithiii.com/how-the-word-is-passed
Clint Smith reads an excerpt on *Storybound*.
https://lithub.com/clint-smith-performs-an-excerpt-from-how-the-word-is-passed/

"The Jessica Simulation: Love and Loss in the Age of A.I."
https://www.sfchronicle.com/projects/2021/jessica-simulation-artificial-intelligence/

"Leading Up to 6:01: The Last 32 Hours of Dr. Martin Luther King Jr."
https://www.commercialappeal.com/story/news/2018/03/28/dr-martin-luther-king-jr-last-32-hours-before-assassination-memphis/433749002/
Original layout available at
https://www.niemanlab.org/2013/04/design-isnt-just-for-the-big-guys-in-memphis-the-commercial-appeal-retells-mlks-last-32-hours/

"Love in the Time of Robots"
https://www.wired.com/2017/10/hiroshi-ishiguro-when-robots-act-just-like-humans/

"The Mastermind"
https://magazine.atavist.com/the-mastermind/

"My Four Months as a Private Prison Guard"
https://www.motherjones.com/politics/2016/06/cca-private-prisons-corrections-corporation-inmates-investigation-bauer/

"The Out Crowd"
https://www.thisamericanlife.org/688/the-out-crowd

"Out in the Great Alone"
http://www.espn.com/espn/feature/story/_/id/9175394/out-great-alone

"The Really Big One"
https://www.newyorker.com/magazine/2015/07/20/the-really-big-one

"The Reckoning"
https://www.texasmonthly.com/true-crime/the-reckoning-2/

"Snow Fall: The Avalanche at Tunnel Creek"
http://www.nytimes.com/2012/12/22/sports/q-a-the-avalanche-at-tunnel-creek.html?_r=0
"What the New York Times' 'Snow Fall' Means to Online Journalism's Future." *The Atlantic*.
https://www.theatlantic.com/technology/archive/2012/12/new-york-times-snow-fall-feature/320253/

"'Snow Fall' at 10: How it Changed Journalism." *The New York Times*. https://www.nytimes.com/2022/12/23/insider/snow-fall-at-10-how-it-changed-journalism.html

"Twelve Minutes and a Life"
https://www.runnersworld.com/runners-stories/a32883923/ahmaud-arbery-death-running-and-racism/

"The Uninhabitable Earth"
https://nymag.com/intelligencer/2017/07/climate-change-earth-too-hot-for-humans.html

"Who Is Matty Healy?"
https://www.newyorker.com/magazine/2023/06/05/who-is-matty-healy

Scholarship

Alexander, Robert, and Willa McDonald, eds. *Literary Journalism and Social Justice*. Cham, Switzerland: Palgrave Macmillan, 2022.

American Society of Magazine Editors. *The Best American Magazine Writing*. New York: Columbia University Press, 2005–2022.

Bak, John S., and Bill Reynolds, eds. *The Routledge Companion to World Literary Journalism*. New York: Routledge, 2022.

Berning, Nora. "Narrative Journalism in the Age of the Internet: New Ways to Create Authenticity in Online Literary Reportages." *Textpraxis* 3, no. 2 (2011): 1–23.

Boynton, Robert S. *The New New Journalism: Conversations with America's Best Nonfiction Writers on Their Craft*. New York: Vintage, 2005.

Boynton, Robert S. "Notes toward a Supreme Nonfiction: Teaching Literary Reportage in the Twenty-first Century" (keynote address, International Association for Literary Journalism Studies, Tampere, Finland, May 2013).

Calvi, Pablo. *Latin American Adventures in Literary Journalism*. Pittsburgh: University of Pittsburgh Press, 2019.

Connery, Thomas. *A Sourcebook of American Literary Journalism: Representative Writers in an Emerging Genre*. Westport: Greenwood Press, 1992.

DeGregory, Lane. *"The Girl in the Window" and Other True Tales with Tips for Finding, Reporting and Writing Nonfiction Narratives*. Chicago: University of Chicago Press, 2023.

Dow, William E., Roberta S. Maguire, and Yoko Nakamura, eds. *The Routledge Companion to American Literary Journalism*. New York: Routledge, 2021.

Dowling, David. *Immersive Longform Storytelling: Media, Technology, Audience*. New York: Routledge, 2019.

Dowling, David and T. Vogan. "Can we 'Snowfall' This? Digital Longform and the Race for the Tablet Market." *Digital Journalism* 3, no. 2 (2015): 209–24.

Dowling, David O. "Interactive Documentary and the Reinvention of Digital Journalism, 2015–2020." *Convergence* 28, no. 3 (2022): 905–24.

Dowling, David O. "Toward a New Aesthetic of Digital Literary Journalism: Charting the Fierce Evolution of the Supreme Nonfiction." *Literary Journalism Studies* 9, no. 1 (2017): 100–17.

Fitzgerald, Jonathan D. *How the News Feels: The Empathic Power of Literary Journalists*. University of Massachusetts Press, 2023.

Giles, Fiona, and Georgia Hitch. "Multimedia Features as 'Narra-descriptive' Texts: Exploring the Relationship between Literary Journalism and Multimedia." *Literary Journalism Studies* 9, no. 2 (2017): 74–91.

Greussing, Esther, and Hajo G. Boomgaarden. "Simply Bells and Whistles? Cognitive Effects of Visual Aesthetics in Digital Longforms." *Digital Journalism* 7, no. 2 (2019): 273–93.

Harrington, Walt and Mike Sager, eds. *Next Wave: America's New Generation of Great Literary Journalists*. The Sager Group, 2012.

Jacobson, Susan, Jacqueline Marino, and Robert E. Gutsche Jr. "The Digital Animation of Literary Journalism." *Journalism* 17, no. 4 (2016): 527–46.

Jacobson, Susan, Jacqueline Marino, and Robert E. Gutsche Jr.. "Should there be an app for that? An Analysis of Interactive Applications within Longform News Stories." *Journal of Magazine Media* 18, no. 2 (2018). https://doi.org/10.1353/jmm.2018.0002

Kerrane, Kevin, and Ben Yagoda, eds. *The Art of Fact: A Historical Anthology of Literary Journalism*. New York: Simon & Schuster, 1997.

Kramer, Mark, and Wendy Call, eds. *Telling True Stories: A Nonfiction Writers' Guide from the Nieman Foundation at Harvard University*. London: Plume, 2007.

Kroeger, Brooke. *Undercover Reporting: The Truth about Deception*. Evanston: Northwestern University Press, 2012.

Lindgren, Mia. "Intimacy and Emotions in Podcast Journalism: A Study of Award-winning Australian and British Podcasts." *Journalism Practice* 17, no. 4 (2023): 704–19.

Lowery, Wesley. "A Reckoning over Objectivity, Led by Black Journalists." *The New York Times*, June 23, 2020.

Marino, Jacqueline. "Reading Screens: What Eye Tracking Tells Us about the Writing in Digital Longform Journalism." *Literary Journalism Studies* 8, no. 2 (2016): 138–50.

Marnane, Ryan. "From Print to 360-Degree Immersive: On Introducing Literary Journalism across Media." *Literary Journalism Studies* 11, no. 2 (2019): 136–57.

McHugh, Siobhán. "The Narrative Podcast as Digital Literary Journalism: Conceptualizing *S-Town*." *Literary Journalism Studies* 13, no. 1&2 (2021): 100–29.

McLuhan, Marshall. *Understanding Media: The Extensions of Man*. Cambridge, MA: MIT Press, 1994.

Mitchell, W. J. T. "There are No Visual Media." In *The Visual Culture Reader*, edited by N. Mirzoeff, 3rd ed., 7–14. New York: Routledge, 2013.

Palau-Sampio, Dolors. "Reframing Central American migration from narrative journalism." *Journal of Communication Inquiry* 43, no. 1 (2019): 93–114.

Pavlik, John V. *Disruption and Digital Journalism: Assessing News Media Innovation in a Time of Dramatic Change*. Routledge, 2021.

Pincus, Hanna, Magdalena Wojcieszak, and Hajo Boomgarden. "Do Multimedia Matter? Cognitive and Affective Effects of Embedded Multimedia Journalism." *Journalism & Mass Communication Quarterly* 94, no. 3 (2017): 747–71.

Planer, Rosanna, and Alexander Godulla. "Longform Journalism in the USA and Germany: Patterns in Award-Winning Digital Storytelling Productions." *Journalism Practice* 15, no. 4 (2021): 566–82.

Rauch, Jennifer. *Slow Media: Why Slow is Satisfying, Sustainable, and Smart*. Oxford University Press, 2018.

Richardson, A. (2020). *Bearing Witness While Black: African Americans, Smartphones, and the New Protest #Journalism*. Oxford University Press.

Schmidt, Thomas R. "'It's OK to Feel': The Emotionality Norm and Its Evolution in US Print Journalism." *Journalism* 22, no. 5 (2021): 1173–89.

Schmidt, Thomas R. *Rewriting the Newspaper: The Storytelling Movement in American Print journalism*. University of Missouri Press, 2019.

Schmidt, Thomas R., and Regina G. Lawrence. "Engaged Journalism and News Work: A Sociotechnical Analysis of Organizational Dynamics and Professional Challenges." *Journalism Practice* 14, no. 5 (2020): 518–36.

Sims, Norman. *True Stories: A Century of Literary Journalism*. Evanston: Northwestern University Press, 2007.

Sims, Norman, and Mark Kramer. *Literary Journalism: A New Collection of the Best American Nonfiction*. New York: Ballantine Books, 1985.

Steensen, Steen, and Oscar Westlund. *What is Digital Journalism Studies?* London and New York: Taylor & Francis, 2021.

Sternadori, Miglena, and Tim Holmes, eds. *The Handbook of Magazine Studies*. John Wiley & Sons, 2020.

Tullis, Matt. *Stories Can Save Us: Conversations with America's Best Narrative Journalists Explain How*. Athens: University of Georgia Press, 2024.

Tulloch, Christopher, and Xavier Ramon. "Take Five: How Sports Illustrated and L'équipe Redefine the Long-Form Sports Journalism Genre." In *Changing Sports Journalism Practice in the Age of Digital Media*, 160–80. New York and London: Routledge, 2020. (Originally published in *Digital Journalism* 5, issue 5 (June 2017): 652–72.)

van der Nat, Renée, Eggo Müller, and Piet Bakker. "Navigating Interactive Story Spaces. The Architecture of Interactive Narratives in Online Journalism." *Digital Journalism* 11, no. 6 (2023): 1104–29.

Van Krieken, Kobie. "Multimedia Storytelling in Journalism: Exploring Narrative Techniques in Snow Fall." *Information* 9, no. 5 (2018): 1–14.

Van Krieken, Kobie, and José Sanders. "What is Narrative Journalism? A Systematic Review and an Empirical Agenda." *Journalism* 22, no. 6 (2021): 1393–412.

Vanoost, Marie. "From Literary Journalism to Transmedia Worlds: Into the Wild and Beyond." *Literary Journalism Studies* 12, no. 2 (2020): 34–61.

Wahl-Jorgensen, Karin, and Thomas R. Schmidt. "News and Storytelling." In *The Handbook of Journalism Studies*, edited by K. Wahl-Jorgensen and T. Hanitzsch, 261–76. Routledge, 2019.

Waldmann, Ella. "From Storytelling to Storylistening: How the Hit Podcast *S-Town* Reconfigured the Production and Reception of Narrative Nonfiction." *Ex-centric Narratives: Journal of Anglophone Literature, Culture and Media* 4 (2020): 28–42.

Wolfe, Tom, and E. W. Johnson, eds. *The New Journalism*. London: Picador, 1975.

Other Notable Works of Literary Journalism in the Digital Age

Bruder, Jessica. *Nomadland: Surviving America in the Twenty-First Century*. New York: W.W. Norton & Company, 2017.

DeGregory, Lane. "Girl in the Window." *Tampa Bay Times*, August 3, 2008. https://projects.tampabay.com/projects/girl-in-the-window/danielle/

Dreier, Hannah. "A Betrayal." *ProPublica*, April 2, 2018. https://features.propublica.org/ms-13/a-betrayal-ms13-gang-police-fbi-ice-deportation/

Drost, Nadja. "When Can We Really Rest?" *California Sunday Magazine*, April 2, 2020. https://story.californiasunday.com/darien-gap-migration/

Ehrenreich, Barbara. *Nickel and Dimed: On (Not) Getting By in America*. New York: Henry Holt, 2001.

Elliott, Andrea. "Invisible Child." *The New York Times*, December 9, 2013. https://www.nytimes.com/projects/2013/invisible-child/index.html#/?chapt=1

Finkel, David. *The Good Soldiers*. New York: Sarah Crichton Books, 2010.

Flanagan, Caitlin. "Death at a Penn State Fraternity." *The Atlantic*, November 2017. https://www.theatlantic.com/magazine/archive/2017/11/a-death-at-penn-state/540657/

Ghansah, Rachel Kaadzi. "A Most American Terrorist: The Making of Dylann Roof." *Esquire*, August 21, 2017. https://www.gq.com/story/dylann-roof-making-of-an-american-terrorist

Grann, David. *Killers of the Flower Moon*. New York: Vintage Books, 2017.

Hruby, Patrick. "The Long, Strange Trip of Dock Ellis." *ESPN*, August 24, 2012. http://www.espn.com/espn/eticket/story?page=dock-ellis

Jones, Chris. "Roger Ebert: The Essential Man." *Esquire*, March 2010. https://classic.esquire.com/article/2010/3/1/the-essential-man-roger-ebert

Kisner, Jordan. "Las Marthas." *The Believer*, October 1, 2019. https://www.thebeliever.net/las-marthas/

Lake, Thomas. "The Boy Who Died of Football." *Sports Illustrated*, December 6, 2010. https://vault.si.com/vault/2010/12/06/the-boy-who-died-of-football

Langewiesche, William. *American Ground: Unbuilding the World Trade Center*. New York: North Point Press, 2003.

Laskas, Jeanne Marie. "To Obama with Love, and Hate, and Desperation." *The New York Times*, January 17, 2017. https://www.nytimes.com/2017/01/17/magazine/what-americans-wrote-to-obama.html

LeBlanc, Adrian Nicole. *Random Family: Love, Drugs and Coming of Age in the Bronx*. New York: Scribner, 2003.

Levy, Ariel. "Either/Or." *The New Yorker*, November 19, 2009. https://www.newyorker.com/magazine/2009/11/30/eitheror

MacGregor, Jeff. "Taming the Lionfish." *Smithsonian*, June 2018. https://www.smithsonianmag.com/science-nature/lionfish-invaded-army-divers-chefs-fighting-back-180968999/

Moehringer, J. R. "The Education of Alex Rodriguez." *ESPN*, February 18, 2015. https://www.espn.com/espn/feature/story/_/id/12321274/alex-rodriguez-return-new-york-yankees

Nazario, Sonia. *Enrique's Journey: The Story of a Boy's Dangerous Journey to Reunite with His Mother*. New York: Random House Trade Paperbacks, 2014.

Okeowo, Alexis. *A Moonless, Starless Sky: Ordinary Women and Men Fighting Extremism in Africa*. New York: Hachette, 2017.

Reed, Brian. "S-Town." *Serial and This American Life*, 2017. https://stownpodcast.org/

Saslow, Eli. Pulitzer Prize-winning stories about food stamps written for *The Washington Post*. https://www.pulitzer.org/winners/eli-saslow

Senior, Jennifer. "What Bobby McIlvaine Left Behind." *The Atlantic*, September 2021. https://www.theatlantic.com/magazine/archive/2021/09/twenty-years-gone-911-bobby-mcilvaine/619490/

Sheeler, Jason. "Portrait of the Artist as a Postman." *Texas Monthly*, October 2012. https://www.texasmonthly.com/arts-entertainment/portrait-of-the-artist-as-a-postman/

Sheeler, Jim. *Final Salute: A Story of Unfinished Lives*. New York: The Penguin Press, 2008

Sullivan, John Jeremiah. "Upon This Rock." *GQ*, January 24, 2004. https://www.gq.com/story/rock-music-jesus

Tizon, Alex. "My Family's Slave." *The Atlantic*, June 2017 https://www.theatlantic.com/magazine/archive/2017/06/lolas-story/524490/

Thompson, Wright. "The Secret History of Tiger Woods." *ESPN*, April 21, 2016. https://www.espn.com/espn/feature/story/_/id/15278522/how-tiger-woods-life-unraveled-years-father-earl-woods-death

Weingarten, Gene. "Fatal Distraction." *The Washington Post*, March 8, 2009. https://www.washingtonpost.com/lifestyle/magazine/fatal-distraction-forgetting-a-child-in-thebackseat-of-a-car-is-a-horrifying-mistake-is-it-a-crime/2014/06/16/8ae0fe3a-f580-11e3-a3a5-42be35962a52_story.html

Wilkerson, Isabel. *The Warmth of Other Suns*. New York: Vintage Books, 2010.

Index

A for Anonymous (Kushner) 87
After the Last Border: Two Families and the Story of Refuge in America (Goudeau) 10
　excerpt 95–102
　J. Anthony Lukas Book Prize 94
AGNI 223
AI-powered conversations 69
American Mystic (Mar) 185
animated maps 152
anti-refugee sentiment 94
Arbery, Ahmaud 10, 145, 147–50
Arctic methane emissions, prediction of 206
Arthur L. Carter Journalism Institute 206
artificial intelligence 69–70
The Art of Fact: A Historical Anthology of Literary Journalism (Kerrane and Yagoda) 1
The Atavist Magazine 10, 87, 165
The Atlantic 10, 69, 133, 135, 195
audio journalism 2, 4, 6–8, 10, 15, 87, 118, 133
audio reporting 6, 10, 118

Barbeau, Joshua 70–1
Bauer, Shane 179
The Believer 139, 185
Berning, Nora 16
Berry, Richard 6
The Best American Magazine Writing 2014 (Jannot) 172
Between the World and Me (Coates) 133
biography of Ellis (Hall) 5
Black Classic Press 133
Black Death 139–40, 216
"Black Hawk Down" (Bowden)
　advent of literary journalism 15
　excerpt 16–21

Black Panther (Coates) 133–4
Bly, Nellie 133
"Bodies on the Line" (Schorske)
　Essays and Criticism category of the 2022 National Magazine Awards 139
　excerpt 140–4
"The Bones of Marianna" (Kushner)
　Best Digital Single of the Year 87
　excerpt 88–93
Boynton, Robert S. 7–8, 198
braiding, concept of 2
Branch, John 22–3
BuzzFeed culture 95

Caliphate by *The New York Times* (podcast) 7
Call, Wendy 4
Capote, Truman 1
Captain America (Coates) 134
Cardell, Kylie 7, 8
Carr, Nicholas 15
Carson, Rachel 207
Carver, Raymond 146
"The Case for Reparations" (Coates)
　excerpt 134–8
　George Polk Award 133
　reparations for slavery 133
Catapult 94
civil rights movement 28, 30, 35
Clark, Roy Peter 79
climate change 1, 10, 49, 54, 59, 206–9, 213–16, 218–22
Coates, Ta-Nehisi 10
　"genius grant" from the MacArthur Foundation 134
Colloff, Pamela
　Hillman Prize 80
　reportorial integrity 79
　Taylor Family Award for Fairness in Journalism 80

Columbia Journalism Review 69, 80, 179
Columbia Journalism School 94
The Commercial Appeal 28–9
Connery, Thomas 2
Conover, Ted 1, 179
Cooke, Marvel 1, 133
Corrections Corporation of
    America 179
Counting Descent (Smith) 195
Covid-19 139
*The Covid Drug Wars that Pitted Doctor
    vs. Doctor* (Dominus) 63
Crash Course Black American History
    YouTube series 195
crime and war reportage 1

D'Agata, John 69
Defoe, Daniel 1
DeLillo, Don 146
The Desert One Debacle (Bowden) 16
design
    digital 5, 9, 48, 69, 152
    sound 8
    technique 5
Dickens, Charles 1, 7
digital graphic designers 9
digital journalism 6, 15, 48, 207
digital tools 1
"Dispatches from Ukraine" (Poliukhovych,
    Troitskaya, and Slavinska) 10,
    223
    "Contra Spem Spero"
        (Poliukhovych) 224–7
    "Portrait of Women on Fire"
        (Slavinska) 229–33
    "Who Is to Blame?" (Troitskaya)
        227–9
"The Displaced: Hana" (Dominus)
    excerpt 64–8
    multimedia documentary project 63
Disruptor (Kushner) 87
documentary journalism 6
documentary storytellers 3
Dominus, Susan
    Front Page Award for the
        Newswomen's Club of New
        York 63
    longform storytelling 63

Mychal Judge Heart of New York
    Award 63
Pulitzer Prize for public service 63
Dowling, David O. 3
"The Dream Boat" (Mogelson) 10, 172
    excerpt 173–8

Earth System Science Center 206
Ehrenreich, Barbara 95
Encryption for the Masses (E4M)
    165
environmental journalism 207
Epic 184
ESPN 5–6, 25, 151
Esquire 69, 145

Fagone, Jason
    Deborah Howell Award for Writing
        Excellence 69
    one of "Ten Young Writers on the
        Rise" 69
False Witness (Colloff) 80
Faulkner, William 6–8
Faulkneresque storytelling 6
Fingal, Jim 69
"Firestorm: The Story of the Bushfire at
    Dunalley" (Henley, Topham and
    the international team from the
    guardian.com) 10
    archival photos 48
    cautionary tale 49
    excerpt 49–62
    series of captions 49

game developers 9
Gangrey: The Podcast 80
geoengineering 220
Glass, Ira 118
Goudeau, Jessica 94–5
GPT-3 69–70, 73, 75
GQ 69
Grantland 5, 69, 151
graphics 3, 11, 15, 22, 188
The Guardian 48, 206
Gutsche, Robert, Jr. 4

The Hairpin 103
hand-drawn illustrations 5

Hansen, James   207
Harper   145
Harrington, Walt   184
Hart, Jack   79
hashtag #BlackMirror   70
Henley, Jon   48, 62
Hersey, John   1
Homicide (Simon)   1
Howell, Deborah   69
How the Word Is Passed (Smith)   10
  excerpt   196-8
  legacy of slavery   195
  Times Book Review's Best Books of 2021   195
Hruby, Patrick   5
Huffington Post Highline   69
hyperlinks   15-16

immersion reporting   4
immersive storytelling   9, 63
immigration   1, 126-7
In Cold Blood (Capote)   1
Industrial Revolution   151, 219
The Intelligencer   206
interactive graphics   3
Interactive Narratives, website   3
interior monologue   79
interpretive reportage   151
intimate journalism   184
investigative journalism   69, 80, 165, 179, 200
Irving, Washington   151

Jacked: The Inside Story of Grand Theft Auto (Kushner)   87
Jackson, Mitchell S.   10
  Longform podcast   145
Jacobson, Susan   4
"The Jessica Simulation: Love and Loss in the Age of A.I." (Fagone)
  Deborah Howell Award for Writing Excellence   69
  excerpt   70-6
  first place at 2022 Best American Newspaper Narrative contest   69
  narrative journalism   70
  text messages, letters, and conversations   69

Jezebel   103
Journalism: Theory and Practice   4-5

Kerrane, Kevin   1-2, 11
Kimmerle, Erin   88-9
Kramer, Mark   4
Kushner, David   87-8

"Leading Up to 6:01: The Last 32 Hours of Dr. Martin Luther King Jr." (Perrusquia)
  interactive magazine   29
  2014 Punch Sulzberger Award for Online Storytelling   28
Le Roux, Paul   10, 165-6, 169, 171
Lewis, Michael   16
The Lifespan of a Fact (D'Agata and Fingal)   69
link rot   15
Lish, Gordon   146
literary journalism   1-4, 10-11, 15, 95
London, Jack   1
"The Long, Strange Trip of Dock Ellis" (Hruby)   5
longform audio reportage   118
longform journalism   5, 8-9, 22
Longform Podcast   8, 146, 166, 185
longform storytelling, digital   8, 48, 63, 87, 165, 207
Longreads   184
"Love in the Time of Robots" (Mar)   184
  excerpt   185-91
Lowery, Wesley   9-10

McHugh, Siobhan   8
McLemore, John B.   7
McLuhan, Marshall   2
Mann, Michael E.   206
Mar, Alex   184
Marino, Jacqueline   4
"The Mastermind" (Ratliff)   10, 165
  excerpt   166-71
  Overseas Press Club's 2017 Award for Best Digital Reporting on International Affairs   165
  2016 Online Journalism Award for Innovation in Investigative Journalism   165

Masters of Doom: How Two Guys Created an Empire and Transformed Pop Culture (Kushner) 87
Matthews, Susan 207
Mayhew, Henry 1
media, *see also* multimedia
  audio 6
  cultural shifts in 8
  digital 4, 6, 8–9, 87
  social 4, 104, 117, 165, 215
  technologies 1, 9
medieval dancing mania 139–40
Melnyczuk, Askold 223–4
migration
  forced 140, 215
  mass 10, 172
Mitchell, W. J. T. 2, 10, 145
Mogelson, Luke
  George Polk Awards 173
  National Magazine Award 172
multimedia 3–6, 15–16, 29, 48, 151
  journalism 22–3
  storytelling 87, 118
"My Four Months as a Private Prison Guard" (Bauer)
  excerpt 180–3
  video series and podcast 179

narrative journalism 1, 6, 10, 64, 70, 79, 118
narrative reportage 11, 223
National Book Lifetime Award 16
National Magazine Awards 139, 184
natural disaster 204, 218–19
Newjack (Conover) 179
New Journalism 8, 118
The New Yorker 145, 151, 199
New York magazine 10, 69, 185, 206, 222
The New York Times 63, 69, 79, 139, 172
The New York Times Book Review 87, 94
The New York Times Magazine 79, 139
Nickel and Dimed: On (Not) Getting By in America (Ehrenreich) 95
Nieman Foundation for Journalism 94
Nieman narrative journalism conferences 79
Nieman Storyboard 94

9/11 terrorist attack 199, 218
nonfiction podcasts 118

OpenAI 70, 73
Oppenheimer, Michael 207
"The Out Crowd" (*This American Life* Episode) 6, 10
  Audio Reporting 118
  excerpt from *This American Life* Episode #688 119–30
  importance of narrative journalism 118–19
  serial documentary form 118
"Out in the Great Alone" (Phillips) 5, 151
  digital age travel narrative 152
  excerpt 152–61
  genre of travel writing 152
Outside magazine 87
Outside the Lines 6

parallax scroll 5
The Paris Review 103, 145
Peabody Award 3, 7, 23
People of the Abyss (London) 1
Perdomo, Gabriela 7
Perrusquia, Marc 29
  Punch Sulzberger Award for Online Storytelling 28
  stories on politics and social justice 28
Petersen, Anne Helen 95
Philadelphia Inquirer 15–16
Phillips, Brian 5, 151
photographers 3
The Player's Ball (2020) 87
podcast(ing)
  journalism 6, 118
  serialized documentary 6–7
Poliukhovych, Olha 223
pop culture 84, 87, 113, 152
power dynamics 179
prison 17–18, 33, 47, 92, 169, 179–83, 195–8
ProPublica 79
Pulitzer Prize 3, 5–6, 10, 23, 48, 63, 118, 145, 199, 223

race/racism 1, 5, 18, 41, 88, 145–7
radio 3, 9, 21, 51, 58, 98, 118–19, 148, 153, 182–3, 195, 224, 230–1
Ratliff, Evan 165–6
"The Really Big One" (Schulz)
  excerpt 200–5
  lyricism 200
  National Magazine Award 199
"The Reckoning" (Colloff)
  excerpt 80–6
  interior monologue 79
Reed, Brian 7
Remnick, David 199
reparations 10, 117, 133
reportage for social justice 118
reported essay 2–3, 10, 55, 80, 85, 89, 92, 103–4, 117, 148, 165, 169, 172–3, 198, 212
resettlement policies, America's 94
The Residue Years (Jackson) 145
Riis, Jacob 95
Roberts, Nancy L. 95
Robinson, Jackie 6
Rodrigues-Rouleau, Phillipe 7
Rolling Stone 87, 185
"A Rose for Emily" (Faulkner) 7
The Routledge Companion to American Literary Journalism (Maguire and Dow) 95
Runner's World 10, 145, 147
Russia–Ukraine war 223–32

San Francisco Chronicle 69
The Santiago Times 199
Schorske, Carina del Valle 139
Schulz, Kathryn 199–200
screen-based digital journalism 5, 6
Serial 6, 118, 165
serial documentary form 8, 118
Seventy Times Seven: A True Story of Murder and Mercy (Mar) 185
Silverstein, Jake 63–4
Simmons, Bill 151
Simon, David 1
Slate 151, 207

slavery 10, 133, 195
Slavinska, Iryna 224
Smith, Clint 10
  National Poetry Slam champion 195
Smith Broecker, Wallace 207
A Sniper in the Tower (Lavergne) 84
"Snow Fall: The Avalanche at Tunnel Creek" (Branch) 3, 5
  Branch's literary style 23
  excerpt 23–7
  satellite images and LIDAR elevation data 22
social activism and journalism 95
SonicNet 87
sports 6, 22–3
  journalism 51
  literary sports writing 152
Star Trek: The Next Generation 152
Stead, W. T. 1
Stephens, Mitchell 9
Stories Can Save Us (Tullis) 145
The Storm is Here: America on the Brink (Mogelson) 173
storytelling 10
  conventional devices 5
  Faulkneresque 6
  immersive 9, 63
  longform 1, 5, 8, 48, 63, 87, 165, 207
  multimedia 87, 118
  narrative 4, 22, 64
  nonfiction 5–6
  online 3
  video and audio 2
  web 5
S-Town 6
  Peabody Award 7
  rhetorical techniques 8
supplemental data 16
supreme nonfiction 7–8, 11
Survival Math: Notes on an All-American Family (Jackson) 145
Szalai, Jennifer 206

Teen Vogue 94–5
Telling True Stories (Clark) 1, 79
Texas Monthly 79–80

These Heroic, Happy Dead (Mogelson) 172
This American Life (WBEZ Chicago) 6, 10, 118
Thompson, Hunter S. 151
Thoreau, Henry David 199
360-degree journalism 63
Tolentino, Jia
   2023 National Magazine Award for Columns and Essays 103
   Whiting Award 104
Topham, Laurence 48
Tower (2006) 80
Trick Mirror: Reflections on Self-Delusion (Tolentino) 103
Troitskaya, Tetiana 224
Tullis, Matt 145
"Twelve Minutes and a Life" (Jackson) 10
   excerpt from "Ahmaud Arbery and the White Man's Justice" 146–50
   National Magazine Award 145
   Pulitzer Prize for Feature Writing 145

undercover reporting 32, 179
"The Uninhabitable Earth" (Wallace-Wells) 10, 206
   excerpt from "When Will the Planet Be Too Hot for Humans? Much Sooner Than You Imagine" 207–22
US Drug Enforcement Agency (DEA) 165

video loop 3, 5–6, 22
virtual reality (VR) 63
voice 4, 103, 105, 139, 152, 230–1

Waldmann, Ella 8
Wallace-Wells, David 206–7
war 1, 10, 18, 63, 67, 120, 140, 172, 182, 212, 214, 223–8
Ward, Peter 207–21
The Washington Post 9, 84, 94, 133
"Who is Matty Healy?" (Tolentino) 103
Wild, Jonathan 1
Wired 69, 87, 127, 168, 184
wisdom journalism 9
Witches of America (Mar) 185
Wolfe, Tom 3–4, 16

Yagoda, Ben 1–2, 11